The Nature of Party Government

Also by Jean Blondel

COMPARATIVE GOVERNMENT

COMPARATIVE LEGISLATURES

COMPARATIVE POLITICS (*editor*)

CONSTITUENCY POLITICS

GOVERNING TOGETHER (*co-editor*)

GOVERNMENT MINISTERS IN THE CONTEMPORARY WORLD

PARTY AND GOVERNMENT (*co-editor*)

POLITICAL LEADERSHIP

PUBLIC ADMINISTRATION IN FRANCE

THE GOVERNMENT OF FRANCE

THE PROFESSION OF GOVERNMENT MINISTER IN WESTERN EUROPE (*co-editor*)

THE ORGANIZATION OF GOVERNMENTS

THINKING POLITICALLY

VOTERS, PARTIES AND LEADERS

WORLD LEADERS

Also by Maurizio Cotta

CLASSE POLITICA E PARLAMENTO IN ITALIA, 1946–1976

IL GIGANTE DAI PEIDI DI ARGILLA: Il governo di partito e la sua crisi nell'Italia degli anni novanta (*co-editor*)

MANUALE DI SCIENZA POLITICA (*co-author*)

PARLIAMENT AND DEMOCRATIC CONSOLIDATION IN SOUTHERN EUROPE (*co-editor*)

PARTY AND GOVERNMENT (*co-editor*)

PARLIAMENTARY REPRESENTATIVES IN EUROPE 1848–2000: Legislative Recruitment and Careers in Eleven European Countries (*co-editor*)

The Nature of Party Government

A Comparative European Perspective

Edited by

Jean Blondel
Professor of Political Science
European University Institute, Florence,
and University of Siena
Italy

and

Maurizio Cotta
Professor of Political Science
University of Siena
Italy

First published 2000 by
PALGRAVE
Houndmills, Basingstoke, Hampshire RG21 6XS and
175 Fifth Avenue, New York, N. Y. 10010
Companies and representatives throughout the world

PALGRAVE is the new global academic imprint of
St. Martin's Press LLC Scholarly and Reference Division and
Palgrave Publishers Ltd (formerly Macmillan Press Ltd).

ISBN 0–333–68199–1

This book is printed on paper suitable for recycling and
made from fully managed and sustained forest sources.

A catalogue record for this book is available
from the British Library.

Library of Congress Cataloging-in-Publication Data
The nature of party government : a comparative European perspective /
edited by Jean Blondel and Maurizio Cotta.
    p. cm.
Includes bibliographical references and index.
ISBN 0–333–68199–1
    1. Political parties—Europe, Western. 2. Europe, Western—Politics and
government—1989– I. Blondel, Jean, 1929– II. Cotta, Maurizio, 1947–
JN94.A979 N37 2000
320.3'094—dc21
                                                        00–033337

10   9   8   7   6   5   4   3   2   1
09 08 07 06 05 04 03 02 01 00

Printed and bound in Great Britain by
Antony Rowe Ltd, Chippenham, Wiltshire

Contents

List of Figures and Tables

Figures

Table

Preface

Of the relationships which characterise the institutions of Western European democracies, that between governments and the parties which support them is perhaps the most intriguing as well as the least well-known. We may or may not like parties – usually we do not – yet we are convinced that parties should have a large influence in democratic politics. It seems to follow that they should greatly influence the way governments are shaped and take their decisions. Except, however, that we are only half-convinced when we come to this last point, because we also believe that governments should not be the 'prisoners' of parties: we therefore quickly join our voice to the concert of those who attack 'partitocracies' and their cortege of unsavoury camaraderie, favours and corruption.

Such a set of rather contradictory standpoints does not help much, if at all, in a quest for the understanding of what the relationship between parties and governments *is* or of what that relationship *should be*. Contradictions in attitudes about the relationship echo the apparent impossibility of finding an acceptable 'niche' in which both government and parties which support them can comfortably live together. Hence perhaps the huge gap in this field of political science; hence, too, in a more mundane fashion, the fact that this book has taken so long to appear after a first effort was made in a volume entitled *Party and Government*, published in the mid-1990s, which described how the two sets of bodies – parties and governments – seemed to relate to each other, *seriatim* so to speak, in a number of countries, mainly of Western Europe.

This is not a hugely valid excuse to justify the fact that this book has taken so long to emerge: the data had been collected; the will to tackle the problem was there. Yet the problem became increasingly daunting as we came closer to confronting it. Difficulties relating to data seemed to pale and to pale more and more by contrast with the difficulties which the normative and the analytical questions posed. What do we really mean by 'party government'? Is it that the government *should* be dominated by the parties in a democracy? Yet if it should not be *dominated*, what should the mode of influence be? And should not the government also exercise an influence? We knew we had to navigate between two extreme, equally unacceptable solutions: yet only these unacceptable solutions seemed to provide answers which had a minimum of 'substance'. Nor was this normative puzzle the only one: the analytical difficulties posed by the two entities, parties and government, were equally daunting. For what is, indeed, a party? Everyone knows that a party is not (just) a set of men and women bound together to promote a cause and that there are many 'parties' within each single party. If so, which of these 'parties' should be regarded as the 'real' one? Is it the parliamentary party, the party in the constituencies, the broad mass of supporters? Nor is it easier to describe what we mean by governments. Is it just the ministers? Do we include 'aides'? Do we even include civil servants, at any rate top ones?

More than once, the temptation to abandon the 'quest' was great: we did not succumb and we hope we were right. We know that we do not give, by any stretch of imagination, definitive answers: but we hope that this volume will at least trigger theorists – not just empiricists but normative theorists and analytical theorists – to begin to raise what are unquestionably key questions for modern democracies. How should parties behave in relation to governments? How should governments behave in relation to parties? And how can the goal of a satisfactory relationship be achieved?

As the other studies of this series on cabinets and governments, this work would not have finally emerged, even if after much delay, had it not been for the generous support of the European University Institute, the Italian Consiglio Nazionale delle Ricerche (contract no. CNR 97.00650.ct09), the foundation Monte dei Paschi di Siena, the Dutch Science Foundation (NWO) which provided support for a meeting at the University of Leiden, as well as of the research councils of the countries of the contributors to this volume. We wish to thank them most heartily. We must also remember that the data on which this work is based were collected, several years ago, by a number of researchers who studied appointments, patronage practices and a number of detailed policies in the countries on which this book is based: we wish to thank them all, even if belatedly. Whether we have begun to render justice to the magnitude of the problem is not for us to judge: but what we can say is that we have been intrigued by the problem and that one of the main purposes of this volume is to communicate the feeling that there is here an intriguing situation about which much will have to be done before a solution appears.

JEAN BLONDEL
MAURIZIO COTTA

Notes on the Contributors

R. B. Andeweg is Professor of Political Science at the University of Leiden.

J. Blondel is External Professor at the European University Institute in Florence and Visiting Professor at the University of Siena.

M. Cotta is Professor of Political Science at the University of Siena.

A.-P. Frognier is Professor of Political Science at the University of Louvain.

W. C. Müller is Professor of Political Science at the University of Vienna.

J. Nousiainen is Emeritus Professor of Political Science at the University of Turku.

1
Introduction

J. Blondel

This work examines the relationship between governments and the parties which support these governments, a relationship which has been summarised by the expression 'party government'. It focuses on eight Western European countries for which detailed empirical data have been collected, Britain, France, Germany, Italy, Belgium, the Netherlands, Austria and Finland. But the purpose of the study goes beyond these countries: it is to begin to answer questions about what is the nature of party government by using the reflections which the analysis of these eight Western European countries suggests. There are many reasons why a reflection on party government needs to be undertaken: they all stem from the fact that party government, surprisingly perhaps, has been grossly understudied and therefore remains nebulous if not wholly obscure as a concept.

A first examination was undertaken in a previous volume, *Party and Government* (Blondel and Cotta, 1996) which analysed on a country-by-country basis the same eight Western European polities as well as the United States and India. The empirical data which form the basis of the present study are broadly similar, but the analysis here is cross-national, which makes it possible to draw conclusions, albeit tentative, about current trends in the nature of party government in Western Europe, conclusions which could not be reached on the basis of the country-by-country approach adopted in the earlier work.

Moreover, alongside the empirical analysis of party government, common to this and the previous volume, the present study also explores a number of theoretical ramifications, as party government raises general questions about the scope to be given to its two components as well as about the normative implications of the concept. Perhaps one of the most surprising aspects of this sub-field of political science is the fact that, except for very few authors and, above all, except for one in particular, R.S. Katz, the notion of party government seems to have been regarded by those who have written about it as so simple, so obvious, that its true meaning did not appear to deserve to be closely investigated. The truth is the opposite: the concept is of great complexity, a complexity which stems from the fact that it attempts to 'marry' two components which are also highly complex, are organised on the basis of different principles and pursue different aims. Thus the link between party and government is often contrived; it may even be regarded as being somewhat artificial; but the reasons for the artificiality of this link have not been explored and have even been almost entirely ignored. This may account for the fact that, in many and perhaps the majority of cases, the 'marriage' has been unhappy and even acrimonious.

To understand a little better why what is inherently a highly complex relationship has been considered to be straightforward, it is necessary to go back a little into the way in which the concept has come to be used since the nineteenth century to describe the characteristics of parliamentary systems: the first section of this chapter will be devoted to this historical detour. This will make it easier to discover why the notion of party government raises difficulties at three levels, normative, analytical and empirical, and to begin to survey in the second section following the nature and extent of these difficulties.

The concept of party government in historical perspective

As one examines how the concept of party government began to be used to describe political life in parliamentary systems, the first surprise comes from the marked discrepancy between the part played by parties since the early nineteenth century in and around government, and the limited importance, not to say almost total lack of concern, displayed by observers of political life, both at the time and much later, about the *way* these parties related to the governments with which they were associated. On both sides of the Atlantic, from rather early in the nineteenth century and at any rate in several countries from the 1830s and 1840s, parties came to play a major part: yet there was no apparent realisation that the idea of party government was likely to cover many different situations. The notion that there was 'party government' was therefore not discussed as such in the nineteenth century: even after the Second World War, the concept continued to be regarded as rather unproblematic for several decades. Rose's *The Problem of Party Government*, published in 1974, was probably the first work which used the expression in the title of a book: yet the emphasis was not in this work on the problems posed by the concept: the title is therefore somewhat misleading. The first time that the concept began to be examined more systematically was in the studies directed by Wildenmann and others in the 1980s: but, although the first of these works, entitled *Visions and Realities of Party Government* states that 'we shall here have something to say about the historical development of the party government form of democratic organisation...', almost nothing at all is mentioned on that point subsequently in the chapter (Castles and Wildenmann, 1986, 4–5).

The discrepancy, indeed the dissonance, between the part played by parties in government and the lack of analysis of that part is intriguing as a phenomenon of the history of ideas. This is especially so if one contrasts the dearth of analyses in this respect with the huge literature on such topics as presidential and parliamentary systems, cabinet government or the separation of powers from the eighteenth century, while, at least from the end of the nineteenth century, studies of party organisation and party development began to emerge in earnest. This lack of interest in party government thus did not form part of a general lack of interest in the structure of governments; by the turn of the century at least, the role of parties in modern societies and especially in democratic societies had come to be analysed. What there was was a kind of blind spot about the links between governments and the supporting parties.

This discrepancy or dissonance is not only interesting to analyse from the point of view of the history of ideas. It also needs to be examined as it can provide a key to the way in which observers of politics, including political theorists, have tended to regard the role of parties in society in general and in government in particular. By not mentioning, let alone discussing, the role of parties in government, political theorists were indeed making a 'statement'; if we analyse this 'statement' more closely, we may understand better some of the problems posed by the relationship between parties and government.

To begin examining the nature of this 'statement' about parties and governments and in particular about party government, we must first briefly examine the part parties did indeed come to play in Western government from the early decades of the nineteenth century; we then need to examine what was said about 'parties and governments' and about 'party government' throughout the nineteenth and twentieth centuries; this will suggest some of the reasons for the discrepancy between the fact of 'party government' and the observations made of this fact.

Parties and governments: emergence and development

From the early part of the nineteenth century, the part played by parties in government came to be rather large in a number of countries. This was first and foremost the case in the United States, where, as Bryce points out, 'the great moving forces are the parties'; the author then points out that: '[i]n the United States, the history of party begins with the Constitutional Convention of 1787 in Philadelphia' (Bryce, 1891, I, 5). Clearly, with Andrew Jackson, elected President in 1828, parties had become a key feature in American politics and in particular in American *government*: the 'spoils system' is manifestly a key element of the role of parties in government.

At about the same time, parties were beginning to become important in parts of Europe and in particular in Britain. Mackintosh, for instance, sees elements of party government in the 1830s: although he states that after the 1832 Reform Act, 'few liked to be termed "party men"' and '[p]arties were thus loose entities', he adds in the same sentence that parties 'grew up around Cabinets rather than [be] well-defined organisations which could produce them' (Mackintosh, 1962, 72). It is difficult to imagine a clearer way of saying that parties and governments were already closely connected to each other in Britain in the 1830s. Moreover, while Britain was 'in advance' over other European countries at the time, parties were already beginning to play a part in the governmental life of several of them, France and Belgium in particular. To say that France had 'party government' in the 1830s would of course be an exaggeration, given the part played by civil servants in supporting the governments of King Louis-Philippe and given what was to happen in the country in the 1850s and 1860s: but party was there and historians have repeatedly pointed out the role of 'legitimists', 'orleanists', and 'republicans' in political life at the time, while, in Belgium, conservatives and liberals were key forces in the development of the country.

The role of parties is also noted by historians in other countries, if not from the 1830s, at least from the second half of the nineteenth century. Clearly, by the 1890s, parties had therefore come to have a key role in the life and even composition of governments of many Western European countries; this role even seemed to be extending gradually to those empires which had managed to maintain monarchical rule longer. In Britain, from the time of the Second Reform Act of 1867, 'party government' had become a feature of the executive: the battles led by Disraeli and Gladstone which took place from the late 1860s therefore had a similar 'party' character as the 'party' battles which were to be led by

Churchill and Attlee in the 1940s and 1950s and similar contests later on. While it is therefore important to determine the moment at which governments and parties became intrinsically (and one would add indissolubly) linked in the case of each European country, the reality of party government, in some countries at least, dates back from early in the second half of the nineteenth century.

The lack of analysis of the characteristics of party government

Yet there was at the time little or no interest in observing the nature of these developments. The theory of government continued to be based on eighteenth-century concepts drawn from Locke and Montesquieu and 'modernised', so to speak, by Burke and the authors of *The Federalist Papers* (Hamilton *et al.* 1911). Burke was the great protagonist of the idea of independence of Members of Parliament, an independence which was indeed restricted in the 1770s given that most British MPs were in effect controlled by members of the aristocracy, as Namier (1957) pointed out: but the government did not then (yet) depend on parties. Similarly, nearly two decades later, in Letter X of *The Federalist*, the 'dangers' of 'faction' were being stressed and it was argued that only a federal arrangement could limit the effect of these dangers (Hamilton *et al.*, 1911, Letter X).

This way of looking at government was probably justified at the beginning of the nineteenth century. That they should have been in vogue then is not surprising; nor is it surprising that, therefore, the main debate should have continued to be about the relative powers of executive and legislature. What is more surprising is that the debates should still have been along the same lines decades later; it is indeed particularly surprising that Mill and Bagehot, whose *Representative Government* and *English Constitution* were published in 1861 and 1865 respectively, should scarcely mention party in the context of government. Mill states almost as an aside that the prime minister is appointed by parliament and that that person 'is the candidate of the party whose general policy commands its [parliament's] support' (Mill, 1957, 234). The case of Bagehot is perhaps even more surprising, since that author's object was to examine how the constitution actually worked: yet, as Crossman states in his 1963 Introduction: 'Of the modern party, Bagehot had not even a premonition' (Bagehot, 1963, 39); and he quotes Bagehot who writes: 'At present the member is free...' (Bagehot, 1963, 168).

The first author who did discuss party government at some length was Bryce, especially in his *The American Commonwealth*, published in 1891; but even he does so in a somewhat negative manner, asserting more the

ineffectiveness of government without parties than the specific characteristics of party government. His best description of what party government consists of, according to him, is to be found in his chapter xxv of
part I:

> Party government in France, Italy, and England means that one set of
> men, united, or professing to be united, by holding one set of opin-
> ions, have obtained control of the whole machinery of government,
> and are working it in conformity with those opinions.
>
> (Bryce, 1891, I, 284)

He then contrasts the British case with the situation in America where

> men, no doubt, talk of one party as being 'in power'... But they do so
> because that party enjoys the spoils of office, in which to so many
> politicians the value of power consists.
>
> (*Ibid*).

It is noticeable that, in neither case, Bryce asks himself what exactly
party government did in reality consist of.

Bryce was writing at the same time as Ostrogorski, who wrote the first
(voluminous) work on parties (1903): Ostrogorski was not concerned
with party government, but only with organisation. So was Michels
three decades later (see Michels, 1962 edition). Both exercised considerable influence on thought about parties, including the fact that the
study of party organisation became divorced from the study of parties
in government. In the case of Michels this was perhaps understandable,
since his aim was to look at the way in which socialist parties (who had
not achieved power) were developing. Yet the effect was to draw the
study of parties away from that of government and of the problems
posed by party government.

Meanwhile, two other authors who might have been interested in the
problem of the relationship between party and government did not
address it. Neither Pareto nor Weber seem to have been overly concerned with the problem; Pareto stating that it would be valuable to
see socialists 'coming to power'. As Wildenmann points out, 'Weber's
analysis of the structure of the ruling organisation of the modern state
neglects certain aspects crucial to an understanding of party government, particularly in a contemporary context' (Castles and Wildenmann, 1986, 5). Nor was the notion of party government better
studied in the interwar period, perhaps understandably in view of the

events of that period, or, less understandably, in the early post-Second World War period. Thus, as pointed out earlier, the first work which refers to the matter in its title is that of Rose (1974), yet his *The Problem of Party Government* is scarcely about the problem of party government as such: it is essentially about the problems of British government, as if one could equate the expressions British (or cabinet) government with party government. The author only begins to examine some of the aspects of the problem in a very interesting chapter 15 (Rose, 1974, 371–416), where he examines the 'record' of party government in Britain, looking empirically at the relationship between manifestos and record (Table 15.1, p. 403), thus opening a line of analysis which was be subsequently followed by a variety of scholars (see in particular Budge *et al.*, 1976).[1]

The idea that the notion of party government deserved to be studied thus only emerged late in the development of political science. The contrast between the reality of government and the manner in which observers, during a century at least, looked at this reality is sharp. If, to use Richard Rose's expression (1974), there is a 'problem of party government' there is undoubtedly also a 'problem about the lack of analysis of party government' in the scholarly literature.

Five reasons why the notion of party government was not analysed

The lack of serious analysis of the nature of party government appears to have had a number of causes, somewhat contradictory, over the period of a century or more during which parties came to be gradually involved in the lives of Western European polities. There have been at least five elements in the process. At first there was the idea that the matter was unproblematic; if this was the case, there was indeed no need to explore the concept further. Mill's point, quoted above, seems to suggest that he falls in that category. He states that the prime minister is chosen among the parties and so is the ministry: he has no problems about the precise content of such a statement and he prefers to concentrate on electoral systems and the variety of formulas by which representative government can be brought about. Although Bryce discusses party government at somewhat greater length, he, too, seems to have few problems about the content of the concept. He states categorically that party government does exist in Britain, France and Italy, and might have been led to notice that there were various possible interpretations since he himself points out later in the same paragraph that the American conception of party government was different from the European; but he does not delve into the differences and merely states that these are to be found because cabinet government does not exist in America (Bryce, 1891, I, 285).

While the conclusion may be correct, the nature of the differences remains posed: yet Bryce does not seem to be concerned with this matter.

Meanwhile, especially in Britain, a second reason for not analysing the concept of party government seems to have been due to the fact that parties were at the disposal of the government. This may in turn have resulted from the conditions under which party government did emerge in parliamentary countries and even in America. The remark made by Mackintosh is highly relevant at this point. As noted earlier, this author stated that 'parties were loose entities which grew up around Cabinets rather than well-defined organisations which could produce them' (Mackintosh, 1962, 72). Mackintosh says, in other words, that parties were basically 'dependent' on governments rather than the other way around. Only from the 1870s, with the growth of the caucuses which Ostrogorski was to study, did party organisation become important and the idea of 'party-dependent' government begin to emerge. One can indeed understand that if the party is, in practice, a creature of the government or at least does what the government wants it to do, there is little need to worry about the distinction between party and govern-ment (Ostrogorski, 1891). In effect, the same point could be made about parties as has tended to be made about civil services: they are there to obey! Thus the question of party government is unproblematic because the chain of command starts from the government. As a matter of fact, so long as socialist parties were parties of protest remaining, as in Imperial Germany, outside governmental orbit, there seemed to be no need to modify the interpretation.

One should also remember, third, that parties entered gradually and in some countries very slowly into the lives of European governments. Britain and Sweden had known for a long time a 'political' government, if not always a 'party government' in the strict sense of the word, because the King and Council concerned themselves with the 'conflic-tual' questions of the state; but many continental countries had had essentially 'administrative' or 'bureaucratic' governments, that is to say a hierarchy of public servants charged with the management of 'things' rather than with the solution of conflicts. Party came to surreptitiously infiltrate this bureaucratic structure in some cases, but the fiction was conveniently maintained that the government was the King's or the Emperor's government: the nature of the link between government and supporting parties remained, therefore, to an extent deliberately obscure.

It is at this point in time that a fourth reason comes to play a part, namely that these parties of protest, analysed in particular by Michels,

were viewed as rather 'unpleasant' bodies. They claimed to be democratic and to have a series of virtues: in practice, they were oligarchical.
Michels' (and Ostrogorski's) viewpoints link over time with those made
a century earlier by the Federalist papers and indeed by Rousseau: parties
are bad. In Michels' view, the more organised they are, the worse they
are (Michels, 1962, 342–56). This means that there is no case for being
concerned with such a question as the concept of party government.
Whether Michels would have been prepared to agree that party government would be acceptable if it were to be based on 'party-dependence' is
of course unanswerable. What is clear is that he did not like 'proactive'
parties; it is therefore logical to conclude that, according to him, it
would be a catastrophy if party government were to be based on proactive parties making governments dependent on them.

Fifth, while up to the early part of the twentieth century party government was not analysed because parties were either ignored or disliked,
the converse occurred in the second half of the twentieth century. The
idea developed that party government meant that parties initiated policies and programmes which they then implemented when 'in power'.
There was little discussion as to whether such a model was justified or
feasible: the only discussion which took place was whether parties did
effectively succeed in implementing their policies. It was as if it was
assumed that party government entailed such a one-way direction.

By and large, the literature on the subject implied rather than argued
that there was something wrong in parties 'in power' not implementing
the policies which they had previously outlined: democratic rule
seemed to entail that ideas, initiatives and proposals had to come from
the bottom and therefore that groups and parties should be at the origin
of the process which it was the government's role to apply. Thus, perhaps not surprisingly, the first move made was not to discuss whether
such a view was justified in principle, but whether the reality of party–
government relationships in Western Europe suggested that governments did indeed 'implement' the programmes of the parties which
supported them. This was the original aim of the series of volumes on
'party manifestos' published under the leadership of Budge (Budge *et al.*,
1976).

What remains nonetheless surprising is that the problems posed by
the links between parties and governments were almost never considered to be serious: indeed, it is truly puzzling that there even seemed to
be no awareness that there were problems at all. It is perhaps understandable that those who held biased views against parties should not
have been concerned with the difficulties inherent in the character of

party–government relationships; it is less understandable that, by and large, those who were favourable to parties should not have begun to ponder over these difficulties, difficulties to which we now need to turn.

The difficulties posed by the concept of party government: normative, analytical, and empirical

In the earlier volume *Party and Government* (Blondel and Cotta, 1996) an attempt was made to begin to examine the complexity of the relationship between governments and supporting parties by describing the dimensions of party–government relationships and the planes on which these take place: we shall refer to these dimensions and planes briefly at the end of this chapter and more systematically in Chapter 5. Yet the questions posed by party government go beyond a mere determination of the empirical parameters which help to analyse the characteristics of party–government relationships. The determination of these parameters touches some of the empirical difficulties of the concept only; there are two further types of problems, normative and analytical, which are at least as difficult to identify.

The normative problems posed by the concept of party government

These normative problems stem from the fact that party government may well constitute an ideal democratic arrangement, but that this arrangement may also be highly unrealistic. For it may be impossible to reconcile the purpose of parties – to ensure representation and majority rule – with the purpose of government – to provide leadership in the 'general interest' of the nation.

The problems posed by the contrast between majority rule and the 'general interest' have been studied from many points of view, but these studies have not been extended to an examination of the very difficult choices governments have to make in the context of a party–government arrangement. The 'anti-party' line according to which party benefits should be set aside when the public interest is involved is clearly not a solution. Nor is it a solution to refer to a strict concept of the 'mandate' on the basis of which, in Britain for instance, the victorious party is held to have the right to implement its programme. Even if we leave aside the empirical flaws of the notion of 'mandate', flaws which are serious since most electors are known not to have pondered on party programmes before making up their minds on how to vote, the concept, if strictly adopted, constitutes a highly unsatisfactory answer to the question which every government member has to answer each time he or she is about to take a decision 'in the public interest'. Ministers have to decide what relative weight they must give, on the one hand, to what is often a rather vague programme, always elaborated at an earlier period; and, on the other, to the suggestions made, largely under new circumstances, by those who may not have supported the party programme at the time of the election. These ministers thus have difficult practical and ethical choices to make from the moment they attempt to treat fairly both their party and the 'general public': yet no guideline is given by normative theory in this respect, except the blanket but not very helpful statement that 'the public interest' has to be put first. It is because of this difficulty of the 'strict' conception of the mandate that, as we shall see in Chapter 2, the notion of an 'outline' mandate has been put forward as a solution.

At least there has been some discussion of the notion of mandate and of the problems it poses, even if what is being said is only at most tangential to the concrete ethical questions which government members have to face, as we shall see in greater detail in Chapter 2. On the other hand, there is an almost total blank with respect to the even more serious underlying issue, namely whether what should prevail in party government relationships is the *representative* element or the *leadership* element, a distinction which is paralleled by the further distinction between the 'party' base and the 'administrative' base of government. Admittedly, Burke (1770) gives his own blanket answer to this question by stating that he did not consider himself bound in any way by the views of his constituents. While his answer relates to the relationship between electors (that is, the representative element) and the MP (in this case the leadership element), it could be transposed without modification to the relationship between party and government. Burke's blanket response is as unhelpful as is the answer which suggests that 'the public interest' should always be put above the 'party interest': not only is such an answer untenable in practice in modern liberal democracies, it is also not tenable in theory as it does not provide any room for compromise between the two 'sides' and therefore for a genuine link between party and government.

The question of the nature of the link is a key issue: indeed it is *the* key normative issue raised by party government. It is in order to provide such a link that party government exists: with party 'representatives' in the government, the hope is that the government will achieve the desires of those whom it 'represents'. A hope of this kind can become reality, however, only if the government either embarks voluntarily on the same policies as the supporting parties, or is forced to do so. If it *wants* to embark on those policies, the relationship between government and party is indeed highly felicitous; if the government is *forced* to embark on policies it is not keen to pursue, that relationship is obviously difficult and it is improbable that the arrangement will last long. Yet it is equally improbable that the government should always naturally be prepared to do all that the party wants it to achieve and only that. As a matter of fact, if this does occur serious questions will tend to be asked both as to whether the government truly has a mind of its own, and whether, on the other hand, that government is not surreptitiously putting pressure on the party to obtain approval for policies which the party may not have originally wanted.

The fundamental reason for the difficulty stems from the fact that the government cannot be regarded merely as an 'agent' with the party being its 'principal'. At a minimum, what needs to be said is that governments have never been and indeed cannot be merely subservient to the supporting parties. Since the government has to turn party positions into public decisions, it has to show a high level of technical competence and great political skill, that is to say of leadership: the government cannot in reality be expected to display these qualities if it is merely acting as 'agent' of the party. Moreover, the government is also concerned with a host of 'administrative' problems which it has to face and indeed solve. There has therefore to be some leeway, perhaps a lot of leeway between party and government to allow government members to be recognised by citizens as being the leaders of their country while retaining a link with the party to which they belong.

The link between party and government has thus to provide a relationship between the two 'sides' but also substantial freedom for the government if there is to be a satisfactory development of party–government arrangements. There is obviously no easy solution to the problem. The various forms of party government which have existed in Western Europe and elsewhere have all groped, to a large extent in the dark, for a solution which manages to maintain an equilibrium between the formal influence of the party and its freedom of movement. There is no greater likelihood that there will be a 'magic formula' with respect to party–government relationships than there is with respect to the relationship between government and legislature in either the separation-of-powers system or in the parliamentary system, but on these matters at least lawyers, political scientists and indeed political philosophers have made suggestions and proposed lines of conduct: no such development has taken place to provide guidance in the relationship between governments and supporting parties. Yet, in the absence of such guidance, these relationships are more likely to remain in a kind of Hobbesian 'state of nature' and be marked by 'coups' and 'counter-coups' than by an orderly behaviour based on the mutual recognition of a distinction between the domains of one 'side' or the other.

The analytical difficulties of the concept of party government

Assuming that political philosophy might discover in what way representation and leadership can best be optimised, questions remain to be answered about the precise scope to be given to the two components of the relationship between party and government. An analysis of party government implies that these components be distinguished both from each other and from the societal environment which they have to steer and regulate: yet these distinctions are not easy to draw, as Chapters 3 and 4 will show in greater detail.

First, the boundary between *party* and society is rather vague: successful parties have profound roots in society; indeed parties have a political significance only if at least a substantial proportion of society belongs to these parties and, at a minimum, votes for them; this is especially the case in the context of party government, since the parties which are relevant in this context are those which obtain substantial proportions of the popular vote, some of which even succeed in being supported by a majority or a near-majority. Yet, for the expression 'party government' to be operative, the meaning of party must be narrow. A line has to be drawn to distinguish the party from its societal base: the stress is then placed primarily on formal organs of the party and not on the party as a broad socio-political cleavage. However, even if they are viewed only as organisations, parties remain large bodies with many decision-making levels, local, regional and national: some of these levels may not be truly relevant in the context of party government, but they cannot be wholly ignored. Hence the view that it is wholly unrealistic to consider parties as single actors, although it is also unrealistic to treat their various segments as if they were independent units. In some cases this may be so, for instance if 'factions' operate as if they were parties in their own right; but this is unusual, even among parties which are highly divided internally.

Second, the problems posed by the nature of the *government* are at least as complex, not surprisingly given the fact that the government has a 'bureaucratic' or 'administrative' origin as well as, primarily since the nineteenth century in liberal countries, a 'representative' character. In the context of party government, there are thus three possible interpretations of what a government constitutes. There is, first, a highly restrictive definition, as mostly used in common parlance. The government is then regarded as being composed exclusively of a very small group of top public decision-makers holding the offices of prime minister and ministers, but including also the immediate subordinates of the ministers. If this view is adopted, there is *ipso facto* a vast difference in size between the two components of party government, which necessarily leads to a large difference in the nature of the two bodies as well. While parties are pyramidal bodies with tens of thousands, perhaps hundreds of thousands of members who belong, typically on a geographical basis, to numerous branches or sections, above which there are various echelons culminating at the top of the pyramid with a small executive, governments are tightly-knit bodies whose members know each other well, especially in parliamentary systems. Whatever hierarchical structure there is is compensated in part by many informal ties built in the course of a long history of close associations. If party government is to be viewed as linking the two 'sides' on the basis of such a restricted interpretation of the idea of government, there will be a great imbalance between the two components. The imbalance is such that the temptation will be great to take only the top decision-making organs of parties into account, on the grounds that these are the ones likely to have a regular relationship with the members of the government and therefore to be in a position to discuss with them on a relatively equal basis the development of policy-making.

Such an interpretation is not realistic, however, even from the point of view of the government, not just because the government has a bureaucratic origin, but because, currently, it owes its strength in the country and *vis-à-vis* the supporting party(ies) both to the fact that its members occupy a number of prestigious positions and that it is supported by a very large machine without which it would truly be 'naked'! Thus party–government relationships refer in practice to relationships between the supporting parties and a combination of government and public bureaucracy, or at least of those sections of the public bureaucracy which belong to the 'central' apparatus of the state. In this second interpretation of party government, the government does not just include the men and women who are ministers or who directly assist the ministers, but also the bureaucratic network 'below' this group: it would therefore be more realistic to view the relationship as being between party and bureaucracy rather than as being between party and government.

Indeed, the true parallel of the party is the bureaucracy. While the party emanates from society and is deemed to represent society, the 'government', that is to say in this second interpretation the government including the bureaucracy, has to be viewed as emanating from the 'state' and being its expression, if not *stricto sensu* its 'representation'. Such a view corresponds to the historical evolution which led to the emergence of party government. There had been for decades, even for centuries in some cases, state officials under the ministers: 'bureaucratic government' developed in this way. Subsequently, the introduction of the representative principle led to the setting up of legislatures. Two parallel structures corresponding to two different legitimacies therefore came to coexist, a representative structure emanating from society as a whole, with parties capturing the legislature, and a bureaucratic structure with permanent officials expected to act on behalf of the 'permanent interests' of the state. These two structures naturally had to be linked, and one form which the linkage took was that of party government – the 'government' in the restricted sense constituting the link. In this interpretation, the expression party government would thus be in a sense a misnomer, or it should at least be described as 'a set of party–bureaucracy arrangements or a combined partisan and administrative structure presided over by a government'.

This second interpretation results in a more balanced relationship between the two components: the bureaucracy parallels the party and both sides are large pyramids which end up with few people at the top. Yet, while this description is apparently more realistic at one level, it is still not entirely satisfactory because it is just not the case that the government can be regarded as a kind of arbiter sitting above party and bureaucracy. The 'government' in the narrow sense does proceed, in most cases at least, from the party or parties which are about to support it. Admittedly, some ministers may well come from the bureaucracy, but their appointment has to be 'blessed', so to speak, by the supporting party or parties, while the converse does not take place.

Hence, a third interpretation which takes into account the points just made. On the one hand, the government in the narrow sense can be regarded as a Trojan horse inside the bureaucracy, designed to ensure that the bureaucracy obeys or at least does not act only according to its own wishes; conversely, while the government proceeds from the party and receives its authority from the supporting party or parties, it is also helped by the bureaucracy against this party or these parties as the bureaucracy is the element which gives that government its technical competence and administrative power – the weight, in a nutshell, with which it can if necessary confront the supporting party(ies) and decide that it will undertake policies which may be at considerable variance from what they might wish to see undertaken. Thus, the party infiltrates the bureaucracy by means of the government, but the government can use the bureaucracy (though cynics would say that the bureaucracy can use the government) to limit the influence of the party on public decision-making.

The expression party-government may therefore be the correct one after all, since the government is a key element in the 'game' being played; but this element does have a highly ambiguous character. Given this ambiguity, the relationship between party and government is likely to take many forms. Not only the defining characteristics of the protagonists, supporting party(ies), 'government' and, in the wings, bureaucracy are likely to be diverse, but, and to an extent consequently, the characteristics of the relationship will be viewed differently depending on prevailing ideologies about the nature of the state, about its role, and about the extent to which the government can carve for itself a special position using the state as a prime basis for its strength.

*   *   *

Given what government is, given also what parties are, given the complex questions posed by the contrasts between representation and leadership, between the 'party side' and the 'administrative side' of government and between majority (party) rule and the search for the 'general interest', it is surely right to question the notion that supporting parties are the 'principal' and governments the 'agents'. The answer cannot be so simple.

As a matter of fact, empirical studies show that party government corresponds to a large variety of situations. This is why, as mentioned in our 1996 volume, the nature of party government if it is to be fully assessed needs to be considered in terms of its two dimensions and of the three planes on which it takes place. The two dimensions refer to the extent to which there is autonomy or interdependence between governments and supporting parties and, if there is interdependence, to the extent to which the government tends to be dependent on the supporting parties or the supporting parties dependent on the government. The three planes of the analysis concern the fact that governments and supporting parties relate to each other in different ways with respect to appointments, to policies and, as was argued in the 1996 volume, to the distribution of patronage. If we add these empirical aspects of the analysis to the normative, analytical and empirical problems posed by the assessment of what constitutes party government, it follows that the investigation of the topic, far from being straightforward, is both difficult and intriguing. The present study starts, therefore, from the hypothesis that in party government the relationship between the two sides is bound to be complex, indeed also varied, and that these variations are not just to be expected but are the consequence of the very nature of the concept. The general analysis of the problems posed by party government is thus the object of the four chapters which form Part I of this volume. Part II then examines, on the basis of the empirical findings relating to the eight Western European countries which were mentioned earlier, the characteristics of these polities with respect to appointments, patronage, and policy-making: the findings on the three planes are then considered jointly in the final chapter in order to begin to identify what could be the broad characteristics of the link which exists between the three planes of the party–government relationship. The conclusions of Part II are inevitably tentative: they are concerned with a few countries over a limited period (from the mid-1970s to the early 1990s). As we noted, difficulties of measurement are substantial and difficulties are even greater when one attempts to combine the findings relating to the three planes of the relationship. Given the fact that very little work, either theoretical or empirical, has taken place in the field so far, the present study therefore has to be viewed principally as endeavouring to map out the characteristics of the problems which have to be overcome, while indicating the broad lines along which party–government relationships have developed in contemporary Western Europe.

Note

1 See also the other works written or edited by Budge and his collaborators in the bibliography.

Part I

2
The Normative Foundations of Party Government

A.-P. Frognier[1]

Party government and the return to the principle of concentration of powers

The emergence of party government in democracies had the effect of enabling parties to exert their influence over both the executive and the legislature, as well as, occasionally at least, over the judiciary. Thus, two or even all three of the powers which, on the basis of the principle of the separation of powers, should remain distinct, came to be united. This evolution has occurred in contemporary parliamentary polities, but no similar trend has taken place in the United States: the parliamentary system ensures that the same majority rules in both parliament and cabinet, whereas the direct election of the US President makes it possible for different majorities to control the executive and the legislature.[2]

Should one therefore refer, in relation to contemporary parliamentary democracies, to a 'return' to the concentration of power which characterised absolutist regimes, as was the case when in most Western European countries monarchs took over the prerogatives of the parliaments of the Middle Ages? All power was then concentrated in one of the organs of government. Both the notion of representation which parliaments embodied and that of leadership which was the function of the monarch were in the same hands; the distinction between legislative and executive action disappeared.

The French Revolution stopped this development. It dissociated representation from leadership and strongly emphasised the predominance of the legislature over the executive. The former was regarded as expressing the will of the Nation (and, later, the will of the People), while the executive was described in negative terms: it should not legislate, as it did in absolute monarchies. The details of the arrangement were not considered important. Mill, for instance, strongly believed that the people should be able to grant its consent to laws, whereas anyone could elaborate and formulate these laws. He even thought that it would be bad for parliament to take part in the elaboration of legislation, because it would distract that body from its fundamental task which was to adopt or reject bills: the preparation and the implementation of these bills could be left to non-representative individuals (Manin, 1995, 244–5). This view of extreme separation of powers had some impact, mainly in France, but under the influence of the French Revolution the principle had come to be adopted in many countries.

This was to be for a transitional period only, however. Whatever the principles, the need to ensure a smooth functioning of the system led to a gradual return to the concentration of power in one organ as a result of the development of political parties and of cabinets. This concentration benefitted the party-based executive which 'confiscated' most of the legislative power for itself. Parties and cabinets came to be associated to each other, either by being wholly 'fused' in British-type two-party systems where the cabinet and the party leadership which holds the majority in parliament are one and the same, or close to each other in multiparty coalition systems in which the cabinet is under the control of the leadership of the government parties. In both cases, the importance of parliament became secondary. This led to the rise of 'partitocracies' in some countries, Italy or Belgium for instance: yet party government is not intrinsically undemocratic as long as two key conditions are met, namely that elections are free and the rights of the opposition are respected (Ferrero, 1988, 288).

While such an evolution was taking place, almost nothing was said on the subject by normative political theorists; almost nothing was said either on the way executives operated in practice. This was due mainly to three reasons. First, according to Ranney (1962), who largely followed Schattschneider (1942) on this point, the lack of interest in the way executives functioned and as a result in the way party government operated stemmed from the fact that the 'classics' were mostly concerned to identify the rights of the people, but devoted little attention to the way in which these rights could be implemented.

Second, where a discrepancy exists between the proclaimed norms and the reality, there can be a variety of reactions. There may be a move to modify the norms; but there may also be a tendency to deny that there is any such discrepancy. In the particular case of party government, the (symbolic) cost of modifying the norms would probably have been too high: the formal structures and the political values which predated the party-based type of representative democracy continued to hold, despite the fact that the key part played by parties had long been recognised, whether by those who (for example Schmitt) viewed such a development as a sign of decay of the political system or by those who, as Kelsen, argued on the contrary that parties were one of the prerequisites of democracy (Schmitt, 1988).

The third reason relates to the negative way in which parties are perceived, a point which has been touched upon in the previous chapter. This negative approach to parties has more often resulted in critical attitudes than in efforts designed to discover new norms which might correspond better to the fact that parties exist. According to Daalder (1992), four main types of criticisms have been directed against parties over more than a century. A first has consisted in rejecting parties altogether, either because of the traditional belief that they threaten the political order or because of the liberal and individualistic belief that parties limit the freedom of individuals. A second criticism consists in regarding parties and in particular mass parties as ideologically-based oligarchical machines. According to a third, the party systems which deviate appreciably from the British model should be rejected. According to a fourth, parties have become less crucial in societies in which other actors can play a part, for instance in the context of neo-corporatist arrangements or in new social movements. One could further add the many criticisms levelled against parties and against parliamentarism between the two world wars on the grounds that liberal democracies were unable to maintain peace or prevent the coming to power of authoritarian and even totalitarian single-party systems in fascist and communist countries.

Yet party government has survived and even triumphed. Moreover, in spite of the criticisms levelled against it and the obstacles which it encountered, it did reestablish the old political formula according to which all powers are concentrated in one organ. A number of questions therefore arise: Why did this occur? How did this occur? What problems have to be solved? What are the normative principles on the basis of which party government operates?

Party government as a solution of the problem of governance: representation without leadership

The question of the distinction between representation and leadership is crucial for political systems because it is linked to a further matter, namely the extent to which the legitimacy of political action depends on the representative character of the decision-making process. The people will more readily accept decisions, including harsh ones, if they are taken in their name and according to principles in which they believe: the legitimacy of political authorities is therefore closely associated to the extent to which these are representative.

Yet, in a complex society, political power is shared by a host of different bodies of which the most important are undoubtedly the legislature and the executive – that is, the organ which, in theory, determines policy guidelines and which takes concrete decisions. For a political system to function satisfactorily, these bodies have to be both representative and legitimate, but this result may be obtained on the basis of different arrangements. The legislature and the executive may both be legitimate, a point which relates to a finding of Almond and Verba (1963) in *The Civic Culture*: the more the participatory and the 'subject' culture are in equilibrium, that is to say the more the input and output functions of the political system are implemented concurrently, the better the functioning of society. Where there is no such equilibrium, the same body has to be both representative and legitimate: thus a charismatic leader may compensate for a weak and/or unpopular legislature, a situation which is the exact opposite of what the French revolutionaries attempted to do, since they wanted to locate the source of all legitimacy in the legislature and take it away from the executive. However, there are doubts as to whether that scheme was sensible. A powerful and popular legislature will never be able to govern: it tends to suggest alternative modes of actions; and it faces conflicts which it cannot settle internally. This leads to blockages which affect the legitimacy of the political system. Hence a power structure in which leadership is given little importance is an unbalanced power structure and runs the risk of resulting in a deficit of both representation and of legitimacy.

Gauchet (1995) expresses clearly the need for a global vision of representation which is not restricted to representation through a legislative body:

> The stabilization of representative regimes has indeed, at one of its main points, passed through the rise and the predominance of the executive. This phenomenon still needs to be reflected on. To elaborate a theory of democracy today means to explain in what respect the body which decides and acts is intrinsically as 'representative' as, if not even more 'representative' than the body which expresses the general will by means of the 'production' of laws. One should explain even more why this is the case when one notes the personified

character of the executive organ, a state of affairs which is most shocking as it contrasts sharply with the point that the law should be depersonalised, anonymous, and general, a point which has been so celebrated by revolutionaries for its liberating value. Why does the power vacuum, which results from the fact that it is delegated to another body, entails nonetheless that it be identified with an individual? These are the mysteries which, if one tackles them, clearly demonstrate how little we know what 'representation' really is.

(pp. 15–16)

Party government gives an answer to this question. It makes it possible to reconcile in an original manner the two requirements of representation and leadership, at least up to a certain point. In short, it links the representation of the general will – obtained by means of representatives of the people elected on the basis of programmes – to effective non-dictatorial leadership (that is, one in which there can be peaceful alternation in office) obtained by means of the accession to power of a team which will lead the country as long as it enjoys a parliamentary majority. According to Ranney (1962, 12–14), party government is the only system in which the democratic principle is operationalised in three different ways. First, parties simplify the choices to be made and, for this reason, it is better that there should be two only. Second, parties are able to mobilise the electorate, which might be apathetic otherwise. Third, the control of government by the people can be achieved through the parties: in this way the group in power is rendered collectively responsible.

This is true only up to a point, however. Indeed, the two requirements of representation and leadership, although they are both necessary, are also opposed to each other to an extent in a representative democracy. First, representation is typically linked to particular interests and is geographical as well as social, at least when elections are held on a constituency basis. As a result, decisions are not likely to be optimal for the whole society. To solve this problem, liberal constitutions have maintained the fiction that MPs are deemed to represent the whole population, except in some federal systems. Second, the executive aims at maintaining the loyalty of its majority and/or at ensuring its reelection. Thus, because of the difficult coexistence of the two principles of representation and leadership, party government limits its own room for manoeuvre; but accurate and permanent representation is also hard to achieve, because representatives have to govern and make choices which will lead to sacrifices among some segments of the population. Hence, party government provides a solution to the problem of the relationship between the two elements, but at the cost of some limitations.

To be effective, party government requires a degree of consensus within society – a sufficiently developed civic culture in order that the particularistic interests do not too often predominate over the common good and in order that pluralism and the rights of the opposition be respected. This means that, in particular, the maintenance of a given team in power should not be considered as a matter of life or death by the members of that team. Such an equilibrium between the functions of the legislature and of the executive is better achieved in a presidential system in which the head of government is also elected and thus becomes a representative in his or her own right; in such a case, however, the relationship between executive and legislature is likely to be more conflictual than in parliamentary systems, unless these conflicts are reduced as a result of the existence of a 'civic culture'.

How political representation is achieved in the context of party government: the 'outline mandate'

Party government fulfils the representative function by means of both programme and team, the task of the team being to implement this programme within the framework of democratic rules, including elections, the peaceful alternation of power and the respect of the rights of the opposition. The true nature of these representative arrangements can only be understood if programme and team are seen as being linked. Party government cannot be defined by programme alone, although the idea of a programme is also specific to party government. To concentrate exclusively on the programme would be making the same mistake as that which liberal thinkers made with respect to democratic systems: they considered the collective will only and not the individuals whose task it is to implement that will. Programmes are presented by individuals at elections; they are also applied by individuals, who have some room for manoeuvre to implement and sometimes modify those programmes. In the party representation model, trust with respect to programmes and trust with respect to teams cannot be dissociated, even if the mix is different: thus programmes are more important in a mass party context than in a 'cadre' party context and individuals are more important in the latter situation than in the former.

The parliamentary history of Great Britain shows how the link between programme and individuals slowly emerged and how the two elements could no longer be separated. There were divisions in British parliament before the eighteenth century: these were constituted by 'factions' consisting mainly of 'connections' of a local and family character. Whigs and Tories were more ideological, but with great plasticity and much movement of individuals from one to the other, this plasticity and the key part played by personal interests making it difficult for modern analysts to grasp the way parliament operated at the time. Something closer to a modern idea of a political party emerged when the King's government began to have to 'manage' majorities on important occasions: such a 'management' of the majority, which is described in great detail by Namier (1965) in the context of the role of the Duke of Newcastle, consisted basically in offering advantages to those one wanted to rally round. According to Jennings (1961, ch. 1), political considerations were secondary. The links between party and executive had already by then become tight: to define these links, Namier refers to a 'non-Euclidean' conception of politics (Namier, 1965, x).

For Jennings (1961), Burke was the first to elaborate the doctrine of party government. He did so in 1770 on the basis of the idea that politics must be practised according to principles which bring the population together. Hence, a party becomes a gathering of individuals who share the same principles. He stated that a party is 'a body of men united for promoting by their joint endeavours the national interest upon some particular *principle* in which they are all agreed' (our italics). It is therefore normal that politics should become a struggle between parties whose leaders try to place their friends in public positions. Burke's only error was that he thought he was describing politics at the time of Queen Anne, while party alignments were in fact still unclear at the time.

Jennings places the threshold of party government in 1783, when a vote of censure in parliament brought down the King's government. At that moment,

> these were no longer party connections; they were parties based on principles. The principle of the Whigs was that the personal power of the King...had increased, was increasing, and ought to be diminished.
>
> (Jennings, 1961, 49)

In 1790, the conflict between Pitt and Fox was also based on principles: '...Pitt and Fox were party leaders to whom loyalty was due, not manipulators of aristocratic connections' (*ibid.*). As it became a 'matter of principles', the party has gone over to parliament's side and it was no longer the instrument of the royal executive. Furthermore, the party's strength was increased by the weight acquired by its leader, who automatically became the prime ministerial candidate.

This wholly parliamentary phase of party power was to be short-lived, however. The logic of the British system rapidly led the cabinet to control the party throughout the life of a parliament and of a government. The cabinet became the mechanism linking principles to individuals and above all to the party leader, as elections clearly indicated both which programme was to be that of the government and who would form the government.

In England as elsewhere, the extension of the franchise made parties even more crucial: they became 'mass parties' and their principles were adopted on a mass basis. Parties were indeed the only groups able to manage large numbers of members. As the electorate becomes very large, voting decisions cannot be primarily guided by personal relations: they have to be based on organisations built around general messages. Programmes therefore began to be essential. Furthermore, parties came to develop internal procedures to elaborate these programmes and to present them to the members. Yet the dimension of personalities did not disappear, as votes are also cast for individuals, but these individuals tended to be regarded less in terms of what they are in themselves rather than as the mouthpieces of the party programme. Constituency influence also declined, an evolution which may ultimately result in the whole country becoming one large constituency.

Obviously, the greater the likelihood that the party programme becomes the governmental programme, the more what is said in the programme is important: this is what occurs in British-type two-party systems. Conversely, in multiparty systems where coalitions prevail, party programmes are less central in so far as compromises must be reached among the parties during the elaboration of the governmental programme. The governmental agreement or 'pact' then becomes the cabinet's main instrument. There is a double programme, so to speak, electoral and governmental, and political action is rendered more complex as a result.

However, party programmes are in a process of change. Analyses of the functioning of parliamentary systems at the end of the twentieth century suggest that individuals have become more influential once again and that power is becoming more personalised. It also seems that party programmes have become more undifferentiated than in the years after the Second World War. This is linked to the increased tendency of voters to move towards the centre of the political spectrum, a development reflected empirically in the decline of polarisation. Party identification also appears to be decreasing as modern techniques of political marketing tend to reduce the importance of the intellectual content of programmes and to increase the role of emotional messages.

If the relative weight of programmes compared to individuals were indeed to diminish, there would be a partial return to a previous state of affairs. Yet some findings appear to contradict this tendency: for example the development of issue-voting, mainly but not exclusively for 'post-materialists' or for those who vote for new parties. Issue-voting is based on concrete preoccupations which are targeted directly at the government and at its policies, a development which would appear to encourage parties to concentrate on more 'concrete' programmes than broadly 'ideological' ones. All these characteristics may not be mutually exclusive. On the one hand, some parts of the population may prefer to base their decision on personalities and on messages of a 'marketing-type'; on the other, other parts (most often younger and more educated) may be more interested in concrete policies. Moreover, as the empirical investigations conducted by the Manifesto Research Group have indeed shown, electoral programmes have an impact on policy-making, even a major impact on the actions of the parties when in power. Programmes are therefore not electoral gimmicks (Budge, Robertson and Hearl, 1987).

The type of representation based on programmes on the one hand, and of individuals on the other, can be defined as characterised by an 'outline-mandate', at some distance from both the 'imperative' mandate, whereby electors choose delegates in the strong sense of the word, and the 'personal' or 'trusteeship' mandate which maximizes the autonomy of the representative. The 'outline mandate' gives those who are elected the right to carry out in parliament and, if they become the government, in the executive, the policies which have been formulated in the programme in broad terms, but also leave the government some room for manoeuvre. Depending on the circumstances, the relative part played by the programme and by the individuals does vary.

Deviations from the 'ideal-type' party government can be identified by reference to the extent to which the mandate which prevails in a given situation is at variation with the characteristics of the 'outline-mandate'. If cabinet leaders have little room for manoeuvre with respect to the party programme, the result is 'immobilism'. Representatives of large mass parties such as socialist parties have often been criticised on this point: they are alleged not to be able to adapt to new circumstances and to respond to new challenges. This suggests a deviation in the direction of the 'delegate' mandate. On the other hand, if leaders are not constrained at all by the programme, or if parts of the programme are inconsistent with each other, power becomes personal and the overall function of representation is not fulfilled adequately: this situation could be referred to as one in which there is deviation towards the 'trusteeship' mandate.

How the programme can help representation

Since the programme constitutes the most specific element of the representative aspect of party government, there are normative implications both in terms of its elaboration and in terms of its implementation.

Representation and programme elaboration

For parties to be able to help the process by which inputs are converted into outputs, the inputs must reflect accurately the demands of the population: only then can political decisions reduce the pressure exerted on the system. The way aggregation is performed is therefore crucial. If the parties, in their programmes, do not accurately reflect the preoccupations of the population, the political process as a whole does suffer. As a matter of fact, many contemporary criticisms of the action of parties concentrate on this point.

The links between parties and population are expressed differently according to the way in which society is structured. In polities in which interest groups are strong, parties primarily tend to aggregate the demands made by organisations which, according to Almond's and Powell's framework (1966), tend to articulate interests. Where interest groups are weak, the strength of the links between party and population depends primarily on the extent to which parties are able to feel the 'pulse of the nation', so to speak. This was achieved in the past by local constituency organisations, which transmitted the views of citizens to national party leadership. Although contemporary parties still have local branches, there are other, ostensibly more 'scientific', means of discovering what citizens want: political marketing emerges at this point.

When groups are relatively weak, attention has to be paid to the 'base', even if, as occurs in many cases, parties are rather centralised. The 'surgeries' of MPs and ministers continue to provide means by which some information is obtained about citizens' desires. For, while political marketing is important, a party is not a survey institute. It not only has to reflect the desires of its electors as it sees them; it also has to be concerned with the future, notably with respect to matters of which the population may not always be aware. Moreover, opinions tend to change when problems cease to be considered in the abstract and become concrete: parties have to take these changes into account. This is why communication within the party is essential, even if active members tend not to be representative of the views of electors and may often be more radical.

In societies in which groups are strong, on the other hand, parties play an effective part if these groups also articulate interests effectively. However, groups may be more concerned with their own interests as organisations than with the needs of the section of the population they are deemed to represent. An even greater danger for party government lies in the fact that political decision-making may be carried out by the groups themselves, as a result of 'neo-corporatist' arrangements, thereby excluding parties from the game, in part, admittedly, as a result of the sheer inefficiency of these parties. Yet 'neo-corporatism' did not develop as widely as some had predicted: parties regained control in the polities in which they once flourished, thereby compensating for the instability which they experienced as a result of greater electoral volatility by a stronger grip on political decisions.

Representation and programme implementation

It seems unnecessary to suggest that party programmes should be implemented; it also seems obvious that implementation should consist in translating the programme into governmental decisions whilst in government, although a programme can also be a platform for the opposition. What this means is that the programme should not be a kind of hopeless dream or merely an electoral plank.

Yet there are manifest problems. First, the government must have enough freedom of manoeuvre to be able to implement the programme; and both internal and external factors can limit this freedom. Since party government is based on the notion that the parties in power control both the legislature and the executive, it follows that these parties not only have to govern, but that they have to retain their majority in parliament and be concerned with the fate of that majority at the next election. Party government cannot therefore be detached from down-to-earth preoccupations. What is now at stake is not the 'management' of the majority in parliament in the way Newcastle did in eighteenth-century Britain, but the 'management' of the majority in the country in order to obtain an electoral result which enables the governing parties to carry on being in power. This leads to the development of patronage activities which can consume a substantial amount of energy and go against the drift of programmatic politics. As a matter of fact, there seems to be an increase in patronage activities in contemporary Europe. The room for manoeuvre of executives is thus bounded by the requirements of electoral politics and by the patronage linked to it.

The room for manoeuvre of the government is also limited by international constraints, a point which is increasingly relevant as the 'globalisation' of the economy and the process of integration have come to severely restrict the scope of decision-making powers of Western European states. To be effective, government parties must not foster policies which they are unable to implement: they should concentrate on the fields in which they have influence and, for instance, develop conditions which will enable the polity to cope with the international situation in which it finds itself.

Implementation is also possible only if there is coherence, both in the programme and in the party itself. Programmes should not contain contradictory proposals: they should not advocate, for instance, a lowering of taxation and promise at the same time to increase social benefits. Admittedly, individuals often hold such contradictory views, and parties might be tempted to do the same, but programmes should not be mere translations of the state of public opinion, they must endeavour on the contrary to create a framework for action.

Programmes can enable parties to be representative only if the parties structure has a number of characteristics. According to Ranney (1962, 16–20), the party organisation and its members must be 'responsible'; it must be relatively united as too much factionalism impedes the implementation of the programme. According to Katz, the party must be prepared to act as a team, whether it wins or loses the election (Castles and Wildenmann, 1986, 40). This has consequences for intra-party democracy, as Schumpeter (1947) pointed out: if a party must be responsible and cohesive, the scope for internal democracy is markedly reduced, as cohesion might be affected otherwise. The party is the main instrument of democracy in the country: yet it cannot itself be democratic. Katz argues, however, that intra-party democracy does not prevent cohesive action from taking place outside the party (Castles and Wildenmann, 1986, p.40), while Budge notes that the parties which have the most democratic structures, the Scandinavian parties, are not examples of anarchy and that parties remain committed to their ideological *raison d'être* (Budge, 1996, 130).

Besides, since programmes have to be implemented, complex problems arise in relation to the circumstances within which this implementation is to occur. A programme is elaborated in a given context and, if the context is modified, it seems to follow that the programme should be modified as well. This raises questions about the idea of rationality in relation to promises: these can be regarded as being likely to be irrational since they are concerned with future action and circumstances are also likely to change, especially if the time span between the promise and the potential implementation is long. This might lead to the conclusion that there is little value in elaborating political programmes at all.

Tentative solutions to this difficulty can be put forward at two levels, however. First, the programme should not be too precise as, then, its validity will not depend so closely on circumstances. This does not mean that the programme should be so general that it becomes meaningless: what is required is that the fundamental principles of the programme be clear. Second, it is preferable that changes in programmes be legitimised through adequate procedures, a satisfactory procedure being one which requires the approval of party members. In Belgium, for instance, in the event of a substantial change of the governmental programme, the leadership of the parties agrees to this change and then submits it to their party congresses. Such a procedure, even if it takes place exclusively within the parties, does have a democratic dimension as the party congresses accepted the programmes in the first place, before they were submitted to the electorate. The fact that this programme was approved by a proportion of electors sufficiently large to allow the party to participate in government confers certain rights and certain responsibilities on to the party members. Admittedly, there could be other means by which to test the views of members and of electors – referendums, for instance – and these might be more democratic, but they would also take more time and be more disruptive.

Similar arrangements can be adopted when governments face new problems. If they are able to find solutions based on the same principles as those proposed in the programme, the difficulty ceases to exist. If that is not the case, however, procedures similar those just mentioned could be adopted within the party.

The limitation of the power of party government: the need to respect party pluralism

There have to be mechanisms preventing party government from abusing its power, given that there is no effective separation of powers which might limit the potentially authoritarian actions of the executive. As Schmitt put it:

The participation of popular representation in government, by means of parliamentary government, has proved to be the means *par excellence* to put an end to the separation of powers and, along with it, to the old idea of parliamentarism. (1988, 63)

Indeed, the simultaneous control of two 'powers' – executive and legislature – in party government, and sometimes of the judiciary as well, at any rate in partitocracies, can enable one or a few parties to entirely control the polity, a situation which is obviously unacceptable if it is not compensated by the respect of party pluralism and in particular by the respect of the rights of the opposition. This is therefore a central requirement where there is party government; there is no other way in which the power of the government party(ies) can be limited.

The idea of respecting party pluralism has a normative origin; but it also has a practical aspect. The idea is normative in the sense that it stems from the values which have been adopted gradually in the West and which include such notions as freedom of speech and freedom of association. In Britain, in particular, respect for the opposition has been linked to the concept of 'fair play' which has prevailed in the relations among political actors (Jennings, 1969, 16). Yet it is also practically useful for the government to respect the rights of the opposition, so long at least as elections are held regularly. By protecting the opposition, a party protects itself against not being given the same rights in any subsequent legislature in which it would be the opposition.

The respect of the principle of pluralism entails that some conditions be fulfilled. First, the opposition must have the means of expressing its views freely: it has indeed been suggested that one of the remaining functions of British parliament is to provide the opposition with a platform, as the status given to the leader of the opposition in the House of Commons emphasises. This role is now one which the mass media are increasingly taking upon themselves: the respect of party pluralism has therefore to extend to the mass media and in particular to television, a condition which, however, is not fully met in many western democracies.

The respect of the opposition also implies a fair electoral system. The artificial creation of majorities by manipulating electoral rules, as has occurred occasionally in France, infringes this requirement. In general, the many obstacles which are built against new parties, such as thresholds or non-proportional formulas, are highly questionable.

Respect for the principle of alternation of parties in power also stems from the same general idea. Yet the movement of electors towards the ideological centre and the increased similarity of programmes reduce the significance of this alternation and consequently the genuine character of party pluralism. As electoral programmes resemble each other more and more, voters are less able to distinguish among the electoral messages, except in relation to new, marginal or anti-systemic parties.

Although the matter is not typically raised in a democratic context, there is also some ground for questioning the ways in which majorities are built in multiparty systems. In such cases, parties which have lost substantially at an election may be able to remain in power if the arithmetical majority in parliament allows them to do so. Meanwhile and conversely, the protection of the opposition also implies that the opposition abide by a general code of conduct: it should not block the workings of parliament in a non-constructive manner, for instance. However, it is nonetheless difficult in practice and can also be politically dangerous to attempt to formulate general rules in this respect.

The difficulties and the future of party government

Parties and party government are not fashionable. Surveys conducted in western countries show that traditional parties are the object of much popular criticism and that confidence has become low. Thus, the Italian partitocracy has been transformed dramatically and that of Belgium experiences serious difficulties with citizens massively protesting against the malfunctioning of the police and of the judiciary, as well as against the shortcomings of the partitocracy itself.

Mair (1995) believes that parties have a vast power within the state – a power which has never been as large – and yet are the object of widespread criticism which has seldom been as strong. He argues that the combination of these two characteristics is dangerous, as parties are in a privileged position but the population no longer finds any justification for such a position: this can only encourage disaffection:

> The disenchantment with parties and even the resentment against parties should therefore not simply be read as a symptom of party decline *per se*; indeed, were parties to be wholly in decline, as public-office holders as well as representative agencies, then the sense of discontent might well evaporate. Rather, the problem appears to lie in a set of contradictory developments, in which parties are at once less able but more visible, less relevant but more privileged.
>
> (Mair, 1995, 55)

Mair's analysis has the merit of not focusing only on the decline of the legitimacy of parties, but on their paradoxical situation: parties are at the same time strong and weak. No solutions to this 'crisis of representation' of parties is being proposed by him, but one may imagine that such solutions could be found by closely examining the representative role of parties and in particular the extent to which they help to formulate demands as well as ensuring that their grip on the state and on society is reduced.

Not all agree with this pessimistic analysis. Budge (1996) is more optimistic and advocates a solution which is based on the view that party government is well-established. His concern is primarily that contemporary representative democracy is not geared to responding to citizens' growing aspirations for more direct forms of participation. The main target of his criticism is therefore parliament: he believes that new communication techniques should increasingly enable citizens to decide on policies – for instance to approve or reject bills from their homes via internet computer terminals. Parties would continue to put forward programmes; and elections would determine the composition of the government, which would remain a party government. Within the framework of its programme, the government would offer opportunities to the population to debate legislative proposals on-line and to adopt or reject them. In such a context, the role of parliament would essentially be to formulate legislative proposals and to discuss the ways in which these could be implemented. Parties would campaign on a regular basis to make a case for their policies each time a legislative proposal was placed on the agenda.

It is rather interesting to see direct democracy proposals of Athenian origin return to the fore, in the context of a party democracy which has replaced classical representative democracy. It is also paradoxical to note such a development since the founding fathers of representative democracy, with the exception of Rousseau, aimed at preventing the development of 'demagogy' and of popular control![3]

Yet the problems of party government remain, and also problematic is the question of the relationship between representation and leadership both at the level of the political system as a whole and, within parties, between the role of programmes and the role of individuals. The solution is to be found somewhere between the extremes in order to ensure that the system be representative and efficient, so that it can be fully legitimate. The 'global representation' which has been advocated by Gauchet (1995) and which includes both legislature and executive can be adequately achieved by means of party government, but only provided the main parties put forward programmes which truly aggregate interests and the leaders of these parties can implement what was described earlier as an 'outline mandate' coherently, that is to say without deviating towards immobilism or towards personal power. Such a solution is perhaps more a hope than a reality, as demands push the decision-makers, in part at least, in different directions. But the regime will tend to be viable if it does not deviate too much from the central position in which the 'outline mandate' can be implemented. If this occurs, it will be possible for the government to govern without being rendered inefficient as a result of having to make too many concessions to its allies and to voters. Without doubt, this is the key challenge which party government has to face.

*   *   *

Party government is flexible: this is its great value. It has indeed survived all the crises of the twentieth century and proved highly adaptable to new circumstances. The question which now arises is whether it will continue to be able to adapt to new social and political situations and, in particular, to increasingly sophisticated electorates asking for more issue-based programmes and better and more direct participation; and whether this can occur without making it more difficult for governments to govern. Above all, what is at stake is whether party government will continue to cope in a context in which there is no general recognition of the true characteristics of this type of rule and of the way it can best be inserted in contemporary political life.

Notes

1 We wish to thank B. Rihoux for the translation of this chapter.
2 'Power is unified', wrote J.L. Sundquist about the parliamentary system (1986, 14).
3 Manin (1995) explains why the Greek system of direct democracy based on the direct participation of citizens in the elaboration of policies, on drawing lots to select the holders of most public offices, and on the rapid rotation of incumbents, is inherently rational. He also shows that, for some aspects, the rejection of direct democracy in the contemporary world is more due to normative than to technical reasons.

3
Party Government, State and Society: Mapping Boundaries and Interrelations

R. B. Andeweg

Two unconnected debates

The idea of party government is to bring together, to unify two different spheres, as argued in chapter 2. Often this unification is incomplete and tensions remain between the two. Even if unification were achieved, it would still be important to know what exactly is unified, and what is not. In other words, the next step in the exploration of the relationship between governments and governing parties is to clarify concepts. In this chapter we shall attempt to distinguish *party* and *government* by relating them to the cognate concepts of *state* and (civil) *society*. In doing so we shall, for the moment, treat these four elements as if they constituted unitary actors: in the next chapter the concepts of party and of government will be examined in more detail and will cease to be viewed as unitary.

As already noted, the question of 'party government' has a strong normative dimension, with (primarily American) advocates of 'responsible party government' on the one hand, and (primarily European) critics of 'partitocrazia' on the other. It has an empirical dimension, with scholars trying to measure the extent of party government and the 'partyness' of governments (Rose, 1974; Castles and Wildenmann, 1986). In the debate 'society' does not feature, other than as 'the electorate'. The 'state' is mentioned more often, but primarily as a set of resources for a party to be captured through its control of the government, or as an outright synonym of government, as when the German 'Parteienstaat' is translated into English as 'party government'.

Elsewhere in the discipline, a debate is going on about 'state vs (civil) society'. The distinction is an old one and it has been rediscovered often both in the academic community and in political discourse, as by key-players in the transition towards parliamentary democracy in Central and Eastern Europe. In this debate the concept of 'government' is virtually absent, but 'party' is mentioned almost as a synonym of the state, as by critics of the communist 'one-party states' before 1989.

Each of these two debates has been pursued by its own community of political scientists, without much contact between them. Although the two debates are clearly distinct, the common use of at least some of the concepts suggests that they are closely interrelated. In fact, both the party/government distinction and the society/state distinction can only be properly understood by combining them. To be able to show why this is so we must first define the four concepts.

The concepts

Unfortunately, the search for generally shared definitions of each of the four concepts has been as long as it has proved fruitless. Dyson (1987), for example, succinctly summarises the most important dimensions that separate more than a hundred definitions of 'state'. The elusiveness of 'government' as a concept is best illustrated by the many attempts – eventually all in vain – to gain precision by the use of different labels: 'cabinet', 'cabinet system', 'central executive territory', and the currently most fashionable 'core executive' (Rhodes and Dunleavy, 1995). In the search for a definition of 'society' there is common ground in that all definitions are negative, but they do differ on the question of what (civil) society is not: the state, the party, the market, the individual (Dekker, 1995).[1]

There are many reasons why state, society, government and party are all originally contested concepts. Prominent among them is that these have not been developed by scholars to be used in empirical research, but that they play an important part in political discourse. Consequently, their meaning is affected by historical connotations that vary across (and even within) countries. A legal system based on Roman law, for example, appears to lead to a different conception of the 'state' than a legal system based on common law, a distinction itself the result of military events of many centuries ago. Experience with a totalitarian one-party state cannot but leave an imprint on the social meaning of the concept of 'party', to give another example. Their role in political discourse also entails that the concepts are rhetorical weapons, and any definition seems to involve an ideological choice: the 'state' as embodiment of the 'volonté generale', or as an instrument of the dominant interests in society, for example.

Another reason for the confusion about definitions is that the concepts are interrelated. It was already difficult to disentangle them completely in the past: yet Berger rightly asserts that today 'there is no longer any conception of a stable division of labor among parties, interest groups, and government' (cited in Koole, 1996, 509). The work on neo-corporatism, iron triangles, policy networks and so on testifies to the blurring of the distinction between state and society, just as discussions on partitocracy indicate that the lines between party and government are difficult to draw.

Political scientists have reacted in various ways to this lack of conceptual clarity and precision. One strategy has been to replace the concepts that play a part in political discourse with new, 'scientific', terms. An example is Dahl's (1971) replacement of another contested and ideologically charged concept, 'democracy', with 'polyarchy'. The attempt failed because it proved impossible for a social science to isolate itself from society and its commonly used terms. Another example of this strategy is Easton's initially successful rejection of the term 'state', in disgust over its myriad definitions, and his introduction of the term 'political system'. Although that term has become widely accepted, it proved as difficult to separate the 'political system' from its 'environment', as it is to distinguish 'state' from 'society'. As late as 1981 Easton still warned that advocates of 'Bringing the State back in ... threaten us with a return to a conceptual morass from which we thought we had but recently escaped' (Easton, 1981, 322); but recently even he came to acknowledge '... that the "structure of the state" is indeed a central phenomenon worthy of investigation if we are to understand political outputs and outcomes, or policies and their consequences' (Easton, 1990, 11). If we are allowed to generalise from these two examples, current attempts to introduce alternatives for the term 'government', as mentioned above, are unlikely to succeed either.

A second strategy is to take for granted the impossibility to delineate the concepts and to study instead the political struggle which takes place to draw lines between these interrelated concepts. As Mitchell argues with regard to the definitions of state and society,

> Rather than searching for a definition that will fix the boundary, we need to examine the detailed political processes through which the uncertain yet powerful distinction between state and society is produced.
>
> (Mitchell, 1991, 78)

However worthwhile such a meta-perspective may be, it presupposes that the political actors involved in the production of the distinction assume that it matters where exactly the boundaries are drawn. This inevitably leads to the question why it matters, and brings us back to the search for definitions.

The approach of this chapter consists in accepting that the four concepts overlap empirically to such an extent that it is impossible to draw clear and unambiguous borderlines between them, while at the same time acknowledging that, at its core, each of the concepts is distinct. We deal with these assumptions by developing ideal types (in the Weberian sense) of state, (civil) society, government and party. The deviations from these ideal types, over time and across polities, can then be used to study the interrelations between the concepts.

Fortunately, an ideal type of the *state* is provided by Weber himself. He describes the state as a compulsory association, constituting an administrative and legal order that has a monopoly of the legitimate use of physical force in the enforcement of its order within a particular territory (for example, Weber, 1966, 154). Other definitions may emphasise different aspects, but do not really offer a different perspective. Nettl differentiates the state from other states (the state as a unit in international relations), from society ('... the autonomy of the state is reflected by areas of exclusivity as well as primacy in all societies that have a well-internalized concept of the state', Nettl, 1968, 565), and from government:

> If the notion of the state is to be at all meaningful, and not merely a ragbag synonym of government, it must be divorced from and even opposed to personal power.
>
> (Nettl, 1968, 563)

We need not here go into the sources of what has sometimes been called 'internal sovereignty' in terms of justification (*droit divin, raison d'état*, popular sovereignty, and so forth) or historical origin (but see Spruyt, 1994), but other questions cannot be ignored. The state is often depicted as a unitary actor, for instance in the study of international relations, in Marxism or in German and French legal philosophy, and even by Weber when he describes the state as

> based on the idea of a powerful corporate group whose membership either closed or limited outside access and whose functioning

accorded with norms that corporate groups regarded as valid.

(Bendix, 1992, 1007)

However, the assumption is not only empirically untenable: it is also unnecessary. Interactions within the state and within society may provide explanations for the interactions between state and society.

Moreover, Weber's administrative and legal order lumps together two longtime rivals in the search for a definition: the state as a coercive instrument, an organisation for making binding decisions (*Machtstaat*), and the state as a legal order, as law (*Rechtsstaat*). However, this combination may nonetheless actually be helpful, as it makes it possible to define the *government*. In studies of party–government relations, the government is often left undefined and the concept is implicitly used as a synonym for the state. Building on the two aspects combined by Weber, however, the government can be seen as part of the state. It is the *Verwaltungsstab*, the highest executive giving direction to the state apparatus (bureaucracy, army, and so on), both in its relations with other states and in its relations with society. As Rockman puts it: 'In the sense of a condition of ordered rule, government is the authoritative expression of the state' (1987, 257), but as such it is constrained by the state as a legal order. That legal order may restrict the government's scope by recognising other institutional jurisdictions within the state, such as parliament, the judiciary, independent regulatory or administrative bodies, and so forth. As long as these other jurisdictions exist, the government cannot monopolise the resources of the state: *Machtstaat* and *Rechtsstaat* remain distinct.

From attempts to define the state and to differentiate it from *society*, some aspects of a definition of society may be derived: if compulsory membership defines the state, voluntary association and plurality characterise society. Next to the state's public (that is constitutional, administrative and criminal) law, relations within society are governed by private law. What is morally acceptable in society, such as a trade, may be corrupt within the state (Jacobs, 1992). It appears difficult to define society without reference to the state, as something other than a state-free sphere or as a non-territorial unincorporated area. Lately, the term *civil* society has become fashionable once more (Keane, 1988, 1998). There seems to be, however, but little added value in the adjective 'civil' in terms of conceptual clarity. It has been used as a synonym for democracy where years of 'people's democracy' had contaminated that concept, for the representation of society by other voluntary organisations than political parties ('*Bürgergesellschaft* versus *Parteiendemokratie*'), especially in Germany, for the part of society that is not affected by economic calculation, especially in the United States or for organised society, that is the part of society that does not consist of egotistical individuals, as in many communitarian writings (Dekker, 1995). These definitions are all part of normative debates, but occasionally of empirical endeavours as well. Linz and Stepan, for example, distinguish civil society (interests, values), political society (elections) and economic society (market) as three of the five arenas (in addition to the state apparatus and the rule of law), the developments in which determine the transition to, and consolidation of, democracy (Linz and Stepan, 1996, 3–15), but the three seem to overlap appreciably. If interests and values are key variables in civil society, economics and politics seem to be part of that arena, rather than different spheres.

Another usage of the term civil society, older and ideologically less charged, denotes that part of society that is entitled to interact with the state, that is that consists of citizens rather than subjects (Koole, 1996). This definition includes not only individual citizens, but also the corporations and associations that these citizens can choose to join or leave voluntarily. As this study is confined to liberal democracies, however, this distinction between society and civil society is also redundant.

One of the voluntary associations within (civil) society is the political *party*. Defining political parties as part of society is controversial, and not just by those whose very definition of civil society is anti-party. Parties are usually seen as a linkage mechanism between society and state, and hence can belong to both, or to neither. Studies of the organizational structure of parties, as will be discussed in Chapter 4, usually distinguish four major dimensions of the party: the party in government (unless the party is in opposition, of course) consisting of the party's ministers; the parliamentary party group, consisting of the party's MPs; the extra-parliamentary party organisation, consisting of the party's members and officials; and the most elusive of all, the party in the electorate, consisting of its (potential) voters. Only the latter two seem to be located unequivocally inside society.

Studies of the historical development of parties add to the ambivalence. What Duverger (1964) labelled the *parti de masse* was indeed created outside the state, in society, or even in non-civil society, as these parties often had to fight for the enfranchisement of their supporters first (Koole, 1996). Yet, preceding this type of political party was the *parti de cadre* which usually started as a loose grouping of like-minded MPs, as such having its roots in the state rather than in society. These are important considerations, to which we shall return; they refer to the empirical variety of political parties, rather than to the ideal type, however.

In Sartori's survey of definitions of political parties (1976, 58–64), not a single one sees the direction of the linkage mechanism as going from state to society; it always goes the other way around: parties link society to the state, as in Sartori's own often quoted 'minimal definition' of a party as 'any political group identified by an official label that presents at elections, and is capable of placing through elections (free or non-free), candidates for public office' (Sartori, 1976, 63). Just as government is part of the state, so the party is part of society: it is that part of society that seeks to capture the government in order to get access to the state's resources and/or to change the direction of the state in its relations with other states and with society. To the extent that parts of the party structure are located on the state-side of the border, it is there temporarily, as a bridgehead.

Sartori's 'minimal definition' was designed primarily to distinguish parties from other organisations in society that 'are intent upon gaining and maintaining control of the instrumentalities of government' (Sartori, 1976, 61), such as movements, churches, interest groups and so on. Thus, political parties are not the only parts of society that seek to influence the state by influencing the government. These points can be summarised as in Figure 3.1.

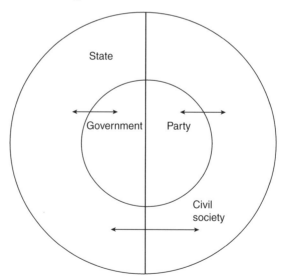

Figure 3.1   A conceptual map of state, society, government and party

Boundaries and relations

Figure 3.1 presents an over-stylised and over-simplified picture. It is confined, for example, to one territorial 'level' of the polity, the national level in this case, and it does not deal with the complex interactions between local, regional, national and supranational state, government, parties and society.

The figure may also give the wrong impression that the four concepts are part of a zero-sum game. Putnam (1993) argues instead that a well-organised civil society (that is one consisting of more than atomistic individuals in clientelistic networks) actually enhances the capabilities of state institutions. With the exception of some anarchist theorists, most would agree that this works the other way as well: society, left on its own, is not a haven of choice and voluntarism, although it is some-times suggested that it is. The state is the body which has to ensure equality and freedom within society for workers, women and ethnic or religious minorities; it is the body which has to guarantee economic choice through anti-trust legislation, and so on. If society were to destroy the state, it would eventually destroy itself; if the state were to capture society, it would also, eventually, implode. As Van Gunsteren puts it:

> It is in civil society that people form their ideas and organise them-selves. When ideas and concerns have grown and become robustly organised, citizens may effectively present them in the public–poli-tical sphere. The vitality of citizenship is fed by the vitality of civil society. Given this connection it is understandable that politicians who are interested in citizenship try to bring state and society closer together and to use state power to strengthen civil ties. In doing so, however, they often undermine what they want to foster. This is so because civil society usually remains vital as long as the state keeps its proper distance from it. When state and civil society get too close or become identical, they both lose vitality.
>
> (Van Gunsteren, 1997, 158–9)

We shall argue that the same paradoxical logic can be made to apply to the relations between party and government.

This does not mean that the boundaries between the four concepts cannot vary or shift appreciably, however. The appropriate drawing of each of these boundaries is the subject of normative debate. Where government has taken over the state completely, history books speak of *absolutism* (*'L'Etat c'est moi'*). More recent echoes of the debate on absolutism take the form of controversies over the politicisation of the civil service *('L'Etat Mitterrand')*, over the political control of public broadcasting (Italy, France), over the independence of the central bank (UK), and over ministerial control of criminal prosecution (the Netherlands).

The strongest recent debates and the most significant boundary changes have taken place with regard to the distinction between state and society. The developments also show an intriguing parallel between liberal democracies and communist systems. Where the state has taken over society completely, there is *totalitarianism*. Spain under Franco, Portugal under Salazar or Greece under the colonels were absolutist regimes, not totalitarian ones. Most communist regimes were both absolutist and totalitarian. The distinction between the two situations has even played an important part in US foreign policy (although the word 'authoritarian' was used for what is described here as absolutist). Even in communist regimes, however, there has always been variation in the degree of totalitarianism: in Poland society was kept alive by the church and regularly clashed with the state; in Hungary, society, especially in its economic manifestations, was allowed to exist so that the state could survive. Meanwhile, the development of a welfare state in liberal democracies led to an ever greater intervention of the state in society. Some have proclaimed the 'etatization of western societies' (Chodak, 1989) and even the word 'totalitarian' has been used by those who are anxious about Orwell's 'Big Brother' or Hayek's 'Road to Serfdom'.

More recently, both in Western and Eastern Europe, the trend has been in the opposite direction. The collapse of the communist regimes has been interpreted by some as being caused by (civil) society reasserting itself through social movements, but even if it has not always been the prime mover of change, society has certainly been its beneficiary. The crisis of communism in the East was accompanied by a crisis of the welfare state in the West. Already before 1989, western governments had embarked upon more or less ambitious programmes to 'roll back the state' through privatisation, deregulation and marketisation. Rhodes (1994) called this process 'the hollowing out of the state' (because of privatisation, replacing departments by agencies, transfer of powers to the European Union, and the 'new public management'). Although some of these developments may hollow out the government rather than the state, through agencies or Europe for instance, others can indeed be seen as a contraction of the state and an expansion of society.

The observation of such boundary shifts is being hampered by the fact that the boundary itself has become faint. During the expansion of the welfare state in the West, state and society interpenetrated and the border became a corporatist blur populated by quangos. A more recent phenomenon is the 'emigration of politics' (Huyse, 1994) – the fact that companies, electronic media, science (all actors within society), take decisions that present governments and states with *faits accomplis*. At the same time, state institutions are assumed to increase efficiency by adopting market-logic from society (Osborne and Gaebler, 1993).

The debate on the relation between party and society centres on the decline of parties ('the party's over!' exclaimed the American columnist David Broder in 1971). It is often suggested that parties have lost many of their functions in recent decades: communication from state to society is via mass media rather than via the party press; communication from society to the state is via opinion polls and increasingly through referenda, rather than through party meetings; political socialisation takes place in the state education system, not in party summer schools or youth clubs; interest articulation is taken over by lobbyists and interest groups, interest aggregation by policy units, think tanks or royal commissions; parties see their membership dwindle while new social movements and organisations thrive, Greenpeace or Amnesty for instance. Parties still enjoy a monopoly on recruitment to positions in state institutions such as government and parliament: this leads some observers to speak not of a decline, but of a transformation of parties, for instance into electoral-professional parties (Panebianco, 1988). In both interpretations, however, the common denominator is the fact that the relation between parties and the rest of society is being eroded.

Towards a typology

Having thus introduced the four concepts and explored the boundaries between them, we can now discuss their relevance for the theme of party–government relations. As a first step, a rather crude typology can be constructed by looking at the variations in the relations between the government and the greater state and between parties and society at large. For that purpose these two relations are regarded as dimensions. The poles of these dimensions are logical extremes, unlikely to exist in the real world (Figure 3.2).

Where the party has captured society, and government is in complete control of the state, party government has the *potential* to develop into the party state, once approximated by the Soviet Union, the People's

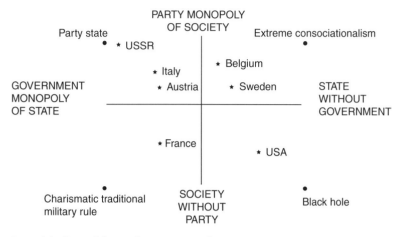

Figure 3.2   Potential party/government relations

Republic of China, and their satellites. The word 'potential' is emphasised in this and the following cases. After all, the term 'party government' assumes that the direction of influence is from party to government, while the opposite direction is also possible. It depends on the party's use of appointments, policies and patronage, whether or not the potential for party government is realised. Not as close to the extreme of 'party state', but still in the same quadrant, one finds countries such as until recently Italy and to a lesser extent Austria, with parties that play a prominent role in society and governments that have brought large sectors of the state under their control. It is here that terms such as *'partitocrazia'* or *'Parteienstaat'* apply. The opposite extreme is where both the role of party in society and of government in the state are negligible. The closest approximation to this 'black hole' situation is constituted by the United States, where political parties are more important as labels than as real organisations and where commentators have lamented the lack of a centre in Washington.

At the upper right-hand of the figure are situations in which party equates society while the government is not a significant part of the state. There are no close approximations to this extreme situation, but it does resemble an extreme case of consociationalism: the 'pillarisation' of society in countries such as Belgium in the recent past did mean that most organisations within society (churches, trade unions, schools, mass media, housing associations and so forth) were closely linked to one of the major parties (Luther 1999). The government was primarily a clearing house, distributing resources to the 'pillars' according to fixed legal criteria (proportionality). In a different way, Sweden can be located in this part, as its parties are privileged representatives of society and its royal commissions (for policy-making) and independent agencies (for policy-implementation) reduce the role of the government within an otherwise strong state. Finally, at the lower left-hand corner are governments dominating the state with a society without strong parties. The extreme case is constituted by charismatic, traditional or military autocratic rule, but France is also in this part of the figure, although far removed from its extreme position as it has a strong government and parties that are weakly integrated in society, the Communist party being a partial exception.

One dimension is missing in the figure, that of the relationship between society and the state. How the polity is divided between state and society may not affect the degree of party government, but it does affect its scope or relevance. Katz is probably the only one who took into account both the party–government and the state–civil society debates when he made the

> distinction between *partyness of government*, referring to a narrow institutional sense of party government as party control of the formal governmental apparatus, and *party governmentness*, referring to a broader sense of party government as a general social characteristic. For example, in a *laissez-faire* economy, high partyness of government would still leave parties in a relatively marginal position in the authoritative allocation of economic values. Correspondingly, if the power of government grew whilst the party politicians' relative ability to control it shrank, parties might become absolutely more important in the overall allocation of values even whilst the partyness of government declined'.
>
> (1986, 45–6)

The complete pattern of potential extents and scopes of party government is illustrated by a cube in Figure 3.3.

The lower left-hand space at the front of the cube represents the extreme form of party government in which there is a total merger of party, civil society, state and government. If one moves up within the cube, the party's potential for capturing the whole state apparatus declines; if one moves to the right-hand side of the cube, the party's potential for representing all of civil society declines; and if one moves to the back of the cube, the potential for 'party-governmentness' declines, to use Katz's expression. The upper right-hand cell at the

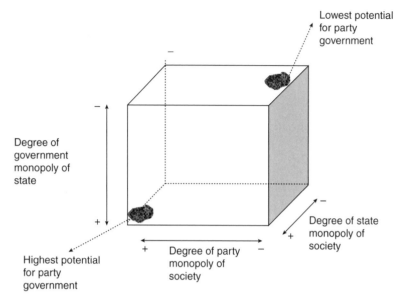

Figure 3.3   Potential extents and scopes of party government

backof the cube offers the least potential for the authoritative allocation of values by parties.

Direction of party–government relations

Influenced by the normative debate on responsible party government, empirical studies have sought to ascertain the degree to which, and the conditions under which, the potential for party government is materialised. There is not just one 'potential' but a range of 'potentials', depending on the nature of the relations between party and society, government and state and state and society. This project also adds to the existing literature by noting that the relationship between party and government is two-way. In the terminology of Figure 3.1, the boundary between government and party can shift in both directions. The government can become the party's bridgehead in the state, but the party can also become the government's bridgehead in society. We must gauge not only the *partyness of governments*, but also the *governmentness of parties*. In addition to the extent and scope of party government, the direction of the relation between government and ruling parties is also influenced by the other relations, namely between state and society, between state and government and between party and society.

The relation between society and state

Katz argues that partyness of government and party governmentness are inversely correlated. Paraphrasing his argument, one can say that a large public sector (big state, small civil society) makes the party(ies) more dependent on experts, many of whom are bureaucrats; it diminishes the span of control over a government apparatus that has grown as a result of state interventionism; it gives rival organisations in society a stake in politics; it encourages parties to shift the responsibility (but thus also power) to independent agencies (Katz, 1986, 58). Especially the first two elements of his argument (reliance on government experts and increasing span of control) could lead to the capture of the party by the government, rather than the other way around. The contraction of the state and the mood of crisis of the welfare state characterising the 1990s may reverse this direction, and make the government more dependent on the party, although this view is not shared by Müller (1993, 426–7).

At first sight, this hypothesis runs counter to one of the very few discussions of the relationship between state and party which have taken place so far in the literature. Nettl has argued that,

> It can be shown that where states exist, parties tend largely to be the institutionalization of social cleavage – and this usually means a multiparty system. Where no state exists, however, parties carry a much larger functional weight. They become engines of authority-legitimation (not then provided by the state); where this is the case the structured articulation of interests and/or cleavages in party terms is inhibited.
>
> (Nettl, 1968, 581; see also 588)

As a result, 'The very absence of the state has often been largely responsible for transforming parties of representation into vehicles of government in societies like England and Sweden' (*ibid.*, 581–2). In other words: where the state is strong, parties remain representatives of society; where the state is weak, parties become agents of the government. The argument is compelling and highly relevant to a discussion of party–government relations, but it does not necessarily contradict the hypothesis advanced here. Nettl discusses the state as a sociocultural phenomenon, the effects of the state being a salient cognition to people (as in France, Italy, Germany), or not (as in the UK, and the US). Nettl admits that a high level of cultural stateness needs to coincide with a high level of empirical stateness (*ibid.*, 586–7) and, similarly, a culturally weak state may go together with an emprically strong state: the state may be relatively absent from American or British culture, but the state is by no means absent in American or British society. It is with the state 'in practice' rather than with the state 'in culture' that this chapter is concerned.

The relation between state and government

Katz (1986, 55–62) listed a range of conditions that affect the strength of party government. Many of these are on the state side of the border with society (system of government, electoral system, centralisation). Müller sees such conditions as mechanisms for the state to manipulate parties:

> The state may influence party and party system change in three broad ways: (1) by those regulations which affect political parties in a direct fashion, that is party law, electoral law and state party finance, (2) by regulation and control of those parts of civil society which are of particular relevance for political parties, namely mass media, interest groups and the economy and (3) by the nature of the institutions of the state and the power relations between them. The latter includes the state structure, the executive, the parliament, the bureaucracy, constitutional courts and the scope of direct democracy.
>
> (1993, 420)

Müller acknowledges that the impact of the state on the parties is less now that parties are in a position to change the very features of the state that affect their room for manoeuvre. One can even go further on the basis of the distinction which has been made here between state and government: as parties can only directly capture the governmental part of the state, it follows that the smaller the government – that is the greater the jurisdiction of less-permeable state institutions (the courts, independent committees, 'inquiries' into the conduct of politicians) – the more likely it is that the state's impact on the parties outweighs the parties' impact on the state, and vice versa. In other words: the direction of the relation between government and parties is dependent on the size of the government within the state.

The relation between parties and society

This relation is the most important in influencing the direction of party-government relations. We saw that many of the parties' roots in society (through membership, communication, socialisation, interest-articulation and aggregation) are withering. This has two effects that both tip the balance between government and parties in favour of the government. First, many party functions which have just been listed have not disappeared: they have been taken over by rival organisations within society (social movements, interest groups, think tanks, independent media, pollsters). These rivals now address government directly and no longer through the intermediary of parties. Government pays attention to these new representatives of society, as parties have progressively less to convey in terms of ideological direction or information. Second, the government may even set up its own links with society, bypassing parties completely, as through the increasing use of referendums or of 'tele-democracy'.

However, at the very moment when parties see their relationship with society weakening, their relationship with the state is strengthening:

> Paradoxically, amidst a growing literature on the 'decline of party', one can hear warnings of a *'Parteienstaat'* (Germany), *'partitocrazia'* (Italy), *'partitocratie'* (Belgium) . . . As mechanisms for elite–mass linkages, parties have taken up a position closer to the state: this is epitomised by their increasing reliance on public funding rather than on membership fees.
>
> (Andeweg, 1996, 157)

These paradoxical developments are in fact logically related, as Katz and Mair explain:

> . . . the sheer size and commitment of party memberships have generally failed to keep pace with the growth in electorates, on the one hand, and with the rapidly escalating costs of party activity, on the other. Parties have therefore been obliged to look elsewhere for their resources, and in this case their role as governors and lawmakers made it easy for them to turn to the state.
>
> (Katz and Mair, 1995, 15)

These resources consist of subventions, privileged access to electronic media, opportunities for party patronage, and so on. This insulates the established political parties against new challengers (which do not yet have access to these resources) – adding to the 'freezing' of the party system – but it also makes the parties dependent on the state for their survival. As a result 'No longer simple brokers between civil society and the state, the parties now become absorbed by the state . . . . parties have now become semi-state agencies' (Katz and Mair, 1995, 16).

In his challenge to this type of analysis, Koole points to the blurring of the distinction between state and society which was referred to earlier:

> Both the expansion of the state and the diffusion of power create problems for party scholars. When state and society overlap to a large extent due to increased state intervention, a phrase like 'No longer simple brokers between civil society and the state, the parties now become absorbed by the state' loses much of its meaning. And when state power is no longer concentrated in one place (unilocus), the image of a state as an 'institutionalized structure of support [for parties], sustaining insiders while excluding outsiders' takes too much for granted that the state acts as a monolith (quod non).
>
> (1996, 514–15)

This is an important observation, but also an exaggeration: state and society have not (yet) merged completely and the kind of resources that the parties are increasingly dependent upon (positions in the bureaucracy, tax money, regulation of party access to electronic media) are not located in the blurred no-man's-land where state and society overlap. Writing about the Dutch case, Koole's position is not altogether different from Andeweg's and Katz and Mair's: his coining of the term 'modern cadre party' is no accidental reference to Duverger's party type with origins in the state rather than in society. Pointing to the shift in power within parties to the parliamentary party, he argues:

> To be sure, Dutch parties are moving closer to the state in the sense that they have developed what I have referred to as the parliamentary party complex, but their financial situation in particular prevents them from removing themselves entirely from a membership base.
>
> (1994a, 300)

*   *   *

Katz and Mair warn of the dangers inherent in parties turning into para-statal organisations: this may block or limit feedback from society reaching the government and the state, leading to an eventual implosion of the state, or allowing dissent to accumulate until it finds an ugly outlet. For empirical examples of a more and a less extreme nature, one need only to refer to the collapse of the Soviet Union and of most parties in Italy. The state, as argued above, cannot survive its usurpation of society, and the party cannot survive its usurpation of the state's resources either. The parallel with the aristocracy's political fate, especially in France, is striking: once autonomous landowning feudal lords represented their part of the empire to the monarch. Whether because of agricultural crises or monarchical manipulation, they gradually developed into a court elite, increasingly dependent on and under the control of absolutist monarchs. Other forms of representation of civil society emerged, and the aristocracy faded away or ended under the guillotine.

Note

1 For an overview of the many definitions of 'party' as well as his own 'minimal definition', see Sartori (1976).

4
Defining Party and Government[1]

Maurizio Cotta

Conceptualising party and government

An examination of the relationship between government and party implies that the meaning of the two concepts and the two phenomena is made clear. It also means that we must have the instruments enabling us to discover variations across countries and over time with respect to these phenomena. We are still far from having reached this point. Most discussions which take place in this respect are based on oversimplifications. There is a strong temptation for instance to use holistic interpretations: both phenomena are commonly analysed as if they were unitary actors – values, perceptions, goals, actions are ascribed to them. While this view may be close to reality in some cases, though probably for only one of the two phenomena at a time, this is not true in most cases. Party and government are more likely to be either arenas where a variety of actors compete or cooperate among themselves or systems, that is to say composite entities, which result from interactions among their components. Which view best fits reality cannot be decided in advance: it is, rather, an empirical matter.

Moreover, the viewpoint adopted in the discussion of the relationship between party and government tends to be tilted in favour of one of the two terms: and there is indeed a pendulum movement over time in the choice of the dominant viewpoint. In the past the focal point was generally the government, though exactly how far back depends to some extent on cultural differences among countries, as well as on differences in disciplinary traditions within the same country (for instance between the tradition of constitutional law and of political science). In this perspective the government was conceived as a part of the state, in fact as the top institution of the state, its 'head'. The main (normative) preoccupation was often the defence of the autonomy of the leading organ of the state from external influences and in particular from parties. The long anti-party bias noted in Chapter 1 and which counted so much in analyses of political life relates to this point. The dominant question was then how to 'save' the government from the 'evil' influence of parties aiming at conquering the allegedly impartial and nation-minded institution of the government and at subordinating it to their allegedly factional and particularistic goals.

The other point of view is exactly the opposite, the starting point being the party viewed as a crucial element of the representative process. Normative and empirical points reinforce each other in this respect as well. On the empirical plane a long tradition of studies on elections under the conditions of mass participation showed to what extent parties with a well-defined identity and a strong organisation came to control the representative process. On the normative plane democracy became the predominant political value and it was interpreted as a process centred on competitive representation. Thus parties gained, both in theory and in practice, the status of crucial 'transmission belts' of the democratic will. The 'normal' expectation was therefore that parties should gain an upper hand on the government and use the government to implement the popular will. The dominance of party over government – party government – far from being an 'evil' became a critical condition of true democracy (Ranney, 1962). In such a perspective there was obviously little point in studying government *per se*, except to determine the conditions under which parties could control the instruments of governance. Thus, as it was noticed once (King 1975), for a long time little attention was paid to cabinets in political science studies. More recently, however, the rise of anti-party feelings and the signs of a decline of organised parties shifted attention again in the direction of governments.

These two rather crude interpretations of the party–government relationship are not altogether unrealistic, but their relevance is greater at some specific stages of the evolution of democracies. The first interpretation has tended to correspond to early parliamentary government, the second to coincide with the apex of the mass ideological party. However the situation is often more complex. At present, the notion of a state as a unitary actor with a single 'will' of its own simply cannot be sustained; at the same time changes within parties may not always have reduced the political role of these bodies but have certainly eroded the rigid mould of the membership party and increased differences among various components of the party itself, for instance between the group in power and the membership at large (Mair, 1994). One must therefore go beyond the simplified views of party and government and of their relationships: this requires a more detailed analysis of what is party and of what is government. In the first section of this chapter I will therefore concentrate on the party, and in the second I shall examine the government.

What is party?

The simplest view of party is one that pictures it as a unitary actor with a well-defined set of political goals and policy preferences. If matters were as simple, the problem of party–government relations would be relatively easy to solve: it would entirely depend on whether the government can be taken over by party men and party women and be guided by the preferences of the party, or vice versa.

Things are normally not as simple. Parties are internally articulated and complex dynamics take place within them. The single-actor image is perhaps more the conclusion of the process than its starting point, an exception rather than the norm. We must therefore 'unpack' the party as, later, we shall have to do with government, although we can already assume that there will be differences as the organisational format of parties varies more than that of governments, not just across countries and within countries but even more over time if we adopt a long-term view.

First, parties are sets of individuals with common interests, values, ideals and programmes; they are also sets of individuals with personal ambitions (Burke, 1770; Sartori, 1976; Ware, 1996). Yet a party is more than a set of individuals: it is an organisation which transcends these individuals. For most of these, the party existed before they became associated with it and it will remain in existence long after they will have left it. The organisation constitutes a resource for all those who belong to it: because and as long as it exists they can achieve results which they could not achieve otherwise. The party also has a collective identity: it evokes a tradition, an ethos, a 'we-feeling' which comes to be valued in itself and must be preserved (Panebianco, 1988). In this sense the party is a source of both instrumental and expressive benefits for those who belong to it. As a result, it is permissible to say that the party is a tool of those who are associated to it but that they are also to an extent the tools of the party. There are enormous variations, of course, from loosely-organised parties which come to be the prey of the instrumental strategies of those who work within them, to totalitarian parties in which members are wholly expendable. Yet both aspects probably coexist in almost every party.

Second, parties adapt to the different arenas and settings in which they operate: as a result, they cut across and link the various institutions of the political system. This has two consequences. On the one hand, parties are a unifying factor within the pluralism of institutions typical of liberal democracy; for instance they can bring parliament and government closely together, whatever views there may have been about the separation of powers. On the other hand, they are involved in different political games and they operate at the same time under different sets of constraints and opportunities. This results inevitably in an internal differentiation of components of the party and creates tensions among these components, which may even come to be viewed, to an extent, as different 'parties'. Thus one refers commonly to the parliamentary party, the membership party, the party in government and even the party in the electorate; one could even go further and speak of the party in local government, in the bureaucracy, and so on. Let us therefore first analyse in some detail the nature and the meaning of the most important of these components before returning to the overall picture, discussing the relationship between the various components and attempting to answer the question: 'who is (or who owns) the party ?'.

The party as a parliamentary organ

The party in parliament, made of the representatives sharing the same partisan identity, was often historically the earliest component, as it grew from the need for collective action within parliament. An obviously important aspect is to support the government if and when its very existence depends on such a support in parliament; but when this is not the case, as in presidential systems, there is a need to reduce conflicts and to organise the competition for leadership positions within the legislature, from those of speaker to the chairmanships of committees. The parliamentary component of the party is obviously the one most directly subjected to electoral influence. On the one hand, this is a constraint, as the party depends on electoral results for its strength; questions of reelection become a dominant preoccupation for members individually and for the parliamentary party as a body. On the other hand, the electoral connection is obviously also a resource: elections provide members of the parliamentary party with a democratic legitimacy and an authority that other components of the party do not so clearly have. The extent to which that electoral resource is 'owned' by members individually or by the parliamentary group as a whole, or by another entity such as the membership party, does vary markedly, however. The electoral system and the whole election process, from the selection of candidates to the campaign, are important factors influencing this relationship and thus increasing or decreasing the autonomy of parliamentarians. A combination of single-member constituencies, primaries for the selection of candidates, the absence of membership parties, an open and rich market for campaign resources and weak ideological cleavages has rendered American congressmen both very strong and very independent. On the other hand, multi-member constituencies, closed-list systems, strong membership party organisations, relatively limited markets for campaign resources and strong ideological cleavages have resulted in members being markedly dependent on the party organisation in many European countries, in the past especially in the case of parliamentary parties of the working-class left.

In general we can expect a significant degree of internal pluralism in a parliamentary party given the strong contacts its members have with the many interests of the electorate. The more individual members 'own' the electoral resources, the more the parliamentary party as a body will be relatively independent from the other components of the party. However, if MPs are too independent, the parliamentary party as a whole comes to be at risk and can become a loose confederation of powerful and independent barons, thus being little more than a tool in the hands of the parliamentarians. In the age of the notables, who indeed individually owned the electoral resources, parliamentary parties were rather weak. A similar development has occurred in America where the Congress is based upon what can be described as 'neo-notables': congressional parties are weak in relation to individual members. Indeed a strong parliamentary party (as a collective body) can probably be found only where neither the other components of the party nor individual parliamentarians are very strong.

The position of the parliamentary party *vis-à-vis* the government is significantly affected by the institutional structure. In the separation-of-powers model the fact that the executive does not depend for its survival on a parliamentary majority deprives the parliamentary party of a direct influence on the government, but it also frees the party from obligations of loyalty. Government and parliamentary party (except for the existence of coat-tails) have thus two rather independent 'utility functions'. The parliamentary party will try to extract from the government the maximum possible resources that can be used in the parliamentary election campaigns by exerting its influence on bills, on the distribution of funds and on appointments. The government will do the same. The combination of the two strategies will determine the outputs of this form of government. In a parliamentary system the utility functions of the two are much more interconnected. Government is dependent on the parliamentary party(ies) for its survival and it is linked to the same electoral process for its democratic legitimation: as a result the parliamentary party is at the same time more powerful (it can make the government fall) and more constrained because the success or failure of the government will have a greater impact on the election from which the parliamentary party derives its own strength and legitimacy.

There are important variations among parliamentary systems, however, and these have significant consequences for the relationship between parliamentary party and government. In particular the 'proximity' of the government to the electoral result varies: it is at its maximum when the election determines which government will be set up and when the end of the government coincides with a new election; it is at its minimum both when the electoral result leaves space for various solutions, which result in bargaining after the electoral outcome, and when the end of the government does not necessarily entail a new election. The position of the parliamentary party *vis-à-vis* the government varies accordingly: when the electoral 'proximity' of the government is at its maximum the position of the parliamentary party tends to coincide with that of the government. Only when the government seems bound to lose the ensuing election can the parliamentary party regain some autonomy; otherwise loyalty is the rational strategy for the parliamentary party, as by supporting the government and enabling it to efficiently pursue its goals the parliamentary party ensures the electoral success of both. When the electoral 'proximity' is lower, the parliamentary party becomes less dependent. For instance, if most cabinets do not survive until the elections, the interest of the parliamentary party in electoral success will not coincide with the interest of the government which might be more preoccupied by other short-term problems: the incentives for members of the parliamentary party to fight on their own for their political survival become consequently greater. Moreover, since the cabinet must be formed in parliament and can be unseated in parliament, the parliamentary party has at its disposal a powerful instrument for exercising influence. Yet a paradoxical effect occurs: when the link between government and parliamentary party becomes too loose, the cohesion of the parliamentary party is also undermined because one of the strongest motives for unity disappears.

The electoral connection is not the only factor affecting the parliamentary party: the structure of parliament also plays a part. Generally speaking, parliaments are among the least hierarchical institutions. There is a leadership constituted by the speaker and the committee chairmen but the bulk of the internal structure is fundamentally egalitarian: each member has equal weight as he or she can cast a vote. Yet the organisation of parliament is an important intervening variable: where parliament has a strong committee structure the members of the parliamentary party operating in each committee, especially those with seniority, acquire autonomy as a result of their specialisation or their links with interest groups. On the basis of the power they hold in these positions they have greater opportunities to challenge the government.

The parliamentary party has a leadership of its own when the party is in opposition, a leadership which may be more or less autonomous *vis-à-vis* the membership party, a point which we shall discuss later. What then happens to that parliamentary party leadership when the party enters government? It may become (part of) the government, as in the British case: to quote Blondel, the parliamentary party once it has won the elections is 'beheaded' (Blondel, 1996) – its leaders move in the cabinet and leave the parliamentary party without its head. A different image could be used, however: by winning the election the parliamentary party and its leadership obtain the 'crown' of government. Instead of losing something, it gains a new authority and new resources that are built in the institution of government and which will benefit the whole party in the electoral competition. The possibility of using two opposite images for the same situation hints at some of the ambiguities of this relationship.

To some extent, given the strong linkage existing in the parliamentary systems between cabinet and parliament, one can view the (party in the) cabinet as a component of the parliamentary party; yet the new institutional position gained by the party leadership creates a greater gap between backbenchers and leaders than when they all sat in the opposition benches. The party leaders in government have the prestige and also the distance that result from the responsibility of running the country.

There are different arrangements, however. The parliamentary party leadership may stay out of the government and maintain an identity of its own. The leadership of the party in parliament thus becomes to some extent bicephalous: one head is in the government and the other in the parliamentary party. The relative importance of the two heads may also vary: *vis-à-vis* a strong and durable government one would expect the parliamentary party leadership to be reduced to a rather dependent role of 'agent', but in the case of unstable cabinets a lasting parliamentary party leadership might gain a much stronger role (and appear rather as the 'principal'). The weaker and the more indirect the linkage between government and election results, the more this second type of situation is likely to arise. If the government does not proceed 'automatically' from the election, but only comes into being possibly after lengthy negotiations (inside and outside the parliament) and/or if the fall of the government does not necessarily entail the dissolution of parliament, the leadership of the parliamentary group is likely to be longer lasting than the government.

Party as a membership organisation

Parties, particularly in the European experience of the twentieth century, have typically had significant membership organisations. In extreme cases this organisation has come close to being a self-contained and self-sufficient world for important sections of the population. The party then constituted not only the focal and rallying point for citizens actively interested in politics, but also a 'community' taking care of many needs ranging from social protection to education, to leisure activities and even to personal relationships. Some European socialist and communist parties are examples of such a development (Roth, 1963). In other cases the membership party has been merely an organisation of variable strength designed to mobilise the people at and between elections.

A vast literature on parties from Ostrogorski (1903) and Michels (1915) to Duverger (1964), from Kirchheimer (1966) to von Beyme (1985), from Panebianco (1988) to Katz and Mair (1995) and Scarrow (1996) has illustrated the various organisational models adopted by membership parties. A number of key points emerge. First, the membership party itself must be seen as a system within which different actors are at play. Members who subscribe to the party platform and pay dues are the 'population' of the party. As is the case with the population of a country, a large proportion of members is passive; a minority, however, the militants, contributes markedly to the life of the party during and between election campaigns and helps to keep the organisation alive. In terms of time and efforts freely given to the distribution of party propaganda, to contacts with potential voters, to the running of the activities of the party, from congresses to banquets, they form a crucial resource. As many studies about parties have shown, militants strongly defend the ideological purity of the party. This is understandable: given that their efforts do not have instrumental goals, they must be sustained by a strong faith. Symbolic incentives, such as the defence of party identity have a large part to play.

National party rulers can differ markedly from the militants, but this is not so of lower-level rulers, which are typically recruited among the militants. Of the latter some will move to the top but most will remain confined to the bottom steps of the ladder. At the top of the party, a relatively small group of national leaders holds offices, such as those of secretary or president, while a few more sit on committees and councils without holding a specific office. These represent the membership party *vis-à-vis* other actors: what they say *is* the position of the party. They are also the most obvious candidates to occupy positions outside the party, for instance in parliament or in the government. In Europe, national party leaders are generally elected on the basis of an internal democratic system: their legitimacy derives more or less directly from party members. As a matter of fact, the role of rank-and-file members is substantially reduced as a result of the presence of strong oligarchical elements within the party organisation: the selection of party leaders tends to stem from the ability of these leaders to enlist the support of the relatively small group of middle and top-level elites in control of the organisation at national headquarters and in the provinces.

The goals of leaders differ from those of militants: for these the party is an end in itself; for leaders it is an instrument in their bid for power in the democratic polity. Offices, policies and patronage (in variable combinations) are the stakes in that game. Internal party cohesion, electoral victories and strategic positioning in the coalition-building process are the conditions of success. Party leaders can be assumed to want to maximise their gains, although it is not possible to know the terms of the trade-offs which they make. For them the party organisation (members, militants, staff) is a resource to be used in that game (Scarrow, 1996). But it is also a constraint: they can use it, but not beyond a given point. In order to preserve their power in the party they must respond to some extent to the demands of members and even more of militants and middle-ranking leaders. Finding a balance between the preservation of the identity of the party (as required by the rank-and-file) and adapting it to the needs of the national political game is one of the crucial tasks of the party elite. To put it differently: the party elite will pursue the maximisation of its goals to the extent that it does not endanger its position within the party.

Leaders can obviously miscalculate. They may underestimate the dissatisfaction of the rank-and-file *vis-à-vis* their choices and lose support to competitors (the fall of Margaret Thatcher shows that this is not a theoretical point). On the contrary, they may overestimate the needs of the party and become unable to effectively play the part they have to play in the nation. It is sometimes truly difficult to find a balance between the two requirements.

Within the group of national leaders a distinction not to be forgotten is that between *the* leader and the other members of the top elite. The competition between them for the top position, albeit combined with the necessary amount of cooperation, may be extremely robust.

Variations in party structures are obviously critical for the relationships between the different components of the membership party. From the highly ideological and densely organised mass parties, such as some of the socialist parties of the early part of the twentieth century, to the more pragmatic catch-all parties with a leaner organisation as exemplified by some bourgeois parties or by 'reformed' left parties (Kirchheimer, 1966), to what have been described as 'cartel' parties by Katz and Mair (1995), organisational transformations are significant and we may expect an equally significant impact upon the relations between the party elite and the other strata of the party.

We can assume a diminishing weight of the rank-and-file and a correspondingly greater freedom of action for the party leadership *vis-à-vis* the rank-and-file as one goes from the mass party to the 'cartel' party. The action of the leaders is gradually less constrained by the militants. Paradoxically, however, the less constrained the leaders are from within the party the more they are vulnerable to external pressure. If they cannot oppose the wishes of the party base, they will be under greater pressure to adapt to the will of other actors. If the atrophy of the membership party goes beyond a given point we may ask whether it is still relevant to talk about a membership party. One might further ask what happens to the party leadership. Can it still find its basis in the membership party or must it transfer its foundations somewhere else (typically in the party in public office)? And in that case can the election of the leaders through the party maintain any substantial meaning or rather will it become simply a ritualistic cover for the real nomination processes that take place behind the scenes?

The relationship between the membership party and the parliamentary party is crucial. These are not two separate parties, they share the same political identity. Moreover, with few exceptions, members of the parliamentary party are also (and indeed were beforehand) part of the membership party; and, vice-versa, the higher ranks of the elite of the membership party tend to sit in parliament. In fact the party leadership often plays under both hats at the same time. Yet the two components of the party are involved in different 'games' each of which is characterised by different opportunities and constraints, in particular the electoral 'game' for the parliamentary party and the organisational 'game' for the membership party. Each segment of the party is therefore to some extent viewed by the other as an instrument to further its particular aims. For the parliamentary party, the dominant goal being reelection, the membership party will be seen as a resource: its help during election campaigns is obviously important. Meanwhile, for the membership party and especially for the militants, the parliamentary party and electoral success are valued as instruments helping to strengthen the organisation and pursue its goals. Through a strong parliamentary party the membership party can obtain some of the policies it wants, important positions for its members and the goods that patronage can offer; above all, it can gain access to the government which plays a crucial part with respect to these benefits.

For each component of the party the instrumental use of the other may not be without problems. The membership party may be to some extent a handicap for the parliamentary party in its quest to win the support of sections of the electorate which are more distant from the party core and may be very distant from the party's more dogmatic elements. Conversely, 'true believers' within the membership party may find the parliamentary party lukewarm in its defense of party identity and too open to compromises with party enemies.

There is more than one equilibrium point in this relationship. At one extreme, the parliamentary party dominates and the external party is reduced to an ancillary role, the British Conservative Party being an example. At the other, the membership party dominates the parliamentary group, some socialist and communist parties having adopted this model in the past. The resources available to each of the two components and the importance which each has for the other determine the point at which an equilibrium is reached in a particular case. The availability and importance of resources depends in turn on a mix of internal and external factors. Broadly speaking, where the membership party holds the keys of electoral success the parliamentary party tends to be dependent; where the parliamentary party controls the electoral process it will be able to assert its autonomy from the membership party. The resources the membership party may have under its control are both material and symbolic: it may have the financial means and the manpower to run an electoral campaign; it may also play a crucial part in the production and upkeep of the values and ideals which appeal to the voters and induce them to vote for the party. The party as a membership organisation may thus contribute significantly to producing long-term loyalty among voters. It is more doubtful whether to consider the selection of parliamentary candidates as a resource, as it is probably more the consequence of the control exercised over other resources than a resource in itself. Historically the membership party has acquired a voice in deciding who the candidates will be when it showed that it was able to mobilise other resources. But the fact that the party 'produces' as a byproduct of its activities skilled politicians (who are ready to become candidates) means that the party controls another specific resource.

Studies of parties have shown that not all of them have controlled these resources to the same extent: less ideological parties have not had a monopoly of symbols, and some parties have been unable to mobilise a large manpower. Moreover, with the passing of time some of the original resources have been exhausted or have lost their importance: the ideology of a party may have decreased in intensity, and the need to mobilise many people to distribute leaflets and posters may have declined. New resources, such as the media, or means coming from other sources, for instance public financing, may have gained in importance making the role of the membership party less crucial (Katz and Mair, 1995), though Scarrow takes a somewhat different view on this point (1996). This means that parliamentary parties after a long period of subordination to membership parties may be again gaining greater levels of autonomy.

The party in the electorate: does it really exist?

From time to time a further dimension of the party is mentioned, that of the party in the electorate. The existence of such a 'party' is less clear than that of the parliamentary or membership party. There is here no formal organisation nor is there a clear leadership: there are only voters whose preferences may prove more or less stable. The notions of party identification, which was developed in America, and that of a subcultural vote based on a strong class, religious or linguistic identity, which is often used in Europe, both referring to a durable link of voters with a party, offer some clues for an understanding of the party in the electorate. By 'party in the electorate' we will indicate that section of the voters that display a stable attachment to a party. The size of this section may vary from country to country and also with time.

The existence of such a stable support for the party is a resource for the other components of the party, the parliamentary party and the membership party. In this way parties have a support base which can be relied on at every election. Up to a point, the stronger the 'party in the electorate' the greater the freedom of action of the other components. But there are limits to this freedom: like the ballast of a sailboat, the 'party in the electorate' enables the other components to fluctuate according to the wind but eventually pulls them back towards the centre which is determined by the position of the ballast: the 'party in the electorate' is thus also a constraint. There are also linkages between this component and the other two: the 'party in the electorate' has a close connection with the parliamentary party which depends on it for its power, but the strength of the party in the electorate depends in turn to a large extent on the membership party which builds and preserves the identity of the whole party. The 'party in the electorate' is thus different in kind from the other components as it does not produce significant actors in the party–government game, despite the fact that it gives resources to, and produce constraints for, the other components.

The bureaucratic party

A similar conclusion can be drawn about the bureaucratic component of the party. Parties often have a professional, paid staff appointed to run a substantial part of their activities at central and local levels. This bureau-cracy may come to be very significant in party life: it then becomes a substantial resource for the component which controls it. The link is usually with the membership party, as the professional bureaucracy has typically been set up to help organise and run the membership. But other solutions are also possible. In the British Conservative party, for instance, the central professional staff has a significant autonomy with respect to the other components of the party and is controlled by the leader. It is then a resource for the party in government. In some cases (Germany is an example) the parliamentary party itself may develop a substantial bureaucratic staff that is separate from that of the member-ship party. The party bureaucracy is not only a resource for the whole party and, within the party, for that component that controls it, but can also be, as any bureaucracy, a factor of inertia and conservatism – party officials come to have interests of their own which tend towards con-tinuity rather than towards innovation.

The party in government

The last component we have to discuss is the 'party in government', which is made of those members of the party that have won a position in the cabinet. Such a component obviously does not exist when the party is in opposition, except to the extent that there is a 'shadow cabinet' which might be described as a 'potential party in government'. But as a shadow cabinet is only a pale image of a cabinet, since it does not control the state bureaucracy, a 'potential party in government' is only a distant approximation of a real party in government as it does not control the machine of government.

The 'party in government' is temporary since no party is sure to govern forever: this places it in a position of relative dependence *vis-à-vis* the other components which are permanent. The 'members' of the 'party in government' come from within the other components of the party and, unless they retire from politics, they have to go back to one of the other components when the party loses power (Blondel, 1991). The duration of the control of the party over the government thus appears crucial in order to assess the strength of the 'party in government'. There are naturally major variations across Europe in this respect: some parties have been in government for very long periods; others had long stints in opposition. In the first case the 'party in government' is likely to be more 'real' than in the second. When a party is in office for many years, the jobs of prime minister, of minister or even of under-secretary become a major political activity for many party politicians and for a further group constitute a realistic goal to strive for. A position in the government may last as long or even longer than a leading position in the parliamentary or membership 'party'. At the other end of the continuum, when the presence of the party in the government is short-lived, a ministerial job is a kind of accident rather than a normal outcome of political activity.

Duration is not the only relevant variable, however: the weight of the party in the cabinet also varies from total control in a one-party government to partial control in coalitions. This leads to different constraints for the party and its agenda, and also contributes to rendering the 'party in government' more or less important *vis-à-vis* the rest of the party.

Members of the 'party in government' come from either the membership party or from the parliamentary party or from both. Except when they are non-politicians or technicians, cabinet members generally have a parliamentary background (De Winter, 1991; Blondel and Thiébault, 1991). Moreover, they may or may not belong to the top leadership stratum of the party: the more attractive cabinet positions are (if the party stays in office for long periods and if the role of the party in that government is strong), the more the leaders of the two other components of the party are likely to want to take over these positions. Attractiveness of government positions is a relative matter, however: it depends also on the attractiveness of other party positions. To be the leader of a party with a strong ideological profile, a massive membership and a large bureaucracy is clearly more meaningful than to be the leader of a party with few inactive members and a weak bureaucracy. When leaders move into the government they will either concentrate both old and new positions in their hands (though they may have to delegate the more routine tasks to a vice-chairman or a secretary general) or abandon their position in the membership or parliamentary party to new leaders.

The question of the relative position of leaders in and outside government has therefore to be raised. At first, leaders in government will have the upper hand as they combine experience and connections gained in the old position with the new institutional role. With the passing of time the distance between government leaders and the various components of the party will tend to increase. A good government performance is, however, likely to strengthen the position of these leaders; whilst on the contrary they will suffer and come to be challenged if the governmental record is more mixed. Where cabinet positions are less attractive because they are short-lived and/or occur in a coalition context, only lower-level leaders or top leaders in decline will be prepared to take them on, particularly if these positions cannot be combined with leading ones in the membership or parliamentary party: the true top party leaders are then those who run the parliamentary or the membership 'party' (or both). In some cases, different leadership positions in the membership party, in the parliamentary party and in the government may coexist and result in a kind of collegial directorate of the party: this was the case in the SPD in Germany during Schmidt's chancellorship; and this occurred rather frequently in the Italian Christian Democratic party before 1992.

The question of the power to control and eventually dismiss members of the 'party in government' is related to factors discussed earlier. The more the 'party in government' attracts top leaders of the other components of the party, the more these can control their stay in power, whatever the formal rules may say. These leaders will also be able to discard ineffective ministers and coopt new ones: the role of the leaders of the membership or of the parliamentary party will merely be to introduce some limits to this power. When positions in the government are more transient and generally less attractive, the leadership of the other components of the party will exercise more power. Indeed, members of the government, including the prime minister, know that their political future lies more in the other components of the party, where they will eventually have to return, than in the present one.

To understand the nature of the constraints and opportunities under which the party in government operates, we have to adopt two different points of view. In the next section we shall adopt the point of view of the party and discuss how the various party components relate to each other. Then, in the second part of this chapter we will adopt the point of view of the government as an institution and take a look at its specific problems.

Parties as complex and diverse systems

Parties, as we saw, are better viewed as 'systems' than as monolithic actors: the complexity of democratic life leads to their internal differentiation. The external action of a party is thus affected by internal dynamics both within and among its parts. Not surprisingly, parties have problems optimising their strategies: different components often attempt to maximise different and at least partially conflicting goals, such as victory at the polls, preservation of party identity or success in government.

The different components provide resources of various types for the party as a whole and for each other; they also constrain each other because of their particular goals and interests (Figure 4.1). The weight and importance of the different components varies significantly across countries, across party 'families' and over time, these variations in turn depending on both societal and political factors. These factors include patterns of social cleavages, forms of social stratification, the availability of alternative resources (especially for the purpose of interests representation and communication), stages of democratisation, configurations of political conflict and mobilisation and institutional arrangements. The position of the party *vis-à-vis* the government also plays a part. As a result, in some cases, one or more components are weak or absent; in other cases, the various components are in equilibrium.

Figure 4.1 Potential relations and exchanges between the party in government, the membership party and parliamentary party

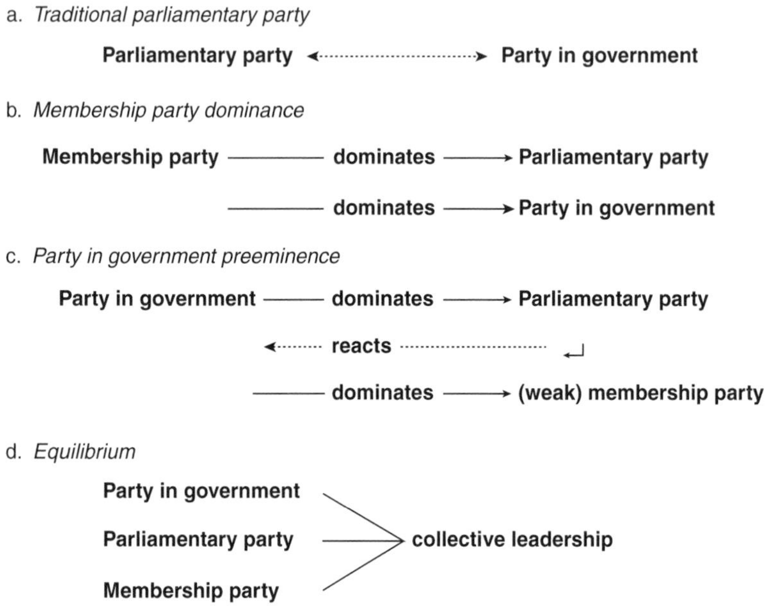

a. *Traditional parliamentary party*

Parliamentary party ◄·······················► **Party in government**

b. *Membership party dominance*

Membership party ———— **dominates** ——→ **Parliamentary party**

———— **dominates** ——→ **Party in government**

c. *Party in government preeminence*

Party in government ———— **dominates** ——→ **Parliamentary party**

◄········· **reacts** ························· ⌐

———— **dominates** ——→ **(weak) membership party**

d. *Equilibrium*

Party in government

Parliamentary party ——→ **collective leadership**

Membership party

Figure 4.2 Types of parties

Let us examine some of these situations (Figure 4.2). At one extreme, one finds the strong membership party (b.) with a clear ideology, a strong bureaucracy under its control and a loyal electorate. The centre of gravity and the top leadership of such a party, which typically comes from a long tradition in opposition, are located rather clearly in the party apparatus. The main resources and constraints derive from there, while the parliamentary component and the representatives in the government are weak and dependent. If we move gradually towards the opposite pole, we find the membership component of the party becoming weaker because members see their affiliton to the party less as a vital engagement and more as a routine linkage, identities are less clear and the ideology is less precise. Meanwhile, the representation of interests is likely to find autonomous channels by which groups come more directly in contact with the members of parliament and with the government. Moreover, the decline in party identification among the electorate means that elections are less predictable: the electoral con- nection becomes therefore more important for the party and the popu- larly elected parliamentary party gains in ascendancy and autonomy. Those party members who are in the government may profit from this

Strength/autonomy of party in government

	low ←————————————————→ high		
a. Vis-à-vis the parliamentary party			
Independent control of MPs over electoral resources	high	medium	low
Strength of committee system	high	medium	low
b. Vis-à-vis the membership party			
Organisational strength of membership party	high	medium	low
Ideological intensity of party	high	medium	low
c. Vis-à-vis both			
Direct electoral mandate of executive	no		yes
Duration in office of government	low		high
Degree of identification of the party with the government	low		high

Figure 4.3 Factors explaining the strength/autonomy of the party in government *vis-à-vis* the parliamentary and the membership parties.

situation if they can count on a kind of direct popular legitimation, not merely in presidential systems but in those parliamentary systems where elections decide who will govern (Figure 4.3). In some cases, as in the British Conservative Party, the parliamentary party and the party in government never lost their prominent position and the membership component has never been able to go beyond playing an ancillary part; in other cases this is a more recent development due to the decline in importance of a previously strong membership component (c.).

When a party has long been in office and the expectation grows that this state of affairs will continue, leaders are likely to cease to view the membership component as an important asset compared to the resources which the control of government offers. The dominance of the party in government may then become overwhelming. However, as in parliamentary systems, the 'party in government' and the parliamentary party are close to each other, and the relationship between these two components becomes crucial when the membership party grows weaker. Yet the nature of that relationship depends in large part on who controls the electoral resources and thus on the factors already mentioned that affect this control.

Finally, when the structures of the party are weak and personal ties are paramount, we may foresee a more fuzzy situation where a small elite occupies the top positions in the different components of the party and moves from one component to another without ever being closely identified with either, but is able to use all of them in an instrumental manner.

What is government?

After having looked into the first side of the party–government relationship we must now take a closer look at the second. The government, too, has many facets. Different meanings of this concept are often used when one discusses its relationship with supporting parties. These relate to the persons in the government, to the institution as a whole or to parts of that institution. There is therefore the need to 'unpack' this concept as we did with the party.

In order to proceed in this direction we must clarify the part played by governments in contemporary democratic systems and this requires us, as anticipated in the previous chapter, to discuss shortly the relationship between representative democracy and the modern state. Historically and structurally, the government, more than any other institution, is at the crossroads between representative mechanisms and the administration of the state.

On the one hand the government is at the top of the representative 'pillar' which is based on elections, parliaments and parties. As Rokkan pointed out, the apex of the democratisation process corresponds to the overcoming of the 'threshold of executive power', that is to say, to the moment when 'parliamentary strength could be translated into direct influence on executive decision-making' (Rokkan, 1970, 79); or, to put it another way, when the government becomes a representative institution. On the other hand, the government is at the top of a huge administrative machine which the modern state developed to perform the many functions concentrated in its hands. Government has the responsibility of steering that apparatus, hence the use of the expression 'administration' in some countries to refer to the government.

Historically, the institution of government developed as a result of the growing expansion and diversification of the state machine and of the need of monarchs to appoint officials to run the organisation.

The cabinet constituted the top group of officials enabling monarchs to ensure that their will would be applied in the different departments. Since the challenge raised by the process of democratisation to the political legitimacy of the monarchy was not accompanied by a similar challenge to the bureaucratic state (Tocqueville, 1856), but rather by the requirement that the bureaucratic state should be subordinated to the new democratic legitimacy, the government as an institution survived and prospered, although it lost its original linkage with the monarchy and established a new linkage with the processes of representation. The institutional forms taken by this new linkage vary. In presidential systems the executive, at least the President, is elected by popular suffrage and subject to the oversight of parliament but cannot normally be dismissed by the legislature. In parliamentary systems the cabinet is accountable to parliament and its survival depends on the support of parliament: this has resulted in the cabinet being the leading element by way of its control of the parliamentary majority. Thus the government continues to head the state bureaucracy while also heading the representative structure.

The nature and role of government has not been shaped only by the separate developments of state bureaucracy and of democratic representation: it has also been shaped by the strong dynamic interactions between these two aspects of contemporary polities, which have produced the rise of the welfare state (Flora and Heidenheimer, 1981) and the growth of the administration which accompanied this rise (Taylor, 1983; Rose, 1984). These developments have in turn greatly expanded the political role of the executive. Moreover, the secular trend of growth of the intervention of the state in the management, regulation and promotion of the economy has increasingly brought the institutions of government to the centre of a two-way flow of communication and influence between the executive and economic actors, individual firms, workers' and business associations and international regulatory bodies. The complex nature of many economic decisions enabled also technicians and experts working for the government to acquire a more prominent role.

Because of this combination of different traditions, it seems more appropriate to view the government as a 'system' rather than as a unitary actor. We need, therefore, to go beyond the outside 'shell' and look at persons, resources, constraints and roles. We must also be aware that the different components which to some extent are part of all contemporary governments do not have the same weight and shape in each country: these components vary across countries and over time.

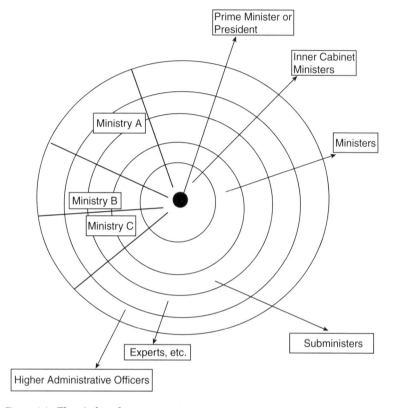

Figure 4.4   The circles of government

First, a government is a group of individuals, but the size and composition of this group depends on the definition given. In a more restrictive definition the government is composed of those, essentially ministers, who attend meetings of the council of ministers or cabinet: this group varies in size but it is much smaller than a parliament, let alone a party. If the focus is the decision-making process, moreover, there is sometimes a stratification between different bodies, with an inner cabinet taking the most important decisions. Yet the borders of the government are not precise. Below the ministerial stratum there is typically a junior ministerial level: members of this level are not normally authorised to attend council of ministers' meetings, but they take an active part in government responsibilities in other ways, sharing some of the duties of ministers with respect to parliament, for instance, by attending committee meetings or steering legislation. They also share some of the administrative business and in particular interact with interest groups. Moreover, each minister is surrounded by a small but important group of advisers and experts. Below these are the top officials of the departments. All of these participate, albeit in different ways, in the activities of government.

Thus what is decided by the government in the narrow sense, by the ministers, has typically been prepared and 'done' by members of the other strata. There is therefore no clear discontinuity between the 'small' and the 'larger' government. It may be claimed that the administrative apparatus is merely the arm of the ministers and should therefore be kept separate, yet public administration and policy studies have shown that not only does the bureaucracy set clear limits to the freedom of action of the ministers, but it also initiates and can promote its own interests and those of its clients. Ministers are therefore only the top of the iceberg, the most visible but not necessarily the most important part. Government is thus constituted in a series of concentric circles (Figure 4.4).

If the study of government consists in studying the individuals of which it is composed, the characteristics of the persons who are part of the government in the narrow sense are only the first step of the analysis: when one moves towards the 'larger' government these characteristics change appreciably. Politicians become administrators; yet there is also some variation in the origins of those who compose the government *stricto sensu*. There are obviously professional politicians, most of whom have a background in electoral politics, some of whom belong to the leadership group of their party while others are less prominent; there are also some top bureaucrats, policy experts and representatives of interest groups (Blondel and Thiébault, 1991). Ministers are therefore likely to have different attitudes, interests and motivations, partly because of their socialisation and partly because of their earlier careers. Moreover, what is true of the government in the narrow sense is even more true of the members of the government in the larger sense: their origins vary markedly. It is a good guess, therefore, that the goals and preferences of those who belong to the same government will also be diverse.

Government members are not simply individuals: they have with few exceptions a well-specified institutional role. Those who have a portfolio – the large majority – are in charge of a sector of the state bureaucracy which is responsible for a defined area of policies. As heads of departments, ministers have major responsibilities; they also acquire in this way important resources for political action. They have at their disposal financial means, expertise and knowledge, although their action is markedly limited by the past policies which they inherit, these being in a sense crystallised in the bureaucracies of the departments and defended by the clients who have mushroomed around them. If one looks at the matter from the point of view of the interests of the departmental bureaucracy, on the other hand, ministers are both a resource and a constraint. They provide democratic legitimacy for the policies of the department; but they may resist these policies. Each department is thus an arena within which different actors – the minister, the undersecretaries, the bureaucrats, the interest group representatives – co operate and compete, while there is also competition and cooperation among the different departments.

In order to understand the resources, the constraints and the incentives which affect the different actors of the governmental game we need to pay more specific attention to the different 'faces' of the government.

The 'representative' face of the government

The 'representative' face is undoubtedly the most visible: as a matter of fact, in democratic political systems the life of the government in the strict sense wholly depends on the electoral process. Governments begin and end because of the direct or indirect effects of this process; their legitimacy stems from it. An important part of the constraints and incentives under which the government operates is naturally linked to this representative character. Yet, as the role played by the government in the representative game may change significantly under the effects of institutional rules and other political factors, there is space here for important variations.

Institutional rules are the first factor in defining the political space within which the representative game takes place and the role the executive plays in it. The choice of a presidential or semi-presidential solution (or, as in Israel, of a directly elected premier), with the popular election of the head of the executive brings the government (or more exactly its upper level) directly into the representative game. The head of the government is 'produced' via the electoral process and, insofar as reelection is allowed and the president or elected premier is willing to run again, the government will participate in the next round of elections. In such a situation the electoral mandate is a resource directly controlled by the head of government who can rely on it to legitimise his or her action without having to 'borrow' legitimacy from other political actors. Yet the electoral connection also works as a constraint: the head of the executive may be held accountable at the next election for past promises and will therefore take future accountability into consideration while making decisions.

In such a system, ministers are only indirectly involved in the representative 'face' of the government: they are wholly dependent on the head of the executive. The team is chosen on the basis of a number of considerations including (a) satisfying the groups and interests which supported the leader, (b) ensuring administrative competence to implement electoral promises, and (c) recruiting personalities with the ability to win support for the leader in the future election. During the first part of the leader's term, more attention is likely to be paid to the previous election and to fulfilling promises or paying political debts; but with the passing of time the forthcoming election is likely to play an increasing part.

In pure presidential systems the separation of powers leads to two distinct representative 'games', that of presidential candidates and that of congressional candidates: in such systems, the government is a representative actor but does not have the monopoly of representation. As a result, whenever the approval of the legislature is required, the government has to confront other representative actors and from this confrontation result various outcomes ranging from stalemate to negotiated agreements.

Government in semi-presidential systems

In semi-presidential systems, the position of the executive in the representation 'game' is less simple. There is a dual executive and there are two parallel lines of democratic legitimation, that of the direct election for the presidency and that of the indirect election by means of parliamentary confidence of the cabinet (Duverger, 1980; Sartori, 1994). There are thus two independent representation games but, contrary to the pure presidential system, here both see a component of the executive involved. In the end either the government manages to re-unify the two games at the top when the president is also the leader of the parliamentary majority and thus dominates the cabinet, or is divided by them when president and cabinet are issued from two different political majorities, the situation referred to as 'cohabitation'. The position of the president *vis-à-vis* the rest of the government changes in a significant way as a result: he or she is either the effective head of the government, at least for strategic decisions, or must retreat to the position of a 'dignified' but less 'efficient' head of state at most concerned with a limited and residual domain. The role of the prime minister correspondingly changes and is either that of an agent or a delegate

– even a scapegoat – of the president or that of the real leader of the government. Why in some cases, as in France, such variations in the structure of the government have taken place smoothly while in Portugal or Poland they have been more conflictual is a matter which awaits empirical investigation. One should note, however, that in France which has since the 1980s been the example *par excellence* of the 'alternating' (Duverger, 1980) or 'oscillating' (Sartori, 1984) semi-presidential system, the president never lost hope of winning back a stronger role as a result of either a subsequent parliamentary or presidential election. In other political systems with similar institutional arrangements such hopes have either never existed (as in Austria), or have ceased to exist (as in Finland and Portugal). In these cases, the presidential election has had a different significance: it is a mechanism of personnel selection rather than the arena of a true representation game. Thus, in semi-presidential systems, the president can be a representative and governmental actor but also runs the risk of losing a significant part of these two roles as a result of other developments in the political system.

Government in parliamentary systems

In parliamentary systems the representative role of the government is in principle less direct. Parliament not the government is elected. The government comes into being only after the representation game has been played and once a majority in parliament has emerged. Moreover, its end comes before the new round of the game which begins when parliament dissolves and new elections are called. Other actors, typically the parties which endorse parliamentary candidates but also more rarely independents, participate more directly in the process. From an institutional point of view, the government derives its democratic legitimacy from these actors; in practice, however, as a result of the format of the party system the government may in fact be elected 'directly' and indeed even run its own reelection campaign. This is particularly the case in two-party systems, but it may also occur in multi-party systems when one party is large enough to win alone or when a coalition of parties fights the election jointly with the aim of forming the government together and facing subsequent elections as a team. In such cases differences with presidential systems have not so much to do with the fact that the representative link is direct or indirect, but with the consequences of other institutional arrangements. In parliamentary systems there is one election only: since there is only one representation game the government may be an even stronger representative actor than it is in presidential systems, where the president has to take an independently elected legislature into account. At the same time, however, in parliamentary systems the election is in a sense collective: the prime minister wins together with the parliamentary party (Rose, 1980a and 1980b; King, 1975). Only together with it can he or she achieve the parliamentary majority which ensures the government's survival.

The representative role of the executive in different types of governments is indicated in Figure 4.5. Type A is a government with a direct representative role in which only the head of the government, the president, is elected directly; the other members of the government derive their representative character from the president. The government however, shares, this representative character with the legislature. In type B the representative character of the government is not direct, but derives from parliament. In type C, because of a special combination of institutional and political conditions, the government is in practice, though not formally, directly elected: its representative character, however, is not separate from that of parliament but on the contrary is acquired in association with parliament itself. No empirical example of type D can be found, and such a type is indeed difficult to conceive even in theory. The mixed type E corresponds to semi-presidential systems in which elements of A and B (or even of C if the prime minister can count upon *de facto* direct electoral support) are combined. Finally, type F corresponds to governments which are not representative and whose legitimacy has a different base: this is the case, for instance, of technical governments.

These types indicate that governments may play rather different parts in the representation game and thus also in winning the political resources produced in that context. Some governments have a more

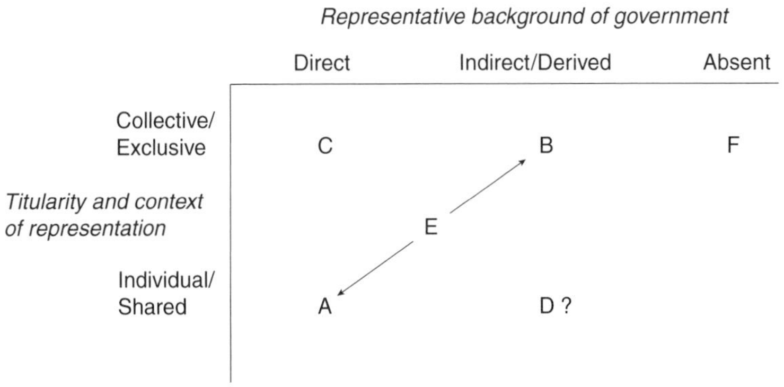

Figure 4.5 The 'representative' face of government: dimensions of variation

direct electoral base than others: they have campaigned in a straight-forward manner and stood in front of the voters, who in turn have been in a position to anticipate clearly what the consequences of their vote would be. Other governments, on the contrary, are dissolved before the election takes place and voters may not have any idea in advance of the consequences of their vote and what the new government will be like. In such cases the government will not have a clear electoral mandate. Yet even when the electoral process leads directly to the formation of a government, the recipient of the electoral mandate may vary: it could be the head of the government alone, all the government as a collective body or the parliamentary majority. In the case of a presidential election, popular investiture goes without any doubt to the head of the executive. In a parliamentary system when there is a 'direct' election the prime minister is obviously a beneficiary of the electoral mandate. But he or she may have to share it with other ministers who are influential in his/her party or who are the leaders of the other parties of the coalition. And the parliamentary majority that supports the government is obviously another recipient of the same electoral mandate. One could refer in a similar way to incentives and constraints. A government which has to win reelection through direct participation in an electoral contest is likely to be under the influence of different incentives and constraints from those influencing a government which knows that it will last or fall because of other factors.

The nature of the representative character of the government may sometimes change with the passing of time. Even when the government did not have a direct mandate from the people but came to power indirectly as a result of negotiations among the parties jointly forming a majority, the government might remain in power up to the next election and then try to win a direct investiture on the basis of its popularity. Such a strategy may or may not be successful; it is almost sure, however, that it will arouse the antagonism of other political actors and of party leaders in particular, as these expect to be the main players. On the other hand, in parliamentary systems in which the government normally receives 'direct' support from the people (C), the parliamentary party(ies) may reassert its (their) right *vis-à-vis* the government by challenging the autonomy of the prime minister and ministers. The government may then come to have the characteristics of a B-type executive at least until it is able to win a new popular mandate.

What difference does it make for party–government relationships whether the government does or does not have a direct representative character? We shall look at the matter in greater detail at the end of this chapter, but it can already be noted that when the government is able to combine the resources stemming from the representation game with those deriving from its administrative role, its authority in front of the supporting party(ies) will increase. The 'party in government' will consequently be in a particularly strong position *vis-à-vis* the other components of the party and will probably attract the top party leaders. At the same time, thanks to its democratic legitimation, it will be able to exert substantial power over the bureaucratic apparatus.

The 'state' face of the government

The government, in first place the ministers, also has a 'state' face as it heads the central bureaucracy. That bureaucracy is composed of a series of organised structures – the ministries – which enjoy a significant degree of autonomy and have grown as a result of decades and in some cases centuries of development. These bureaucratic structures can be said to embody the answers given over the years to the changing and typically expanding responsibilities of the state in different fields (Rose, 1984). The government reflects this increase of the state machinery by its changing composition. In the middle of the nineteenth century there were few ministers and these led the classical departments of the 'minimal state' – foreign affairs, justice, war, interior, finance, religious affairs – while the much larger governments of the late twentieth century include the new functions gradually assumed by the state in the economic sector – such as public works, agriculture, transport, industry, and in the social sector education, health, social security, labour and family (Rose, 1984). Some of these state functions and the bureaucratic organisations that preside over them were created well before (democratic) representative politics developed, while others as well as the extensions of the original ones were the result of the dynamics of democratic politics (Alber, 1982; Flora and Heidenheimer, 1981).

Whatever the factors behind state growth, that process entailed that on becoming more democratic political systems also became significantly more bureaucratic: the government became more closely linked to the representative process and at the same time more heavily influenced by the needs of a huge bureaucratic machine. Once translated into new bureaucracies, into new programmes or into extensions of preexisting bureaucracies, the political inputs coming from democratic politics gained their own independent momentum. The vested interests of strong state bureaucracies ask for representation as any other societal interest: they do so not only by acting through the normal representative processes, but by intervening directly on ministers. Hence the well-known question: do the (political) ministers lead the ministries or are they their captives? (Rose, 1986; Strøm, 1994).

The vested interests of state bureaucracies are an obviously important part of the picture: yet bureaucracies may also defend what they view as the public interest. The two elements sometimes reinforce each other: while serving their private interests bureaucracies may well feel that they are promoting the public interest and vice versa. For example, a move to resist reductions in the number of school teachers coincides with the private interests of the education bureaucracy, but such a policy can also be presented as a battle for the preservation of the strength and quality of public education. Studies have shown that bureaucrats can often enlist the support of their clients to strengthen their demands. When defending an administrative programme the bureaucracy can mobilise the individuals and groups that have profited from it. The government as a whole and individual ministers in particular consequently face a large stream of demands, proposals and pressures from inside their own departments.

More generally as it runs the public administration, the government collectively and ministers individually, as well as the other 'parts' of the government lower down the hierarchy, are constantly confronted with the responsibilities stemming from the fact that in a given country and at a given point in time some activities are expected to be fulfilled by the state and therefore fall under the purview of the central government. These include the responsibilities traditionally associated with the principle of sovereignty, such as taking care of external relations or of law and order, but also the newer responsibilities of the interventionist and social state, such as ensuring economic development and social protection, as well as a whole range of diverse and often petty responsibilities (from providing support for opera theatres to protecting the national movie industry) which have often fallen upon the shoulders of the state by chance and coincidence. The range of such responsibilities varies in a significant way from country to country and over time, but within each country and in the short run it can be considered to a large extent a given.

These responsibilities entail that the government as such is constantly confronted with decisions that need to be taken. Obviously the government has some leeway in its decision-making process, and it can to an extent delay its response and manipulate the agenda, but in the end it is generally less able than other actors, whether parties or parliament, to choose the battles it has to fight. A party may prefer to keep a low profile on budgetary matters when tough and unpopular decisions have to be taken, but finance ministers and governments must present their budget.

When an international crisis requires a decision, a party and even parliament may or may not take a position but the government has to.

Besides being confronted with sectional inputs from within the departments and having to take decisions relating to the life of each department, governments also have overall responsibilities stemming from interconnections among departmental activities, the budget being the clearest example of such an overall responsibility. The government because of its role as head of all the state bureaucratic structures must produce a budget (sound or unsound, balanced or unbalanced) that takes into account all incomes and expenditures. While the minister of finance is more specifically involved in the preparation of that budget, the prime minister and the whole cabinet in the end have to be involved in its approval. The importance of this responsibility (and the pressures and constraints deriving from it) is obviously increased by the size that state budgets have nowadays acquired. The budget is no longer merely an internal matter for the central government but affects the inflation rate, the level of growth, employment and so on, so that the government when managing the public sector also plays a major role in steering the whole economy.

As it is involved in this way, the government comes to be related in a complex manner to a web of economic actors, both internal (trade unions, entrepreneurs, national bank) and external (multinational companies, IMF, WTO, European institutions). These actors are continuously engaged in discussions and deals with the government. Such interactions produce constraints, as the government must take into account the influence and possible reactions of these actors; but the government can also derive from them resources (different forms of support) which can be used with respect to other domestic political actors. We normally expect the government to have a predominant role in this context; however, other actors such as the parties can also play a part, especially if they can show that the government cannot reach any agreement without their consent.

International influences and constraints have become increasingly important in the last decades of the twentieth century in the life of European governments, given the growth in the number of important national policies that have to incorporate consequences of decisions taken at the European level. The implications for national governments are mixed. On the one hand, these governments lose a portion of their autonomy, having to comply with decisions taken in Brussels (Scharpf, 1995); on the other, decisions taken at the European level primarily involve national government representatives as these participate in the various bodies of the European Union – the European Council, Council of Ministers, COREPER, Intergovernmental Conferences. Thus, national governments participate in the decision-making process at the supranational level, while national parties, because of the limited development of their supranational structures (Hix, 1995), are much less able to exert their influence. Since decisions in the European arena are taken under the very special conditions of a cumbersome process involving now 15 countries, national governments are able to point out to domestic dissenters, when it comes to implementing these agreements at the internal level, the enormous difficulties of upsetting agreements painstakingly achieved. The government therefore might well be in a subordinate position on the supranational plane, but it is put in a dominant position internally.

In the fields of foreign affairs and security, external constraints limited the freedom of action of European states to a very significant extent during the long period of the cold war: governments and ministers of foreign affairs and defence were thus in part 'transmission belts' to the national decision-making process of policy decisions taken outside the country.

The state 'face' of government is thus an important source of resources and of constraints: but it is more difficult to assess the variations from one case to another in this respect than it is with respect of the representative dimension, as the dimensions of variation are less obvious (Figure 4.6). A first dimension to be taken into account concerns the strength and professionalisation of the departmental bureaucracies, particularly at the top: some of these are indeed more qualified, more immune to external pressures, more self-confident than others. This is likely to affect the ability of these bodies to 'advise' the government internally and to resist the pressures of the 'representative' elements of government. Given that the central administration is divided into

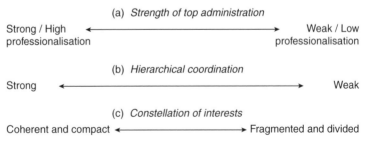

Figure 4.6   The 'administrative' side of government: dimensions of variation

departments which have a different history (old or new ministries), different functions (some being primarily regulatory, other extractive or distributive) and a significant degree of autonomy, we should not assume that all departments will occupy the same position along this dimension of variation. Some – the treasury or the ministry of foreign affairs for instance – are more likely than others – such as the ministries of labour or of agriculture – to exert independent influence on policy-making and to resist political influence.

The strength of the mechanisms of coordination and of hierarchy among the various departments and among ministers constitutes another relevant and partially connected dimension of variation. Presidential or prime ministerial offices and ministries of finance may be more or less involved in screening, prioritising, delaying, vetoing or altering the policy proposals of other departments. This is in part due to factors mentioned earlier as well as to the formal and informal structure of the government (Blondel and Müller-Rommel, 1993); it is also due to temporary or even prolonged circumstances which tend to enhance the role of the 'centre of government' or of particular departments, especially foreign affairs, finance or the interior. If the country plays a prominent international part, the roles of the head of the government and of the minister of foreign affairs will tend to be large; if budgetary problems are overwhelming and there is a pressing need to comply with international economic requirements, the role of the minister of finance will be dominant.

The strength of clients who are directly related to specific departments also has to be taken into account. A coherent and compact constellation of interests may capture a department and lead from within battles for favourable policies while strongly opposing any proposals perceived as hostile. A fragmented and divided constellation of interests will tend to be less effective in supporting independent action by a department.

In order to summarise the points discussed above, resources and constraints dimensions can be identified and used to distinguish among four types of governments (Figure 4.7). Governments of type A have large administrative resources but are also subjected to strong pressures from their 'state' side. The administrative face of the government will have the means and incentives to challenge its representative face. If administrative constraints are weak but resources are strong, as in type B governments, the state face of the government can become a powerful tool of the representative face. Type C governments are those which have relatively weak administrative resources but which fall under strong external constraints and may even succumb to these constraints.

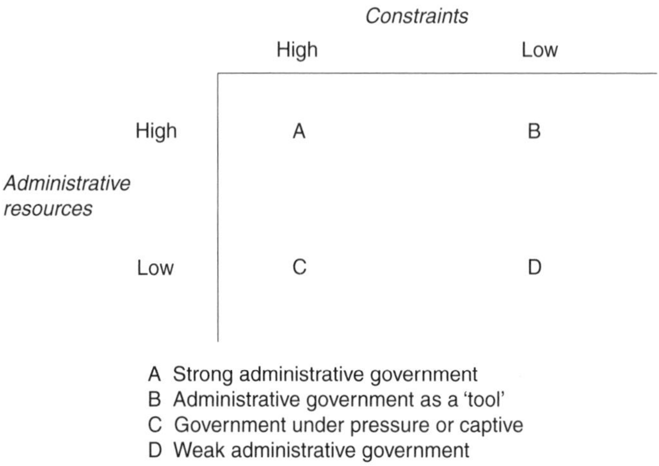

Constraints

	High	Low
High	A	B
Low	C	D

Administrative resources

A Strong administrative government
B Administrative government as a 'tool'
C Government under pressure or captive
D Weak administrative government

Figure 4.7   Types of 'administrative' games

Type D governments operate in conditions in which both administrative resources and administrative constraints are weak: the representative face will therefore dominate but might face difficulties in implementing its political goals. Within this two-dimensional space we can try to place different countries but also different governments of the same country (and perhaps also different components of the same government). If we want to simplify the picture one might just contrast governments in which the administrative component is strong to those in which it is weak, namely governments of types A and D.

The interaction between the representative and the administrative faces of the government

We can now present a general picture of the political context within which the government operates. As we have seen, it operates at the intersection between two types of political 'games', a representative 'game' and an administrative 'game'. The different circles of the government are involved to a varying extent in these games, but the inner core is directly or indirectly linked to both of them.

Figure 4.8 indicates the main lines of interaction between the two games. On the left side of the figure, one can see the role of the government in the representative game. This role is indirect in the case of the ideal-type parliamentary system, and it is direct but played jointly with

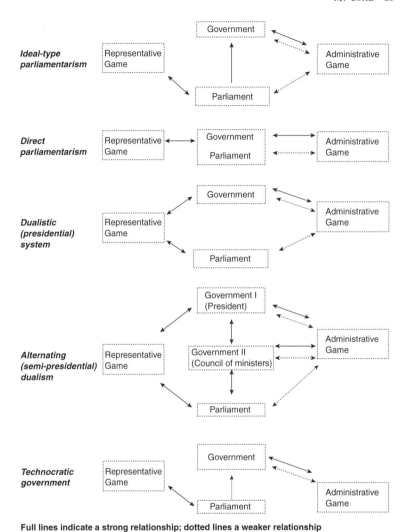

Full lines indicate a strong relationship; dotted lines a weaker relationship

Figure 4.8 Government between representation and administration

the parliament in the case of 'direct' parliamentarism; it is direct but shared with an autonomous parliament in dualistic (presidential) systems; it is both direct and indirect in 'alternating dualism' (semi-presidential systems) where the government is effectively composed of president and council of ministers; finally in technical governments, even the indirect link becomes tenuous. On the right side of the figure

one can see the relationship between the government and the administrative 'game'. For the sake of simplicity this relationship is shown either
as strong (a continuous line) or as weak (a dotted line) in terms of
constraints and resources.

From this graphical presentation we can see that in two cases – 'direct'
parliamentarism and presidential systems – the government directly
plays both games and thus is able to link them. In two other cases –
ideal-type parliamentarism and technical government – the two games
are played by different actors in turn linked to each other (but in the
second case only weakly). Finally, in the 'alternating dualism' of semi-
presidential systems both possibilities exist.

We must now discuss briefly how the two 'games' interact, and how
this can affect the life and workings of the government. We can do this
first by looking at the government from the point of view of the persons
it is comprised of, then from the point of view of the actions (decisions
in the field of policies and patronage) that these persons undertake and
to the resources, incentives and constraints that affect them.

With regard to the first perspective we may start from the persons that
compose the government *stricto sensu*, that is to say those who play the
role of the president (in presidential and semi-presidential systems), of
the prime minister (in parliamentary and semi-presidential systems) and
of the ministers (in all systems). In this perspective the government 'is'
the persons that cover, for the time being, these roles. And we can analyse
the government by looking at the features and background of its members together with the links these have with other institutions and organisations. We can then determine whether the government is made up of
'representatives', of 'state bureaucrats', of 'experts' or 'economic actors'.
The predominance of 'representatives', that is to say of politicians who
have been deeply involved in electoral politics at the parliamentary but
in some cases also at the local level as well, has been documented in the
case of governments of democratic countries; there are also some examples of the other two types, however (Blondel and Thiébault, 1991;
Blondel and Cotta, 1996). The variations are not just across types of
systems (parliamentary or presidential) as might be expected, but also
among governments of the same type: in some parliamentary systems
state bureaucrats or experts of the economy play a substantial part.

The predominance of 'representatives' is obviously linked to the need
experienced by governments of contemporary democracies to have a
popular legitimacy. Yet the linkage of the government with representation processes can take different forms, as we have seen. In some cases,
for example where the head of the executive is linked individually to the

electoral process and is not part of a group which is collectively representative, the other members of the government are more likely to have various origins: a directly elected president, who is a representative in the strong sense of the word, will therefore be able to recruit administrators and experts into the government, together with old friends and a small number of representatives, preferably from special groups, as the American example shows. Other factors also play a part: if parties are temporarily weak or ineffective while there is a need to strengthen the economy, there may be a space for partially technical governments, as occurred occasionally in Finland before the 1980s and in Italy in the 1990s. Past practices inherited from a period when the government did not have an electoral base or the need for governments to preserve some neutrality in highly segmented polities may have led to relatively depoliticised governments such as those of the Netherlands before the 1970s and perhaps of Austria. The administrative 'game' plays a part here: one might expect more technicians in governments where the administration is stronger either for structural reasons – if it is highly professional – or for circumstantial reasons – if some policy or budgetary goals have priority as a result of internal or external constraints. Yet the choice between representative politicians and technicians may not always be clear-cut: technicians sometimes become representative politicians by standing for election. Their original background may still be important but their new posture results in a mixed profile.

The characteristics of the second circle of government, that of the junior ministers and undersecretaries, do not vary markedly from those of the first, but there are substantial differences when one moves to the third circle, that of the top levels of officials. At that level men and women with a bureaucratic background predominate, although persons with a politico-representative background and allegiances are sometimes given positions even at that level. The clearest example of this possibility is provided by the American spoils system where many top positions in the bureaucracy are held by individuals linked politically to the representative side of the government and primarily to the president. Elsewhere, political influence may simply mean that top bureaucrats are selected on the basis of their political leanings.

Yet the government is not just the persons who form part of it at the different levels: it is also constituted by the activities it undertakes, by the policies it decides and by the patronage it distributes. In this perspective the background and personal features of its components are obviously important, but other aspects, too, play a role. It is at this point that the resources, incentives and constraints which derive from the different 'games' the government is playing and which affect its members have to be assessed. The representative game allocates resources of legitimacy, of mandate or of empowerment. The rules of the representative 'game' decide how the government and its members can participate, whether they have an exclusive and direct control, have only a share or are just the indirect recipients of these resources. The government may have to face the competition of other players, such as the leaders of the membership party or parliamentarians, in this game. In order to participate effectively in the representation game the contenders must control some resources in advance. Ideology, political identification and organisational linkages with voters on the one hand, and on the other, charisma, media exposure, policies implemented or promised and patronage distributed to clients are among the resources to be used. With variations, the party as it has been known in the twentieth century, that is to say as a large organisation with a strong political identity, is the place where some of these resources, typically those of the first category, are produced: even if they are not in government, party politicians can control them. Other relevant resources are produced within the government itself via the administration, and politicians in government may win more effective control over them. If it is the case that there is a decline in the control that parties have over the first group of resources as a result of the decline of the ideological mass party, the need becomes greater for party politicians to be in government in order to effectively play the representative game. This might explain to an extent why in some European countries – Finland, Netherlands, Italy – the leaders of parties themselves have had an increasing propensity to enter the government (Blondel and Thiébault, 1991; Blondel and Cotta, 1996).

The role of the government as a key centre of production and allocation of political resources also has to do with the part it plays in what we have called the administrative game. First, the government controls the state administration: this can be used for producing and implementing policies and for producing and distributing patronage. Second, the government occupies a central position in a dense web of internal and international actors, especially in the economic field. This strengthens the visibility of politicians in government and gives them substantial bargaining leverage.

There are, however, not only resources at the disposal of the government, but also strong constraints to be faced. The budgetary ones are the most obvious, but there are many others. The decision and implementation of policies and programmes inevitably meets with all sorts of resistances, complaints and oppositions. Having to face these constraints is a cost for politicians in government which other politicians – for instance leaders of the membership party or parliamentarians – do not have: they can promise more and insist that the government must stick more faithfully to its pure political identity. There are, however, limits to this outbidding: too intransigent party and parliamentary politicians might appear to the majority of voters as unrealistic doctrinaires fighting for a never attainable utopia. The constraints may also be exploited in a more subtle manner by politicians in the government: being presented as 'facts' that cannot be changed they may be used to sell policies to voters and party members that would otherwise have been difficult to accept. The manipulation of economic and international constraints may thus become a resource for the government, the Maastricht Treaty criteria being an example: budgetary restraint which would not otherwise have been adopted was accepted because it was part of the European agreement (which in fact had been pursued by some governments precisely for this purpose). Not all constraints originate from the administrative side of government, however: some are produced by the representative side. It is, for instance, difficult for a government to move against the constellation of interests which was instrumental in mobilising popular support in its favour, or to act when elections are approaching in a direction which it knows will be unpopular.

The two 'games' in which members of government are involved may be in opposition to each other. Thus the extension of pension benefits may help to win support in the representative game, while in the administrative game (perhaps under pressures from international authorities) the need to tighten the budget might require precisely the opposite move. To the extent that it is involved in the two games, the government has to choose or find a middle way. It may use one plane against the other, that is to say the administrative constraints to convince voters or voter demands to keep administrative pressures at bay. Which side will exert the stronger pressure depends on factors which have been examined in the previous pages.

There may also be reinforcement of one game by the other. Demands originating from the two sides may go in the same direction: by responding to electoral demands the government may also please the bureaucracy and vice versa. Thus, a broadening of the provisions of the welfare state satisfies voters' requests but can also find the support of bureaucrats who will have greater resources at their disposal; thus, too, privatisations may please treasuries which under the pressure of European authorities attempt to reduce public debt, but they may also appeal to voters.

The relations between the government and its supporting parties

As we have seen, parties and governments are complex realities: they are systems where different 'games' are played. On the party side one game focuses on the preservation of the identity and of the organisational unity of the membership party; another is the electoral game aiming at maintaining and broadening the electoral following of the party. Yet a third aims at winning control over decision-making processes and in particular over the government. These games are connected to each other but are also partly autonomous. Meanwhile, governments are involved in both a representative game and an administrative game.

Government and party are two systems with variable degrees of overlap. Within them the actors play the political game(s) with the resources available to them and under the constraints typical of each system. The actors of the two systems are to an extent, but to an extent only, identical. Resources are not equally available to the actors of the different systems. The transfer of resources from one system to the other is possible within limits, while each system works under specific constraints. Party–government relationships constitute the intersection between the two systems.

If we concentrate on the representative politicians who compose the government, the government–party relationship is a relationship between these politicians and the other representative politicians who do not belong to the government. To this extent the government, if it is not a government of technicians, is simply part of a larger group of politicians who play the representative game, although different sub-games are also played within it. The role of the government within this larger group depends on the way the representative game is organised and works: the government may be the leading element, a component of this leading element or a mere subordinate body. During the twentieth century, the party has been the 'shell' which has kept all representative politicians together. Party–government relations become in this sense 'within-party' relations between different strata or groups of party leaders: the more the party has a strong organisation with a clearly defined identity, the more the common structure creates a real unity among the different categories of party politicians and reduces the centrifugal effects of the different political games they are involved in. When the distinctiveness of the identity and the organisational strength decline, the 'shell' may become so weak that the meaningfulness of referring to one group (party) of representative politicians becomes questionable. It is common in America to talk of the congressional party and of the presidential party as fairly independent bodies; Mair (1994) suggests that it might be useful to refer to different 'parties' in the European context as well.

Meanwhile, one can view party–government relationships as also taking place within the government between (party) politicians and bureaucrats. The two components are united by the institutional structure of the government and by the responsibilities which flow from the existence of this structure. They are involved in different political games, however. The common institutional 'shell' may be stronger and, if so, the government operates as a unitary body; or it may be weaker and, if so, political and bureaucratic components of the government become distinct.

As a conclusion to these pages we can say that party–government relationships vary markedly because party and government also differ markedly, with particular traditions, specific forms of development, different institutional arrangements and variable internal and external challenges all contributing to the different profiles.

Note

1 The work for this chapter was supported by a grant of the Italian Centro Nazionale delle Ricerche (CNR 97.00650.ct09) and by the foundation Monte dei Paschi di Siena – Istituto di diritto pubblico. I also want to acknowledge the suggestions offered by Wolfgang Müller and the help of Dr Luca Verzichelli in many stages of the research and in elaborating and drawing the figures.

5
A framework for the Empirical Analysis of Government– Supporting Party Relationships

J. Blondel

Party government links the two halves of political life, the half consti-tuted by the inputs of the society brought into the 'blackbox' via the governmental party(ies) and the half constituted by the state outputs organised and controlled in the 'blackbox' by the government. To be understood, the characteristics of party government therefore have to be related to activities taking place within these two halves, indeed not just at the level of parties and of governments, but within the society and the state at large. The aim of this chapter is to provide a framework for such an analysis.

To do so, however, one must move from the general proposition that state and society influence the nature of party government to a practical determination of the mechanisms of this influence. Clearly, in a first and rather tentative examination of the problem, many aspects have to be set aside; moreover, the analysis conducted in this volume is con-fined to eight Western European countries which differ to some extent but also have many aspects in common. The 'societal' half is similar in many ways. These polities are not only all liberal democracies; they are parliamentary democracies, including the semi-presidential French Fifth Republic. This means that government and parliament are closely related, with the parties being central to this relationship. Indeed, par-ties are typically strong, even if Italy since 1992 and to a more limited extent France constitute partial exceptions. Moreover, these countries all have a large number of lively groups and movements which have come to play a major part in the policy-making process.

There is also a substantial similarity in the 'state' half of Western European polities. Whatever may be said about some of these countries and in particular about Italy, the state is 'strong' in the sense that its decisions tend to be implemented: there is penetration of the bureaucracy in the polity at large. Besides, despite the moves towards privatisation which took place from the middle of the 1980s, the scope of the public sector remains large, particularly in the social fields.

All these characteristics mean that many elements which would differ in a worldwide inquiry are simply not variables in the context of a study of eight Western European polities. The framework which has to be adopted for such a study therefore has to be more limited in scope: there are three elements which emerge as key factors likely to account for variations in the relationship between governments and supporting parties in the countries concerned.

- First and ostensibly above all, there are major differences in the party systems of these countries and these differences are linked, to a substantial extent at least, to the cleavage structure of the societies.
- Second, although the state is strong everywhere, its impact on party government does vary, partly because the party system provides more space for administrative-type decisions and less space for partisan decisions in some countries than in others.
- Third, relations between governments and supporting parties are likely to be affected by the fields of policy-making, as some of these policy fields have more of an administrative character than others.

The aim of this chapter is thus to examine the impact which these three variables can be expected to have on the type of party government. Before undertaking this task, however, we need to consider somewhat more closely the character of both the 'dependent' variable (party government) and of the three 'independent' variables which have just been described. It will then be possible to suggest how these independent variables might affect party government in its separate elements as well as overall.

The types of party government and the societal variables likely to affect it

The types of party government

Party government is often mentioned in the singular as if it was of one type only. In reality, there are large variations among different types. This is due to two sets of characteristics which were identified and examined in the earlier volume on *Party and Government* (Blondel and Cotta, 1996, 7–8). First, party–government relationships take place on three planes which are distinct, although they are partly connected. One plane is that of *policy-making*: governments and supporting parties are manifestly both involved in this process and many complex links can be expected to develop between the two sides as a result. The second plane is constituted by *appointments*: this is also manifestly important. The appointments referred to here are at the top of the pyramid of power; they concern the membership of cabinets and of other governmental posts, as well as the membership of party executives. Third, governments and supporting parties also relate to each other in terms of favours and *patronage*. Admittedly, these result in 'mini-policies' and in various kinds of appointments, but both these mini-policies and appointments differ widely from other policies and other appointments: they tend to be undertaken in secrecy and are designed to maintain or increase support for the parties and governments concerned, not to be ends in themselves.

The second set of characteristics on the basis of which party government varies relates to the strength of the rapport between governments and the parties which support them. It can be close, weak or even non-existent; in the last case there is 'autonomy' between government and supporting parties. When there is no autonomy, the direction of the influence can also vary: the government may be dominated by the party or the party by the government. Thus ministers may or may not be appointed at the behest of the supporting parties; thus, too, given policies may be elaborated by the government independently or be the result of initiatives taken by the supporting parties.

If one links these two sets of characteristics, one finds cases in which the government depends on the supporting parties over one, two or all three of the planes of the relationship. One also finds cases in which the government is autonomous or at least relatively autonomous from the supporting parties (and conversely the supporting parties are autonomous from the government), as well as cases in which the supporting parties are dependent on the government. This last situation occurs, for instance, if the government induces the parties, by whatever means, to accept the policies which it proposes, and/or succeeds in ensuring that the party executive is composed of men and women whom it wishes to see appointed and/or decides on favours and patronage.

There is thus a 'pole' of government dependence which is distinct from a pole of autonomy and from a pole of party dependence (Figure 5.1). The relationship between governments and supporting parties

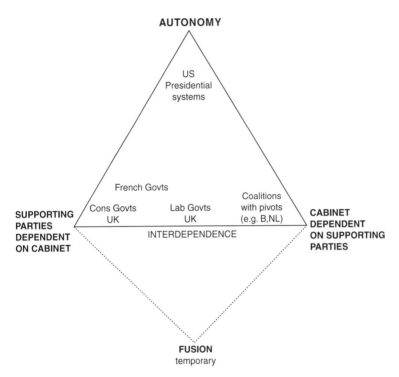

Figure 5.1 Autonomy and dependence in the relations between cabinets and supporting parties

tends, therefore, to take place within a space which has a triangular shape, with the autonomous position at the top and the line joining the two poles of dependence at the bottom, although part of the space below the line of interdependence may also be occupied when there is almost complete fusion between party leadership and government leadership. Such a situation occurs occasionally in some countries, in Britain for instance, in particular during the early period of the life of a cabinet (Blondel and Cotta, 1996, 24–5).

The position occupied in the space by a particular party government is not necessarily the same with respect to the three planes of the relationship between parties and governments. There may well also be changes over time: thus a government may become gradually less dependent on the party(ies) which support it with respect to one of the three planes but little difference occurs with respect to the others.

While the three planes of the relationship are distinct, there are links between them, and these links have a different character depending on the situation. They may result in *reinforcement* or in *compensation* of one type of relationship by another (Blondel and Cotta, 1996, 18–19). Reinforcement occurs, for instance, when parties control government appointments in order to be able to influence government policy-making: supporting parties do indeed often seem to want to take power *in order* to carry out some policies. There is compensation, on the other hand, if parties refrain from participating in government in exchange for exercising influence on policy-making: Strøm (1984) has examined closely this behaviour and views it as a kind of trade-off between 'seeking power' and 'seeking to influence', one type compensating for the other. The party or parties belonging to a minority government thus have to agree to aspects of policy-making with one or more other parties: this interpretation helps to account for cases of 'true' minority governments in parliamentary systems, in particular where these are numerous, as in Scandinavia.

Reinforcement and compensation may also vary over time because appointments, patronage and policy-making are intrinsically different: appointments are made for a period, often a long period; patronage distribution tends to follow a pattern which may have to remain the same, at least in broad terms; policy-making includes a succession of decisions, often unrelated to each other, a characteristic which provides many opportunities for trade-offs. Since appointments are made once-and-for-all, or at least cannot easily be changed, a minister who toes the party line at the time of appointment may not do so to the same extent subsequently: the relationship between the government and the party of this minister is likely to be modified as a result. Moreover, these three planes differ in terms of the extent to which they relate more or less to society at large. Appointments are essentially matters internal to parties and to governments; patronage may affect parties exclusively but it can also and indeed often does concern broader sections of the population. Policies affect potentially, and in many cases in reality, the whole of the polity. Finally, the extent to which patronage exists and even the amount of policy-making undertaken by governments can vary markedly: while in many cases government-supporting party relationships occur 'truly' on all three planes of appointments, patronage and policy-making, in others one of these forms of relationship (patronage or policy-making) is reduced or so limited that it is almost non-existent. These cases of 'incomplete' relationships may play an important part in the life of some party-governments: we shall return to this point in the last section of this chapter.

The societal variables likely to affect party government

Party government depends, as we saw in Chapter 4, on the way supporting parties and governments jointly achieve the double role of representation and of political leadership; but, as was pointed out in Chapter 3, parties and governments operate in the broader context of society and state. Thus the evaluation of the forms which party government is likely to take entails going beyond – or below – the examination of the way governments and supporting parties relate to each other in the specific context of a government. The way parties relate to society and governments to the state needs to be monitored, as also does what may be regarded as the most basic of the relationships, that between society and state. If we were to assess the influences exercised on party government in a comprehensive manner, one would have to find indicators for all these relationships. As pointed out earlier in this chapter, however, in the context of Western European countries the analysis has to concentrate on three key variables.

The first of these is the party system configuration. As we have noted and is well-known, that configuration results in large part from the social structure from which parties have emerged. In Western Europe at least, this occurred often many generations ago; but the configuration of the party system does not lead automatically nor does it lead directly to one type of representation rather than another. An important mediating element is constituted by (often long-standing) political traditions. In some polities, emphasis is placed on a two-block or bipolar view which sharply opposes the 'ins' and the 'outs' or 'government' and 'opposition'. Thus the existing party system configuration becomes reinterpreted, so to speak, in a majoritarian and adversarial direction or in what Lijphart has described, perhaps overfavourably, as a 'consensual' direction (Lijphart, 1984, 1–4). The party system configuration plays a part in this reinterpretation, but in a somewhat indirect and rather complex manner: what matters is not so much whether the system is based entirely or almost entirely on two parties or not; nor is the crucial distinction even whether the government is of a single party type or is a coalition. The key point is whether or not the political battle is regarded as being of a two-block or of a bipolar character. Thus small coalitions, such as those which have prevailed in France during the Fifth Republic, can have a bipolar character as do British single party governments. On the other hand, larger coalitions are typically not bipolar either because they are 'grand' and include all the significant parties, as occurred in Austria, especially before 1966, or because they tend to include a 'pivot' party which is always or nearly always in office, as in Belgium or the Netherlands or Italy (before the nineties).[1] By and large, when the system is bipolar the government is more able to push through policies of a partisan character, while this is not so much or so easily the case where the system is not bipolar.

It is partly because of this difference that the second independent variable, which is constituted by the role of the administrative side of the government, can influence the nature of party government in a given country. The strength of the government in relation to the state, both long-and short-term, depends on the extent to which this government is at the origin of or controls the key decisions within the state as well as on the extent to which public servants recognise that they act on behalf of the government. This is a strength which all governments have in Western European countries, even though this strength is limited to an extent in a number of ways, and in particular by territorial decentralisation, by the existence of independent agencies and by the judiciary. Over and above these limitations, however, as we saw in Chapter 4, the government can use the civil service as an important resource. When the party system is such that the government is unable or unwilling to rely on its strong partisan ethos to develop its policies, it is likely to use – and to have to use – the administrative strength which it inherits from the state.

The character of party government is thus likely to be influenced both by the strength of the supporting parties with respect to the society and by that of the government with respect to the state. If one side is more influential than the other within its domain, party government is likely to depend more on that side than on the other. As a matter of fact, one can see that if the society is appreciably stronger than the state, the government has to rely on the parties in order to be able to act. However, if, in such a case, partly because of decentralisation for instance, the party system is rather inchoate or the parties themselves are rather weak, the government may be unable to rely on the parties to push forward its policies. Such a situation approximates what occurred occasionally in Italy and what often occurs in the United States. If, on the other hand, the state is traditionally stronger than the society, the polity is likely to be ruled to a large extent by a government on which public servants have a major influence: a partial version of this model has often characterised France, particularly under the Fourth Republic and in the early years of the Fifth.

The impact of policy fields on the nature of party government constituted a third independent variable. The administrative function gives
governments a privileged – indeed almost a monopolistic – position
with respect to many aspects of policy-making. Foreign affairs questions,
for instance, are often regarded as being primarily within the province of
the government, which may therefore have a preponderant influence
with respect to these matters, while social or economic questions would
seem more likely to originate from within the supporting parties. This
view may, admittedly, be no longer entirely valid. Some foreign affairs
questions have been hotly debated within supporting parties, in particular issues relating to the European Union; conversely, some economic
matters, for instance questions relating to interest rates, may well be
handled almost entirely by governments alone.

The nature of the policy fields may also affect government–supporting
party relationships indirectly as well as directly, because some types of
issues tend to be urgent or technical. Electoral programmes which – at
least in principle – are elaborated by parties rather than by governments
are unlikely to include technical details or matters relating to implementation: they cannot by definition cover urgent matters. As pointed
out in Chapter 2, some freedom of manoeuvre has to be left to the
government, as programmes anticipate the future but the future can
never be wholly anticipated. It may be that, in practice, these characteristics affect some fields of government more than others, foreign affairs
or aspects of economic policy, for instance.

We have thus identified three independent variables which can be
expected to have an effect on the way governments will tend to relate to
the parties which support them. We can then return to the examination
of the three planes on which the relationship takes place between
government and supporting parties to see in what ways and to what
extent these variables play a part in shaping the nature of party government in Western European polities.

The ways in which the three planes of party government are influenced

To begin with, the effect of the three independent variables which
we have identified is unlikely to be identical on the three planes
of appointments, patronage and policy-making: each of these planes
corresponds to a different reality. In particular, appointments are
primarily an internal matter to parties and governments, while patronage and even more policy-making concern or may concern the

whole polity. Appointments are therefore likely to be affected to a limited extent by the relationship between party and society. Consequently, of the three variables which have been described, only one, the character of the party system, appears likely to have a clear impact on all three planes. The other two, which are related to administrative aspects of the political system, would seem to have their greatest impact on policy-making and a possible minor impact on patronage. The type of influence that might be exercised therefore needs first to be assessed separately on each of the three planes before a global assessment can be attempted.

Appointments to governments and to party leaderships: are parties dependent, governments dependent, or is there reciprocal autonomy?

Appointments to governments and to party leaderships are likely to be markedly affected, in parliamentary systems, by the presence or absence of a bipolar form of political life. Parliamentary systems differ in this respect from separation-of-powers systems, where the institutional structure itself is likely to lead to a degree of autonomy between the two sides. As a matter of fact, the presence or absence of a bipolar division in the political life of a country is perhaps the *summa divisio* among Western European (and other) parliamentary governments: it has a profound effect on the way governments are formed. In a non-bipolar political life, governments are formed slowly, often painstakingly, party leaders being in charge of the operation; in bipolar situations, governments emerge, like Minerva, almost immediately as soon as the electoral result is declared. The consequences are somewhat asymmetrical, however. In non-bipolar systems, appointments to the government can be expected to be entirely dependent on the parties and government members play little or no part in the selection of party executives. In bipolar systems, where governments emerge directly from the electoral process, on the contrary, the role of the supporting party can be expected to be more limited, but still to remain important. Bipolar systems occupy, therefore, an intermediate position between the non-bipolar parliamentary systems and the presidential systems based on the separation of powers where the role of the parties in appointments to the government, and of the government in the selection of the party executive, is almost non-existent.

In the indirectly constituted governments which characterise non-bipolar systems, appointments to the government are thus normally made at the behest of the coalition parties, while government members are not in a position to interfere with party appointments. Something approaching 'fusion' may nonetheless occur when the top party leaders appoint themselves and some of their colleagues to the government – prime ministers or deputy prime ministers for instance. But this is always partial fusion only, especially in large coalitions, since there are not enough posts for the whole leadership of each party to join the government. Moreover, in some cases top party leaders choose to remain outside the government and fusion is explicitly avoided.

The case of directly constituted governments in bipolar situations is more complex. In the first phase of the life of the government, appointments to it are likely to be drawn directly from the party: the result is a kind of fusion as the whole leadership – typically, but not exclusively, the parliamentary leadership – is transferred, indeed 'translated' in the etymological sense of the word, from the party to the government. At that point and for a while, the party is beheaded: it is tied to the government leadership. Yet this fusion is not likely to last. The direct character of the election of the government means that the prime minister can dismiss ministers and appoint replacements without paying attention to other party influentials: he or she is *the* party leader. Moreover, the influence of the leader and of some of the top ministers is such that these will attempt to influence the composition of the parliamentary leadership and of the leadership in the country. Thus the process is one of gradual transformation by which the members of the government, who may be regarded as being to an extent the 'party in government', slowly become more autonomous and indeed may even exercise some reciprocal influence over the composition of the party leadership.

This process can be more or less conflictual, and the relation between state and society has an indirect impact on appointment mechanisms in this way. When a bipolar government is based on a single party, the prime minister is truly in charge of appointments; when such a government is based on a small coalition, the leaders of the coalition parties play a larger part, except for the fact that the leader of the major party is also the prime minister. More generally, the tone of the relationship may be more or less adversarial. In those bipolar parliamentary systems which can be described, following Lijphart, as being truly adversarial, the prime minister decides; in those which are more consensual, as in Scandinavia, appointments are also likely to be made by means of give-and-take between party(ies) and government (Lijphart, 1984, 1–4). Appointments to the government may be ostensibly dependent on the party(ies), but the prime minister is likely to retain a degree of discretion: the arrangement is based on an equilibrium between party and government influence.

Patronage: are parties dependent, are governments dependent or is there reciprocal autonomy?

When representative arrangements are indirect, that is to say when political life is not bipolar, parties not only control appointments, they control patronage as well. The government or individual ministers may have to formally ratify the decisions taken, but these are initiated within the party. Party officials are placed close to ministers to ensure that what is done is what the party favours, on the basis of an overall pattern of allocation agreed previously and sometimes many years previously among party leaders. Patronage tends to be directed at party members and supporters: hence the emphasis on the distribution to the party faithful of public housing, for instance, or of jobs, these jobs being mainly low-grade. The supporting parties are able to maintain their hold on their supporters in this way, and also their superior position *vis-à-vis* the government.

   Where the political system is bipolar, on the other hand, the government is even from the start less influenced by the supporting parties. Patronage is probably less widespread, as it is not as strongly required by the government for its action and as the government is in a position to resist party requests for such benefits. It can play a part, but primarily to secure or maintain the loyalty of key party members and especially that of members of parliament. It tends, therefore, to be targeted at influentials in the parliamentary party(ies) and in the party(ies) in the country rather than at the rank-and-file, as when political life is not bipolar. Both the type and amount of patronage are therefore likely to vary widely depending on whether political life has or does not have a bipolar character, although the situation can vary appreciably as we shall see at the end of this chapter as a result of the extent to which the government is involved in policy-making.

Policies: are parties dependent, are governments dependent or is there reciprocal autonomy?

Policies are typically regarded as the fundamental reason why party government exists: ostensibly at least, the people's representatives are able to transform popular demands into practical action. The reality is somewhat different, however. This is in part because appointments and patronage play a rather independent part alongside policies; and also because governments are often heavily involved in the management of day-to-day problems and may well forget to find much time for party programmes.

Within this general framework, all governments are helped by the fact that their managerial function gives them a privileged position in policy-making, but governments which are not bipolar are more likely to follow the party line than those which are. In bipolar systems, the policy-making agenda is likely to be concentrated in the government, while the parliamentary majority and the party at large are expected to follow. Admittedly, at the time the government comes to power (and, but only to a limited extent, if it is reelected) the supporting party is influential since it is likely to have contributed to the elaboration of the programme: but, even at that point, the government decides on the form and timing of legislation: subsequently, there may be substantial deviations from the programme and even U-turns. Thus supporting parties are more likely to prod, press or grumble than to contribute to law-making.

In systems which are not bipolar, the situation is somewhat contradictory on the surface. On the one hand, policy-making is likely to depend more on the standpoints of the supporting party(ies). Before the government is even set up, a governmental programme is typically elaborated by top party representatives and this programme is enshrined in a coalition pact, as, otherwise, a government would not be likely to last long being composed of and supported by parties which often have different ideologies and always have different electoral programmes. On the other hand, because the parties have had to agree to difficult compromises in order to enable the government to start at all, such a government is likely to tread rather uneasily on fields which are ostensibly highly partisan. The spirit in which it will approach matters will therefore tend to be neutral, so to speak; in other words, the tone will be more administrative than is the case in bipolar systems. What starts as a highly party-dependent form of policy-making gives way in practice to a less partisan approach.

The links between the three planes of government–supporting party relationships: reinforcement, compensation and incomplete relationships

The three planes of party government are not isolated from each other: parties and governments may use the advantage which they draw from their action on one plane to obtain some advantages on another.

These strategies give rise to a variety of types of *reinforcement* and of *compensation*. Moreover, in some cases there may be a total absence or, as is more likely, a near-absence of action on one plane, the plane of patronage or even that of policy-making: the relationships are then incomplete.

The links between the three planes of party government relationships in systems which are bipolar and where representation is direct

In bipolar party governments where representation is direct, the links between the three planes of the relationship can be expected to be close, to begin with at least. The links between appointments and policy-making are close when there is fusion between party leadership and government, as occurs sometimes in the early period of a government.

The links between appointments and policy-making tend to loosen gradually, however, and fusion tends to give way to greater government autonomy, both in terms of appointments and in terms of policy-making. At that point, as noted earlier, governments may have to endeavour to modify party standpoints and to achieve this objective by attempting to influence the composition of the party leadership groups in the country and/or in parliament. These groups, on the other hand, are likely to try and alter governmental proposals and also obtain the resignation of ministers whose policies they particularly dislike. Appointments and policy-making are thus likely to be linked in a continuous manner as relations between party and government become more conflictual during the lifetime of a government.

Some links, both general and specific, also exist between patronage and policy-making. The main link is general since the government distributes patronage such as honours or positions in the public or even private sectors to key members of the party, whether in parliament or in the country, in order to achieve greater support for its policies. Patronage is also sometimes distributed for a specific purpose, for instance when the parliamentary majority is very small or when a difficult vote is to be taken in a party congress or in an important party committee. If, during the lifetime of a government, a gradual split occurs between the views of supporting party members and those of the government, the extent of patronage is likely to increase. Links between policy-making and patronage are thus likely to become closer over time, the key actor in this context being the government, while party influentials are the recipients of the favours. The strength of the links between policy-making and patronage is thus likely to vary in inverse relationship to the strength of the links between appointments and policy-making: the latter decrease while the former increase.

The links between the three planes of party government relationships in systems which are not bipolar and where representation is indirect

In party governments of a non-bipolar character, as representation is indirect, two types of links between governments and supporting parties are likely to take place. First, appointments to the government can be expected to be closely related to policy-making, perhaps even more than where representation is direct. Ministers are appointed by the different parties to ensure that the policies adopted during the discussions leading to the formation of the coalition are followed and indeed carefully followed; ministers may indeed be asked in some cases to report to the party leadership about policy developments. Second, appointments to the government are also linked to patronage. As noted earlier, party officials may be appointed to ensure that patronage is distributed in the way the party wants: the link between appointments and patronage is thus close, and it is also general. However, it is distinct from the link between ministerial appointments and policy-making: action on policy-making is not expected to be necessarily related to activities concerned with patronage.

During the lifetime of the government, the link between appointments and patronage is likely to remain strong, but that between appointments and policy-making may gradually decline as the status of ministers and in particular of the prime minister increases. The government may then acquire some, but only some, autonomy in policy-making, especially since there is little scope for change in the composition of the government so long as the cabinet as a whole does not resign, given that the parties and not the government leader are in charge of government appointments. Ministers are still unlikely to be able, as in some party governments where representation is direct, to attempt to influence the composition of the party leadership: the party leadership remains what it was, a party leadership.

Reinforcement and compensation in the relationship between governments and supporting parties

The links which have just been described between appointments, policy-making and patronage constitute forms of reinforcement or of compensation. There is *reinforcement* if governments and supporting parties build on the strength they have on one of the planes of the relationship to acquire greater strength on another; there is *compensation* where there is a trade-off between actions taking place on one plane and actions taking place on another. In those polities in which political life tends to be consensual, compensation or reinforcement is limited across the various planes: little or no patronage is distributed, and appointments are not directly linked to policies. In the systems which are not so consensual, on the contrary, links of both types are likely to be found. This occurs whether the system is not bipolar and representation is indirect, or whether the system is bipolar and representation is direct. Where representation is indirect, strong reinforcement can be expected to take place as parties tend to control appointments, patronage and policy-making; where it is direct, reinforcement is likely to be found at two different points. At the beginning of the life of a cabinet, the fusion between party and government leaders results in a close link between appointments and policy-making, with the former reinforcing the latter, patronage being limited during that period. Second, but to a more limited extent, there may also be reinforcement if the government subsequently attempts to influence and to an extent succeeds in influencing both appointments within the party and party standpoints on policies: if this occurs, policies are reinforced by appointments in what has become a dependent party.

Reinforcement implies that one of the partners, the government or the supporting parties, is markedly stronger than the other. If this is not the case, reinforcement is replaced at least to an extent by compensation or is accompanied by compensation. Compensation can take many forms, the two main ones being within each plane of party–government relationships or across the three different planes. There is compensation *within* each plane if appointments, patronage distribution and/or policy-making are at the same time in some respects autonomous, in some respects government-dependent, and/or in some respects party-dependent. Thus appointments to the government may be partly made under party influence and partly autonomously; correspondingly, appointments to the party leadership may be made partly under government influence and partly autonomously. Indeed, reciprocal influence in the context of appointments may well occur: the party may influence some ministerial appointments while the government may influence some party appointments.

There can also be reciprocal influence and trade-offs in policy-making and in patronage. In policy-making, these trade-offs are likely to be frequent; as a matter of fact, autonomy in different fields of policy-making can be regarded as instances of trade-offs, the government being 'allowed' by the supporting parties to be involved autonomously in a field (for instance foreign affairs) on the understanding that the supporting parties are autonomous in another field (for instance some aspects of social welfare). Trade-offs are likely to occur within a given policy as well as between policies or between policy fields: a clause of a bill may be reluctantly approved in the legislature by the MPs of the parties supporting the government on the condition that another clause of that bill, wanted by these parties but which the government originally opposed, is accepted by the executive. Trade-offs in patronage are likely to occur to a varying extent, as the control of patronage either by the parties or the government may be total in some countries.

The other broad type of compensation is that which takes place *across* the planes of the relationships (Strøm, 1990). The supporting parties press for ministerial appointments on the understanding that appointees will be fairly free to act in the way they wish once in government. The 'more noble' way of referring to this type of arrangement is to state that the party 'trusts' its 'representatives' in the government to do what is best for the party (and presumably for the country). This trust may be genuine, in the sense that the party recognises that it does not have the technical expertise or the political credibility in the nation to determine what can or should be done. Presumably the party guidelines are vague enough to allow for considerable leeway; but the trust may also be imposed on the party if the government leader or some ministers are regarded as indispensable and can therefore act almost entirely as they please. These forms of compensation can be expected to occur frequently, even if they are difficult to detect, let alone document.

The forms which compensation takes may differ over the lifetime of a government. Ministers may move from being party-dependent to becoming autonomous, as we saw, a change which is likely to be resented by the party leadership in the country or in the legislature – a climate of trust may be replaced by a climate of suspicion. The party might therefore wish to reassert its influence and attempt to impose its views. The situation is then reversed: while ministers have in effect become autonomous appointees by ceasing to be true representatives of their party, the leaders of the supporting party(ies) may seek to establish their influence on policy. These may not be the only examples of compensation in which supporting parties attempt to control policy developments while leaving appointments relatively autonomous: for instance, the head of the government may have considerable scope in making appointments to the government, but these appointees may subsequently have to take the views of the supporting parties into account in developing their policies, perhaps because they feel that they have little support in the nation in their own right and/or because, more concretely, the supporting parties command a majority in the legislature.

Compensation also occurs between patronage distribution and policy-making; but the trade-off probably takes place primarily between supporting parties controlling patronage (a case of government dependence on supporting parties) while (at least as much) policy-making takes place on the basis of government influence (a case of dependence of supporting parties on the government). Supporting parties often display relatively little interest in some aspects of public policy-making, and particularly at the local level party activists may be content to see substantial amounts of patronage coming their way. Favours to the party are then compensated for support (probably mostly passive) given to some government policies.

Divisions among the supporting parties or factionalism within them may also lead to compensation, especially if the government presides over or initiates the trade-offs which occur. One supporting party (or a segment of a supporting party) may thus obtain an advantage while another party (or segment) obtains another. Most, if not all coalitions can indeed be regarded as based largely on compensation-building mechanisms of this kind, since one party receives some advantages while another receives others. In many cases, discussions take place directly among the parties; but in many cases, too, the go-between and indeed initiator of these discussions is likely to be the government. Compensation is thus one of the key mechanisms by which the relationship between governments and supporting parties takes place: it is likely to occur in many different ways in all parliamentary systems although less so than elsewhere where consensus prevails.

'Incomplete' relationships

A link among the three planes of relationships naturally exists only if there is a relationship among all three planes. In some cases, however, the set of relationships between governments and supporting parties is incomplete, one of the three planes of the relationships being non-existent or playing only a very limited part. Appointments have to be made everywhere: there is no incompleteness in this respect, but there may be incompleteness with respect to one of the other two planes of relationships. Admittedly, governments will always be involved in a certain amount of policy-making, but this amount can be very small and almost negligible. Similarly, while there may be little patronage in many cases, it seems unlikely that there should be no patronage at all. The relationship between governments and supporting parties can therefore be regarded as incomplete if the extent of policy-making or of patronage distribution is so small that it is almost non-existent. Finally, there might even be cases in which almost no policies are decided *and* almost no patronage is distributed, but such cases are highly unlikely in contemporary polities, especially in contemporary liberal polities, as the pressure from society at large to undertake policies will tend to be strong.

Relationships of an incomplete character may result in autonomy or near-autonomy between governments and supporting parties, in government dependence on the supporting parties or in supporting party dependence on the government. These situations can be expected to occur as a result of special political characteristics. Thus, the extent of policy-making is likely to be low when one of the partners in the relationship does not wish policy-making to be significant. The government may wish to act, but it may be prevented from doing so because, in coalitions, the parties supporting the government cannot agree or, in either single party or coalition governments, because internal divisions within the parties are large. Alternatively, the government may not want to act because it feels that, if it acted, it would be forced to adopt policies which it does not wish to adopt. A minority government might often behave in this manner, especially if the election is to take place in the near future. This is typically referred to as a 'lame-duck' situation in the context of American presidential government: similar occurrences cannot be ruled out in parliamentary systems.

If the government then wishes to remain in office but is unable to undertake policies, a large dose of patronage is likely to have to be distributed: patronage thus becomes the cement which keeps the system working. There can be autonomy if both appointments and patronage distribution take place in an autonomous manner on both sides. There can be government dependence on the supporting parties, if both appointments and patronage distribution occur on the basis of the supporting parties taking the main decisions; or there can be a mix of both and compensation of one by the other (probably autonomous appointments compensated by patronage distribution taking place under party dominance). Cases of this kind can be said to have a *party-patrimonial* character: policies count little, and the parties are involved in order to obtain a personal advantage for their leaders (who receive government posts) and their supporters (who receive patronage).

Such situations seem to occur in two kinds of situations. On the one hand, particularly in non-bipolar systems, the government may find it difficult to act because parties do not agree on some points. On the other hand, and primarily in bipolar situations, cases in which policy-making is insignificant may occur when the (party in) government has exhausted its programme and/or its imagination: this situation is therefore likely to take place when a government has been in power for a substantial period.

The other type of incomplete relationship results from the absence or near-absence of patronage distribution, with policy-making being on the contrary substantial. If the party-patrimonial system suggests a high level of corruption in political life, the absence of goals and a long period in power on the part of the (party(ies) in) government, cases of incomplete relationships based on appointments and policy-making only can be described as being of a *party-programmatic* character. The government is in office in order to act on the basis of a national platform and little attention needs to be paid to the idiosyncratic requests of segments of the party(ies) or of other bodies supporting the government. Clearly, here too, the relationship can be based on the two planes of the relationships reinforcing each other or compensating for each other. One common type of compensation would seem to be when appointments are autonomous while policy-making is dependent on the supporting parties. There can also be compensation between party dependence on the government (for instance over some policies) and government dependence on the supporting parties (for instance over some appointments and over other policies).

The contrast between party-patrimonial and party-programmatic situations can be paralleled by the contrast between the political situations in which these two forms of governmental rule occur. While party-patrimonial cases correspond to governments having long been in power, party-programmatic cases correspond to the beginning of governments. There is instability in party-programmatic situations as well as in party-patrimonial situations, however, in that the desire to innovate in policy-making almost certainly tends to decline as progress is achieved and results in sheer fatigue among government ministers. A party-programmatic phase may thus gradually give way to a party patrimonial phase unless efforts are repeatedly made to maintain policy-making at a high level.

*   *   *

The relationships between governments and supporting parties take place on the planes of policy-making, appointments and patronage. Substantial differences are likely to be found in the way these relationships emerge, develop and end, differences in the type of party system being those which are expected to play the key part in shaping these relationships on all three planes in Western European parliamentary systems; while the other two factors, which are related to more 'administrative' aspects of political life, appear to primarily affect policy-making processes. Each plane of party government is likely to be influenced separately, but there are expected to be links among them: there can be reinforcement of one plane by another and compensation between one plane and another. In some cases, the relationship is expected to be 'atrophied', so to speak, as relationships may not exist or scarcely exist on one plane: there may be no or little patronage; there may be no or little policy-making. These are the expectations. We now need to turn to an empirical analysis of government–supporting party characteristics to assess whether these trends do indeed correspond to the reality of politics in the eight countries covered in this study. This is the object of the coming chapters of this volume.

Note

1 It would be wrong to equate 'consensual' systems with 'non-bipolar' systems as Lijphart seems to imply. 'Consensual' systems are those in which the relationship between groups, parties and the government are such that decisions are taken on the basis of a genuine and continuous dialogue. This is more likely to occur in systems which are 'not bipolar', to be sure; but this may occur in some 'bipolar' systems, as in Scandinavia and in particular in Sweden. 'Non-bipolar' systems may not be 'consensual', on the other hand, if the relationship between the parties in government and the other parties as well as the groups in the society at large is not, or at least is often not, based on a dialogue.

Part II

6
Political Recruitment and Party Government

R. B. Andeweg

The recruitment of political office-holders has generally been regarded as one of the fundamental functions performed by political parties. Indeed, it is often used as a criterion to distinguish them from interest groups and social movements, as the latter are content to try to influence government policies from without. Thus, Sartori defines a party as 'any political group that presents at elections, and is capable of placing through elections, candidates for public office' (1976, 64) Yet, the relationship between parties, appointments and government is more complicated than such functions or definitions may lead one to suspect. First, theories and empirical accounts of political recruitment look at it as one-way: parties nominating individuals to seats (Norris and Lovenduski, 1995). It is one of the aims of this book to remedy that situation by stressing that governments are not just passive recipients of party inputs, nor mere arenas for the struggle between parties, but also actors in their own right with a vested interest in controlling those who seek to control them. Hence our first complication is that we need to look at party appointments to the government as well as at government appointments to the parties, in particular to the party executive and parliamentary party leadership. As the notion of a two-sided relationship in party government and the different manifestations of this relationship have been discussed in Chapter 5, I shall treat that complication as given in this chapter. Figure 6.1 gives a simplified illustration of how the discussion of appointments in this chapter ties in with the general framework of party–government relationships.

Problems which are specific to political recruitment have to be discussed at the outset. Are appointments a goal for parties in their relationship with the government, or are they an instrument, a necessary

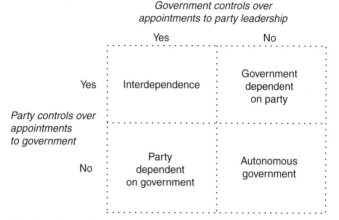

Figure 6.1   Appointments and party–government relations

precondition, for the achievement of other goals the parties may want to achieve? If they are (also) an instrument, how effective are they, how can parties be confident that their appointees will do the party's bidding? How do we operationalise a political appointment? When can we speak of a party appointment to the government, or a government appointment to the party?

Appointments: instrument or goal?

There are two different traditions in political science regarding the relationship between political parties and governments in connection with appointments. In studies of party government so far, appointments have generally been treated as instrumental. Party government constitutes a vital element of parliamentary democracy: it exists in order to transform citizens' demands into the government's policies. Thus Rose, for example, stipulates as two of his eight criteria for party government (in addition to the party having formulated policy intentions and having identified the means to those ends) that '[n]ominees of the party occupy the most important positions in the regime', and that '[t]he number of partisans nominated for office should be large enough to permit partisans to become involved in many aspects of government' (Rose, 1974, 382). Apparently, once the policy goals and the means to these goals have been defined, the party needs to appoint its representatives to key positions in Cabinet or to control departments to see these goals implemented.

Conversely, in the early literature on coalition-building no mention was made of policy goals. Power was measured in terms of government positions; parties were seen as office-maximising bodies. What parties subsequently do with their power and their government positions was of no concern to coalition theory with the exception of an interest in staying in power (hence the interest in cabinet durability). The well-known hypothesis that only minimal winning coalitions will form assumes that governments contain a set of positions and that parties seek to maximise the number of government positions to which they can appoint their representatives. As a consequence, parties will not invite another party to join the coalition and appoint its members to some positions if that is not necessary to obtain a parliamentary major-ity and 'over-sized coalitions' will not form. For the same reason, parties that do not receive government positions will not support the govern-ment and minority governments will not form. In its original form, the theory is policy-blind: it is sufficient to know the parliamentary strength of the various parties to define the set of coalitions that will meet the minimal winning criterion. Once jobs are allocated to the parties and appointments are made, the 'game' is over and the coalition should be stable.

Empirically, however, both oversized and minority governments do form, while some combinations of parties never occur even though they would meet the minimal winning criterion, and coalitions fall apart over policy disagreements. For these reasons, coalition theory increas-ingly incorporates policy considerations. If a party seeks to maximise its stated policy goals, only coalitions of ideological 'neighbours' will form; oversized coalitions may form when a pivotal party in parliament wants to hold on to that position in government, so that it can play coalition parties to its right and to its left off against each other, even when not all of these parties are needed to satisfy the minimal winning requirement; parties without government positions may still support a minority gov-ernment when that government pursues policies which that party endorses. These theories assume that a party is interested in achieving policy goals and that, if it joins coalitions and nominates representatives to ministerial positions, it does so for that purpose.

We thus find both 'office-seeking' and 'policy-seeking' parties in the literature, but do both types also exist in the real world? (Budge and Laver, 1986; Laver and Schofield, 1991, 36–61; Müller and Strøm, 1999). It would certainly fit with psychological studies of politics in which 'power', 'affiliation' and 'achievement' are seen as three drives that motivate different people to go into politics (Winter, 1987). Payne *et al.* (1984) distinguish among seven incentive types which can be grouped into comparable categories. Office-seeking politicians are either power hungry, as in Lasswell's famous formula for the 'political personality' (Lasswell, 1930/1977, 74–7) or seek the recognition and respect that accrues to high political office, while policy-seeking politicians obtain their satisfaction out of achieving particular goals.

The concern here, however, is with bodies – the parties – not with individual politicians. These are often treated as interchangeable: Laver and Shepsle, for example, discuss office-seeking and policy-seeking parties (1996, 25) having established that distinction only a few pages earlier under the heading 'the motivations of politicians' (*ibid.*, 18–20). Yet parties should not be described as if they were individuals: politicians may be purely office-seeking, but it is doubtful whether a party can continue to exist for the sole purpose of having the right to make some 15 to 25 appointments to the core executive, as that is a reward for party leaders only. Even if the desires of some office-seeking party leaders are satisfied by those few appointments, its members and its voters are unlikely to be. In the political systems studied in this book, parties may be less and less dependent organisationally on its militants and financially on its members, but they continue to be dependent politically on the electorate if they are to have the opportunity to make those appointments and indeed if they are to survive. As Budge and Keman put it:

> The most obvious [assumption], given that parties consist not only of leaders, but also of committed supporters and voters, is that conspicuous failures of a party to advance its declared objectives cause it to lose electoral support. (1990, 60)

This is a powerful constraint on purely office-seeking politicians.

The constraint may be relaxed to a certain extent in specific circumstances. A few illustrious positions for their party's prominent politicians may provide a temporary symbolic reward for its voters when the party enters government for the first time or after a long period on the opposition benches; for example Labour in the wartime UK coalition or the German SPD in the 'Grand coalition' of 1967–9. Also, a predominant party in the Sartorian sense may be better able to afford taking its electoral support for granted than parties in a fiercely competitive party system (for a systematic discussion of variables influencing a party's goal priorities see Müller and Strøm, 1999). However, in both cases the relaxation of the constraint is either partial or temporary: the symbolic effects are likely to wear off quickly, and a purely office-seeking predominant party would sooner or later become vulnerable to new challengers.

It could be that a party need not be genuinely interested in policies or patronage, but that these are instruments to achieve the goal of office, rather than the other way around. However, apart from the difficulty in ascertaining the sincerity of a party's proclaimed goals, there remains an imbalance between office-seeking on the one hand, and policy-and patronage-seeking on the other. While it is impossible for a party to be exclusively office-seeking, it is quite feasible to be policy-seeking or even patronage-seeking without the instrument of political office. Sartori's notion of 'blackmail potential' (Sartori, 1976, 123–4) refers to the possibility that in certain situations a non-governing party's mere exis-tence may force the governing parties to adapt their policies: the Italian Communist party for a period, the Liberals or the Unionists in the UK when the ruling Labour or Conservative party had lost its majority in the Commons are examples. Strøm has pointed out that minority gov-ernments are not all that rare, particularly in political systems that provide opportunities for non-governing parties to influence policy (Strøm, 1984). In some consensual democracies, such as the Nether-lands, the opportunities for patronage were not restricted to those par-ties actually holding office: parties representing a major 'pillar' were expected to obtain a share of mayoral or top civil service appointments, even when in opposition. In all these situations, a party is able to 'deliver' to its supporters without holding office.

Leaving exceptional and short-lived cases aside, parties cannot afford to be merely office-seeking unless they aim for many more offices than those within the core executive (Laver and Schofield, 1990, 41–4), but in that case 'patronage-seeking' would be a better description. Parties are constrained to seek the support of voters and they can do so in two ways, by providing them with collective goods (that is, policy) or by providing them with particularised goods (that is, patronage) (Müller, 1989, 328–33). Instead of distinguishing between office-seeking and policy-seeking parties, we should distinguish between policy-seeking and patronage-seeking parties, between 'party-programmatic' situations and 'party-patrimonial' situations as pointed out in Chapter 5, or, to borrow Hume's terms, originally designed for factions within parties, between 'parties of principle' and 'parties of interest' (as used by Sartori, 1976, 76–7).

If this argument holds true for parties making appointments to gov-ernment positions, it is all the more true for governments making appointments to party positions. Such appointments, or perhaps more realistically such an influence over intra-party appointments, are not a goal in themselves. One can imagine that the government occasionally wants to get rid of one of its members by parachuting him into a party sinecure, but that will probably be exceptional as the government has more obvious means to 'promote' someone out of the cabinet room. If governments want to influence the composition of the party leadership, it is because the government wants to make sure that the party will support and defend its policy programmes and/or its patronage in parliament and in the electorate.

The conclusion must therefore be that the recruitment of personnel is not an intrinsically valued goal, but an instrument to other goals. This has two consequences. First, if appointments do become a goal nevertheless, the party no longer functions as civil society's emissary to the state: it has become an organisation to serve the private interests of its leaders that ultimately can only survive if the state's resources make electoral support redundant. In that case, of course, we move outside the realm of parliamentary democracy and outside the purview of this book. Second, appointments are altogether in a different class from the other two aspects of the relationship between government and supporting parties, policy and patronage. This has consequences for the analysis of 'compensation' or 'reinforcement' as described in Chapter 5: in general, appointments cannot compensate for an absence of policy and/or patronage rewards.

Operationalising appointments as party-dependent or government dependent

The distinction between a party appointment to the government and a government appointment to the party is not entirely clear-cut. A parallel can be found with political appointments in the civil service. A political appointee is defined in various ways: (a) someone appointed on the basis of his or her political affiliation; (b) someone appointed by the department's political head; (c) someone appointed for the duration of the tenure of the department's political head; (d) someone appointed to perform political tasks; or (e) someone appointed for political motives. These definitions point to various aspects of the appointment and these aspects can be categorised as being characteristics of the position (temporary or permanent) of the nominee (political background) or of the nominator (motivations and political background). In the case of political appointees to the civil service, the position or task is often only vaguely defined, but this is not the case with appointments to the core executive or to the party leadership; hence, we can safely ignore the nature of the position in our analysis. This leaves two aspects of appointments that are relevant for the analysis, the nominators and the nominees.

Presumably, most appointments can be scored on both aspects, but the relative saliency of the two dimensions can also vary from one appointment to another. Putnam uses a distinction, originally made by Turner, between 'contest mobility' and 'sponsored mobility' (Putnam, 1976, 55). In the first case, candidates for a position more or less nominate themselves and enter into a contest with other self-nominated candidates for the party's seal of approval. In this recruitment pattern, the prototype appointee is a political entrepreneur whose characteristics are more important than those of the nominators. With sponsored mobility the initiative lies with the nominators and the prototype appointee is an apprentice likely to reflect the charactistics of the nominators. Hence their characteristics probably outweigh those of the nominees. In general, European recruitment is characterised by sponsored mobility, and it is therefore unfortunate that most research efforts in the field of political recruitment in that part of the world have focused exclusively on the (social) background of the nominees. Contest mobility best describes political recruitment in the United States, but with modifications can also be applied to some appointments in countries included in this study. In highly factionalised parties, for example, the nominees may not be self-starters, but the initiative for a particular appointment lies with the faction's leadership rather than with the party as such or its leadership. As a result, the factional characteristics of the nominee may outweigh the partisan characteristics of the nominators.

The nominees

The background and previous careers of nominees to political office constitute the aspect of the appointments on which most quantitative empirical data are to be found. Of appointments to the party leadership relatively little is known. To use Katz's expressions (1987), the 'partyness' of an appointee to the government, and the 'governmentness' of an appointee to the party leadership constitute dimensions rather than dichotomies. Appointees to the government, for example, can be non-partisans or only nominally party members; they can be party leaders (that is, leaders of the parliamentary party or extra-parliamentary party organisation), or anything in between. Appointees to the government of the 'non-party' category are theoretically of great interest, but they are rare. There have been a few non-partisan cabinet ministers in the Netherlands, but not since 1956. For Finland, Nousiainen reports only nine non-partisan ministers out of 252 in the 1965–90 period. Apparently, non-partisan ministers have become so rare that De Winter (1991) does not even mention them. There is more evidence of party members who are relative 'outsiders' being nominated to government positions.

The nominators

On the other side of the appointment equation the background of the nominators appears to be most important. Background does not exclusively determine the 'partyness' or 'governmentness' of appointments, to be sure: the freedom of party nominators, for instance, may be more or less restricted by the need to achieve a balance within the total package of appointments, that is to say between genders, regions or, as mentioned above, party factions. Nominators may not always be in a position to refuse appointments coming from other party leaders; especially when they are under pressure to reappoint incumbent ministers, the 'partyness' of appointments is affected.

To answer the question 'who are the nominators', one can use the distinction made in the literature between 'intra-mural' and 'extra-mural' 'selectorates' (Putnam, 1976, 56). This means distinguishing nominators to government positions between 'party' and 'non-party', and nominators to party positions between 'government' and 'non-government'.

There may be, however, a gap between the 'official' and the 'real' story of appointments. Formally, members of the government are not appointed by the party leadership, but in most cases by the Head of State. With the exception of France when the president and the incoming government share the same party colours, this is largely a ritual and information on who makes the actual nominations from which the Head of State will not deviate, is relatively easy to obtain. The problem may be more serious where appointments or elections to the party leadership are concerned. In the United States, the successful presidential candidate is entitled to designate the new chairman of his party. Likewise, a Conservative Prime Minister in the United Kingdom formally appoints the party chairman. In such cases it is clear that the nominator to this position of party leadership resides in the government. In many other cases it is less clear: the party president may be elected by the party conference, but this election may be orchestrated by a small group of 'Kingmakers' or 'men in grey suits' with a high degree of 'governmentness'.

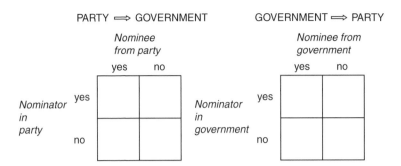

Figure 6.2   The 'partyness' and 'governmentness' of appointments

If the two dimensions are combined and are dichotomised (for illustration purposes only), Figure 6.2 provides the schema for the analysis of appointments in the relationship between governments and governing parties.

If appointments tend to fall in either the 'yes/yes' or 'no/no' category, the conclusion is straightforward: if neither the nominee nor the nominator in an appointment to the government have a party pedigree, and neither nominee nor nominator in an appointment to the party leadership come from the government, there is complete autonomy of party and government; if the appointee to the government and the nominators are party insiders, while neither the appointee to a party position nor the nominators are inside the government, the government seems dependent on the party; if it is the other way around, the party seems dependent on the government.

The most difficult case to interpret is where both the appointments to the government have a high degree of 'partyness' and the appointments to the party a high degree of 'governmentness'. According to Figure 6.1, this indicates interdependence of parties and government, but that characterisation assumes that, when a government official is appointed to a party position, he/she resigns from the government to become the government's agent in the party or that, when a party leader is appointed to a seat in government, he/she ceases to be a party leader and becomes the representative of his/her successor. Such situations do indeed occur, as we shall see later, but often the resignations that are necessary to keep party and government conceptually apart do not follow the new appointment. Finally, with a high degree of overlap or with interlocking directorates, it is no longer possible to distinguish between government and party or to discern which is influencing which. Conceptually, such a case of fusion of party and government is different from the case of interdependence, providing a fifth form of party–government relationship.

So far, only straightforward cases have been dealt with, but there are also likely to be many more ambiguous appointments, as when a party leader appoints a party outsider to the government or when a government official is recruited to the party executive by party nominators, for instance. There is more room for disagreement about the extent of 'partyness' or 'governmentness' of the appointment in such cases, but, as a rule of thumb, the nature of the nominators should usually tip the balance in the diagnosis, given the predominance of sponsored mobility exercised in the political systems which are analysed here.

The unreliability of appointments as an instrument

Moreover, the 'selectorate' does not confine itself to nominations. If, as has been argued, appointments constitute not a goal but an instrument to achieve policy-ends or to obtain access to resources for patronage, appointments are only the start of the relationship between the nominee and the nominators. Having made the appointments, the principal (the party) now has agents in the government, and/or the principal (the government) has agents in the party. To his criteria for party government Rose adds, immediately after the nomination of personnel, that 'partisans in office must give high priority to carrying out party policies'(Rose, 1974, 382). The whole literature on agency, however, centres around the question as to how principals may control their agents.

Laver and Shepsle's (1994, 1996) portfolio-allocation model is designed to answer that question for party appointments to the government, but it can easily be applied to government appointments to the party leadership as well. The portfolio-allocation model assumes a minister to be more or less autonomous and more or less effective in determining his or her department's policies (either directly or indirectly, through the cabinet's collective decision-making). The nominating parties realise this and appoint someone to a particular portfolio whose track record shows that he or she prefers the kind of policies that the party would like to see pursued in that particular policy area. Because the nominee's and the nominator's preferences are identical, there is no need for the principal to control the agent. Thus, the portfolio-allocation model is a neat example of the rational-choice approach to political institutions: the institutions, such as a government or a party, may constrain the behaviour of their inmates through norms, rules and payoff structures, but they do not affect the 'inmates' preferences. Other varieties of neo-institutionalism, however, hold that these preferences can also be endogenous to the institution, namely that the office affects the preferences of the office-holder by setting expectations as to what is appropriate behaviour of a holder of that particular position (March and Olsen, 1989).

In ministerial memoirs and in studies of decision-making in cabinets, support can be found for this last position, a position which implies that parties and governments cannot rely on their appointees sticking to pre-appointment preferences: '*Un Jacobin ministre n'est pas encore un ministre Jacobin*'. First, after appointment, party nominees are often confronted with divergent information and demands, primarily from civil servants and other representatives of the state: this explains the desire of ministers to appoint 'political advisers' to counterbalance such information and demands with party demands and information. In the language of Chapter 4, the appointees have to play both the representative and the administrative 'game'. Second, in coalition cabinets, party nominees have to cooperate with nominees from other parties. This cooperation is necessary for the survival of the government, but it obliges ministers to water down their own party's line. Third and probably most importantly, a psychological tendency exists for individuals to identify with their role, especially when the role is close to a whole institution. 'Ministers go native'; they identify themselves more and more with their departments. This tendency has been observed in many countries. Gordon Walker tells how

> in 1910, Winston Churchill, as Home Secretary, led the attack upon the demand of McKenna, First Lord of the Admiralty, for more ships; by 1913 they had exchanged offices and each, with equal conviction, maintained the opposite view.
>
> (Gordon Walker, 1970, 67)

Or, as a veteran Dutch cabinet minister put it:

> From the very first day the minister is made to understand that he will be judged by the degree to which he is successful in bringing the department more money and prestige. Only the very strong are able to withstand that pressure. In nine out of ten cases the minister returns as a specific defender of the specific interests of the department.

It may take some time for these three developments to affect a newly-appointed minister, but party loyalty suffers from attrition. This attrition can be impeded or temporarily reversed by making the agent dependent on the principal for his/her continuation in office or further career. If the agent is appointed for life, there is no incentive for the agent to do the principal's bidding, as many American presidents have discovered after appointing Justices to the Supreme Court. Among the incentives that principals, such as parties and governments, can use are (the threat of) recall, reshuffle and withholding reappointment (de-selection). The reappointment mechanism is the one that seems most widely used to keep agents accountable, but its effect is probably curvi-linear when the period in office is sufficiently long: after appointment party loyalty gradually declines to revive eventually when the moment of reappointment draws near. The recall mechanism is less universal, but where it exists its effect is more permanent. On the basis of their vulner-ability to removal from office, Weller has argued that of Westminster prime ministers the Australian premiers are the weakest, and the Cana-dians premiers the strongest (Weller 1985, 45–71). A similar permanent effect exists where ministers live in a constant mix of fear and hope with regard to potential cabinet reshuffles.

Thus in order to assess the 'partyness' of an appointment to the government or the 'governmentness' of an appointment to the party leadership', one should not only look at the background of the nom-inees, but at the background of the nominators as well. Further, in party–government relations, an appointment is not a goal in itself, but an instrument. However, appointments are rather unreliable instru-ments by which to control policy or patronage. It follows that one must take into account not only appointments, but also the mechan-isms to keep the nominees accountable to the nominators, that is the mechanisms to alter or quash the appointments.

Patterns of appointments

The recruitment to public offices has not yet been studied systematic-ally. The same applies *a fortiori* to appointments to party positions. As a first exploration we restrict the analysis to six countries for which data have been collected in the course of the project on at least most vari-ables.[1] For these countries, the government in office on 1 January 1990 and at least its two predecessors were examined, but, if these govern-ments were all of the same party composition, one government before the 'alternation' was selected. Thus information has been obtained on five governments in Belgium (Martens V, VI, VII and VIII, Dehaene I 1981–95), three governments in Finland (Sorsa III–IV, Holkeri, 1982–91), four (or six, depending on counting rules) governments in France

(Mauroy, Fabius, Chirac, Rocard, 1981–91), five governments in Italy (Craxi I–II, Fanfani VI, Goria, De Mita, 1983–89), three governments in the Netherlands (Lubbers I, II and III, 1982–94), and six governments in the United Kingdom (Wilson III and IV, Callaghan, Thatcher I, II and III, 1974–90). Information has also been obtained on the party leadership defined as the party executive and the parliamentary party leaders in these countries during the same years. Additional information has been used on political recruitment data found in the various chapters of Blondel and Cotta (1996) and Blondel and Thiébault (1991). For both appointments to the government and to the party leadership, answers to the same four questions are attempted. What is the background of the nominators? What is the background of the nominees? Do nominees combine positions in government and party leadership? Do the nominators have *ex post* control over the nominees?

Appointments to the government

The nominators

Nominations to government posts in Italy and in Finland are closest to the norm of party-dominant governments: between 80 (Finland) and 93 (Italy) per cent of the ministers were appointed by their party's leadership. The same is true of French ministers in the Chirac government, although in this case the reason is probably the fact that this particular government was one of cohabitation than because there was a difference between French parties of the Right and of the Left. Elsewhere, however, variations across parties are significant. For instance, in Belgium the party leadership, or to be precise the party president, plays an important role in the appointment process in all parties, but in the Francophone parties he/she seems to decide alone, whereas in the Flemish parties the party president is part of a small group (often a *troika*) which nominates the ministers, usually including governmental actors such as the incumbent (deputy) prime minister or even influential individuals in the government without ministerial rank, such as Dehaene in 1985. Another party difference is between the British Conservative Party, where the prime minister faces fewer constraints, and the Labour Party, where the prime minister's choice of ministers after a period of opposition is constrained by the expectation that the shadow cabinet, which is to a large extent elected by the parliamentary party, becomes the government. When making appointments later during the government's term of office or when building a subsequent government, even Labour prime ministers are less constrained, however. This phenomenon is more general: of the 42 Dutch appointments studied, exactly half were made by the (parliamentary) party leadership, whereas the nominator was a combination of government and party in the other half simply as a consequence of the party continuing in office. In France, this development went even further: between 1988 and 1992 the president's candidate for the leadership of the *Parti socialiste*, Fabius, was not successful so that, effectively, the leadership of the party and the leadership of the government became distinct and Mitterrand's appointments to the government in those years lacked a party pedigree.

Except in a strictly formal sense, appointments to ministerial positions are rarely in the hands of government actors only, however. In the semi-presidential systems of France and Finland, the President has real (although not exclusive) influence over appointments in the field of foreign affairs. In France, this holds true even during cohabitation: Mitterrand is rumoured to have vetoed several candidates for the portfolios of Foreign Affairs and Defence in the Chirac government. As was already mentioned, in periods other than those of cohabitation, the French president's influence over appointments is more extensive, even when he is not part of the party leadership.

The nominees

With very few exceptions, all ministers are at least party members, but they are not always party leaders. Using a more extensive data set (covering all appointments hetween 1945 and 1984), De Winter (1991, 48) reports that only 9 per cent of French ministers are national party leaders, 20 per cent of Dutch ministers, 24 per cent of British ministers, 38 per cent of Belgian ministers, 46 per cent of Finnish ministers, and no less than 80 per cent of Italian ministers. Our own more limited data suggest similar conclusions: the only exceptions are Italy, where the percentage is much lower (20 per cent), and France where it is higher with 39 per cent of all ministers (and even 55 per cent in the Chirac government) coming directly from their party's executive. These differences may partly be the result from the definitions of party leadership which are used, as the discrepancies all but disappear if the categories of 'party leader' and of 'party insider' are combined. Perhaps the better (converse) measure of the 'partyness' of the nominees is the percentage of relative outsiders. Their number is negligible in the United Kingdom (partly because ministers must be MPs), Italy and Belgium. In the latter two countries the factionalisation of the main governing parties helps to explain this result: the nominators have to achieve a delicate balance between all factions with a limited number of posts, which leaves little room for the appointment of outsiders. Outsiders are more numerous in the Netherlands: they are 19 per cent and even 38 per cent according to De Winter who included earlier governments where the appointment of outsiders was more common. They are also relatively numerous in Finland (20 per cent) and in France (16 per cent): in these two countries, the smaller parties are found to have nominated fewer outsiders and more party leaders to positions in the government. This may be due to the fact that these parties have fewer positions to fill, but it may also result from a feeling that a lack of numerical strength in the government must be compensated by a greater extent of 'partyness'.

Combining party leadership and government

Only in Finland and France do most occupants of leading positions in the party continue in that position after being appointed to a ministerial post. In Britain, the prime minister does not give up the party leadership and in the Labour party members of the National Executive Committee do not have to resign in the rather exceptional case that they are appointed to the Cabinet (for instance Benn in 1974), but ministerial posts cannot be combined with the membership of the parliamentary party's executive committee. In Belgium, Italy and the Netherlands a position in the government is incompatible with a formal position in the party organisation. Obviously, this does not mean that party leaders cease to be influential within the party after having been appointed to the government. Their former position within the party may simply be filled by a loyal substitute. In Belgium, however, in most parties, who suceeds a party president having moved to the government also becomes the true party leader.

Ex post controls over nominees

If, as is assumed, the 'partyness' of ministers gradually decreases after appointment and their 'governmentness' increases, appointment is a less effective instrument of the party control of the government if ministers enjoy long periods in office. This problem is less acute in Finland where the average duration of ministers in power is 2.8 years, or in France where it is 3.3 years, than in the UK where it is 4.7 years, with the other countries being in between: it is 3.9 years in The Netherlands, and 3.7 years in Italy and Belgium (Bakema, 1991, 93). The longer the average duration in government, the more important are *ex post* controls for the nominator, such as the threat of withholding reappointment, a recall and a reshuffle. The power not to reappoint if the party continues in government exists in all six countries, but it does not always reside exclusively with the party. If the nominating party leaders have moved to the government and have not been replaced by effective leaders outside the government, the sword of Damocles is held over a minister's head by another governmental actor (usually the prime minister or, in the case of a junior coalition partner, a deputy prime minister): this does little to guarantee the minister's partyness. Only if the party leader remains outside the government or if the party leader in government has announced his or her retirement while his or her expected successor is outside the government is this power really in the hands of the party.

There are further complications, moreover. The British prime minister decides over the future career of ministers because the prime minister is also the party leader. The very fact that he or she is also party leader, however, renders this same prime minister vulnerable to the party – the parliamentary party in the Conservative party, an electoral college in the Labour party (Punnett, 1993). A successful challenge to the party leadership also implies the end of the premiership. This power is rarely used, but it did cause Margaret Thatcher to resign and John Major to listen to his party's Eurosceptics. Even where the power to reappoint rests with the party leadership, this is not as unambiguously the case with the power to recall. Admittedly, the governing parties in parliament can censure their own ministers, but to do so is like using the atom bomb: not only does it bring down the government, but it usually also exposes MPs to an early election.

Belgian party presidents, and occasionally Dutch parliamentary party leaders, claim the right to replace individual ministers during a government's term of office, but this power seems to be effective primarily in the hands of the prime minister in the UK and of the president and/or prime minister in France. This is even more clearly the case with the power of reshuffle: where it exists, it is not a weapon of the party leadership outside the government. However, Finland seems to be an exception with respect to *ex post* control mechanisms: 80 per cent of the Finnish ministers in the study must anticipate their party's use of re-appointment, recall or reshuffle to make them toe the party line.

Appointments to the party leadership

The nominators

In the six countries, there are very few cases where the appointment to the party can formally be made by the leader of the government: these are that of party chairman by a Conservative prime minister in Britain and appointments of party Whips in both main British parties. Elsewhere, all appointments result from a more or less democratic procedure entirely within the party, such as the election of the parliamentary party leader by the party's MPs or the election of the party president by the party congress. Such elections, however, are not always competitive. Of 27 elections for a position of party president in Belgium between 1981 and 1993, 22 were contested by only one candidate. This candidate is the one previously agreed upon by the party's kingmakers, including governmental actors such as the prime minister or deputy prime minister (De Winter, 1993).

In the French Socialist party, the party executive is appointed by the party, but when Mitterrand was president it was said that 'The president of the Republic and the first secretary (that is, party president) decide the composition of the executive and of the secretariat in order to assure a majority to the Mitterrandists in the same way as the head of state decides with the prime minister the composition of the government' (Thiébault, 1993, 288). However, the party president is formally elected by the executive of the party and by comparable party bodies in most other parties of the Left or by a party congress by most parties of the Right. This means that the President has less control: Mitterrand's candidate to succeed his loyal lieutenant Jospin as first secretary of the party, Fabius, was defeated by Mauroy in 1988, largely because the other party heavyweights' feared that Fabius would turn the party into a machine to support the President. The larger the electorate for such intra-party elections the more difficult they are to control.

In one Belgium party, the Francophone Christian Democrats (PSC), for example, the party president is elected by secret ballot among all party members, and these elections are always contested by more than one candidate. In Britain, the Labour party's National Executive Committee is composed by such diverse nominators (trade union leaders, constituency parties, cooperative societies, the parliamentary party, the party conference), that the prime minister has little control. In Finland, Italy and the Netherlands the effective nominators to the party leadership are, with few exceptions (such as to the leadership of the parliamentary party in the Netherlands) exclusively within the party.

The nominees

In general, the 'governmentness' of nominees to party leadership positions is rather low. In the Netherlands, well over 90 per cent of the nominees had no government experience and the few that had did not come directly from the cabinet, but had some past experience either recently (as with some parliamentary party leaders) or well in the past (as with the few ex-ministers appointed to the party executive). Similarly, in Finland 85 per cent of nominees to party positions had no background in government and only 4 per cent had past governmental experience, but 11 per cent did come directly from the government.

In Britain, there is also little transfer from government to party leadership. The Conservative party chairman has often served in the government, but he only leads the party's national headquarters; the backbench parliamentary party elects its own leadership and the extra-parliamentary party organisation, the National Union, is completely distinct. In the Labour party, there is not even control over the leadership of the national party headquarters, as this control is exercised by the National Executive Committee. This committee contains two members from the parliamentary party and one of these seats is taken by the prime minister, but other members rarely have a background in government.

The picture is different in Italy, where a minority of all appointees to party positions (41 per cent) lack governmental experience, while 33 per cent had served in some past government and 35 per cent came directly from the government. In Belgium, party executives tend to be large bodies, and the majority of the appointees come from outside the government, but many ministers are members and most party presidents have held the office of prime minister or deputy prime minister.[2]

Combining government and party leadership

Here there are marked variations among the countries for which there is information. In the Netherlands, formal interlocking directorates do not exist: the constitution does not allow the combination of the membership of the government with that of parliament, thereby precluding ministers from being parliamentary party leaders. All parties also have rules against the combination of a governmental position with membership of the party executive.

In Britain the combination is also rare, with exceptions such as the Conservative party chairman often being a minister and the Labour prime minister and deputy prime minister being members of the NEC. In Finland, however, a sizeable number of cabinet ministers are also members of their party's executive and in Belgium this applies to most ministers. Even then, however, the 'governmentness' of the party leadership remains limited, as the party leadership tends to be markedly larger than the party's team of ministers. In Finland, although all ministers who are appointed to the party leadership remain in government, only 11 per cent of the party leadership during the period studied were members of the government.

In Belgium, ministers made up 20 per cent of the membership of the Francophone Socialist party's executive and 3 per cent of the Francophone Liberal party's executive, while the figures for the other parties were intermediate.[3]

Ex - post controls over nominees

The threat to withhold reappointment seems to be the only instrument that nominators possess to control nominees. There are very few exceptions: the British Conservative Prime Minister can also dismiss the party chairman, and 6 per cent of all Finnish appointees to party positions face the full array of *ex-post* control mechanisms.

*   *   *

Tentative explanations

Table 6.3 summarises the exploration of the appointment pattern in the six countries. It should be interpreted with some care, as it gives only rough country averages. Thus 'moderate' (mod) can be the result of 'high' in one party or government and 'low' in another. Moreover, it is not always possible to generalise from the data: in Italy in particular, the governments which followed those included in this analysis were of a different nature. They were either 'technocratic' governments without supporting parties, or coalitions including new parties such as Berlusconi's Forza Italia.

In general, there seems to be more evidence of party influence over recruitment to government office than of governmental influence over recruitment to its supporting parties' leadership, but only in Finland does the pattern of appointments fit the model of a party-dependent government almost entirely. In most countries, the parties must at least share their influence over appointments to the government with governmental actors, and in some countries the government is not without influence over appointments to the party leadership. On the basis of this overview, some guesses can be made about the hypotheses advanced in Chapter 5. In that chapter a distinction was made between adversarial and consensual governments, with a further distinction being drawn within the adversarial category between single-party governments and small coalitions on the one hand, and broader coalitions on the other.

Table 6.1   Appointments to government and party leadership in Belgium, Finland, France, Italy, the Netherlands and the United Kingdom

	NL	B	FIN	IT	FR	UK
Appointments to the government						
Partyness of nominators	mod	mod	high	high	mod	low
Partyness of nominees	mod	high	high	high	mod	high
Combination of party and government	low	mod	high	mod	high	mod
Partyness *ex post* controls	low	low	high	low	low	low
Appointments to the party leadership						
Governmentness of nominators	low	low	low	low	high	low
Governmentness of nominees	low	mod	low	high	–	low
Combination of government and party	no	mod	mod	–	–	low
Governmentness of *ex post* controls	no	no	low	low	–	low

It has been hypothesised that the appointment pattern in single-party adversarial situations will be one of initial fusion, soon giving way to party dependence on the government. There is evidence in this direction in Table 6.1: British and French governments (to the extent that the latter can be regarded as single-party) seem to fit the hypothesis. After an election victory, the party leadership moves into the government, leaving the party without a formally distinct leadership. The fit is not complete, however. In the British Labour party, prime ministers-elect are initially constrained by prior decisions of the parliamentary party in their appointments to the cabinet, and their influence over appointments to the party executive remains extremely limited. In France, the party leadership is more influential with regard to appointments during 'cohabitation' periods than when the President is the effective leader of the government.

The next hypothesis is also supported, as cohabitation governments were more clearly coalitions. Coalitions which are not bipolar are expected to show more government dependence on the parties: Italy and Belgium belong to this group and the high degree of 'partyness' of the appointments to the government unquestionably points in this direction. However, the fact that the government does not desist entirely from participating in nominations to the party leadership in these countries indicates that 'interdependence' of party and government best describes the recruitment patterns in these countries.

Evidence for the hypothesis relating to truly consensual governments, such as those of The Netherlands and Finland, is less clear. Governments are expected to refrain from meddling in the recruitment of party leaders, but appointments to the government are a mix of party and government influence. The Dutch case supports this conclusion, but 'autonomy' does not seem to be the best way of describing the Finnish pattern of appointments: compared to the Dutch government the Finnish government contains more MPs and national party leaders and fewer party outsiders. As a result the Finnish case is somewhat closer to a case of government dependence on the parties.

In addition to the composition of the government, other factors also affect appointment patterns. One of them is size. Compared to Dutch governments, Finnish governments of the period of analysis contained more parties: their ministerial teams were therefore smaller which may help to explain the relatively smaller number of outsiders in Finnish cabinets. It was already pointed out that most parties' ministerial teams are smaller than their national party executives: this makes it easier for the party to fill its share of government positions from the ranks of the party leadership than for the government to fill the party executive with ministers. Consequently, and paradoxically, the more appointments a party can make to the government, the more room there is for the appointment of party outsiders and the greater the potential for nominees from the government to dominate the party leadership.

By far the most important factor affecting appointments seems to be time. The grip of supporting parties over the government tends to weaken over time, the Italian Christian Democrats having been an exception. Where the party leadership moves into government (when there is 'fusion'), the party may not disappear, but it becomes so to speak 'beheaded' and is a hostage to the government and its popularity. Even where at least part of the party leadership stays outside the government, the relationship is still unbalanced. When the initial appointments are made, there is not yet a government that may want to influence them, but subsequent appointments are often more based on cooption than that they are party appointments, and the power of reshuffle, where it exists, usually rests with the leader of the government, not with the party leadership. Party outsiders who are appointed to the government automatically become prominent in the party, while the converse is not true. If subsequent election results enable the party to remain in government, the party is so indebted to its ministers for the election victory that it will not be in a position to wield its power of reappointment effectively. The party thus becomes the government's representative in the society rather than the society's bridgehead in the state.

Notes

1   I wish to thank Jean Blondel, Lieven De Winter, André-Paul Frognier, Laurence Morel, Jaakko Nousiainen, Benoit Rihoux and Luca Verzichelli for providing the data.
2   We have no data for France on this variable.
3   We have no data for France and Italy on this variable.

7
Patronage by National Governments

Wolfgang C. Müller

Introduction

Patronage, as understood in this chapter, is the use of public resources in a particularistic manner for political goals. While it is easy to give a general definition of patronage, it is much harder to identify it in practice. After all, technically, patronage is either an appointment (for example to a civil service position) or a policy decision (for example to give a contract or to pass a law). It is only the intention and effect which qualify some decisions as patronage. Thus patronage definitively belongs to the realm of covert politics. In this respect it is in sharp contrast with the other dimensions studied in this volume, 'grand' public policies and appointments.

Many policies are derived from electoral manifestos, and their elaboration often occurs partly under the eyes of the public with policies eventually appearing as laws in the statute book with recognisable impacts on the budget. The process of cabinet recruitment tends to be relatively well-documented by academic and journalistic research and the result of this process, the appointment, is unambiguous. In contrast, the mere existence of patronage is often publicly denied. The evidence of patronage which cannot be disavowed will be said to constitute the exception rather than the rule. Consequently, most information on patronage is soft. Any treatment of it is necessarily based on evidence which does not lend itself easily to quantification and precise comparison. Therefore, the findings reported in this chapter should be seen as even more tentative than those in the other parts of this book. Since the alternative to using soft data is not to study patronage at all, and given that patronage is a relevant but understudied phenomenon, this chapter proceeds from the assumption that even a tentative treatment can enhance our understanding.

Most patronage activities are not one-shot affairs which can be clearly defined in terms of a beginning and an end; on the contrary, patronage often means a continuous stream of actions. Each of these may be relatively insignificant but their total is (or can be) relevant. Patronage, therefore, should be studied as a general pattern of behaviour rather than a number of individual decisions. As differences between different cabinets and parties often cannot be identified precisely, a country-by-country approach is adopted here, the countries being classified according to the dominant patterns during the time of the inquiry, that is to say from the early 1970s to the mid-1990s. The same eight countries are covered as in the rest of the volume, namely Austria, Belgium, Finland, France, Germany, Italy, The Netherlands and Britain (others relevant cases would be Greece, Portugal and Spain. See Mavrogordatos, 1997; Lopes, 1997; Sotriopoulos, 1996; Heywood, 1995, 1997).

Patronage can change over time. The resources available for it may increase as a result of the growth of the public sector or may decrease as a result of privatisation or of the marketisation of government activities. As a matter of fact, the 'selling of the state' (Veljanovski, 1987) may well have a marked patronage potential. One aim may be to maximise government income, to avoid future costs and to create viable firms; on the other hand, privatisation and the contracting-out of services may also trigger party donations and other benefits. Patronage may also be affected by variations in constraints on its exercise as a result of changes in public attitudes, of changes in rules or of changes in the jurisdiction of courts.

The first section briefly examines the extent of patronage exercised by national governments. The second looks at the politics of patronage and discusses patronage style, decision-making and the rationale of patronage. The conclusion relates patronage to other forms of party–government relationships.[1]

The extent and character of patronage in national governments

In order to assess how far patronage takes place in a given country as a result of actions of the national government, a checklist was drawn up of the range of goods and services which might be involved. This range included the following:

1. non-material status improvements
2. jobs in the civil service
3. jobs in quangos

4. jobs in public-sector firms
5. government contracts and licenses
6. subsidies and grants (including tax reliefs)
7. public construction works (as collective rewards for geographical districts)
8. pork barrel legislation

An attempt was also made to assess how relevant these goods are to political patronage in the country concerned. A distinction was made between 'majoritarian' forms of patronage, where government parties take all, and 'consensual' forms where a significant share of the patronage goes to opposition parties, though not necessarily all of them.

Finland

Patronage is not central to party politics in Finland (Nousiainen, 1996, 123–4). Appointments to top and middle-level jobs in the civil service have involved a degree of party patronage, however, as have top positions in quangos, though these are not numerous. Exceptionally, party patronage also takes place for top jobs in public-sector firms. As a rule these appointments are not 'majoritarian': 'established' opposition parties have a share, and they also participate in collective rewards which go to geographical districts in the form of roads, bridges, airfields, schools and ferry connections. These may be valuable from a local point of view but would not have been built or established on a 'rational' administrative basis. Finally, party patronage also occurs in connection with subsidies and grants for various semi-political associations which run welfare and social institutions, such as rehabilitation centres, spas and holiday hotels, and are linked to specific parties. There is seemingly no patronage in relation to party finance (Wiberg, 1991). While Finnish parties have obtained generous public subsidies since the 1960s, there is no evidence of any scandals in this respect.

The Netherlands

According to experts, patronage can hardly be found in the Netherlands (Andeweg, 1996, 148–50). Apart from filling top jobs in the civil service and quangos, as well as those of provincial governors and of mayors of towns with more than 50 000 inhabitants who are appointed by the minister of the interior, patronage by the national government does not exist or is highly exceptional. Moreover, while falling short of full proportionality, appointments subject to patronage are not confined to members of government parties. Party finance is also relatively modest: according to Koole (1994) about 80 per cent of party income comes from members. There have been no major scandals relating to party finance.

Britain

Patronage is not central either in British party politics. It is significant in some non-material status improvements, jobs in quangos and (former) public sector firms (Blondel 1996, 35–7). Non-material status improvements are achieved through the honours system. Honours range 'from lowly medals to peerages giving enormous social cachet and a seat in the House of Lords' (Adonis, 1997, 113). They are awarded by the Queen on the prime minister's proposal. Although opposition parties have a quota, the bulk of honours is reserved for the needs of the government. For the Conservative Party honours are an important means to generate party funds. According to Adonis (1997, 104) 'a few hundred honours' were exchanged for Party donations in the past decade. More specifically, in the 1979–90 period, 174 private-sector industrialists were given peerages or knighthoods. Of those '85 were connected with companies that had given a total of [GBP] 13.6 million to the Conservative Party or front organizations laundering money for the party' (Adonis, 1997, 114). Referrring to the *Guardian* newspaper, Adonis adds that 'industrialists were ten times more likely to be awarded peerages or knighthoods if their firms gave money to the Conservative Party' (Adonis, 1997, 114).

Quangos, that is to say some schools and colleges, health authorities, regional development agencies and so on, have increased in importance dramatically over the last decade as a result of public-sector reform. In 1994, 1444 quangos existed, accounting for a fifth of public spending projected to rise to a quarter by 1995 (Adonis 1997, 115–16). Most appointments to the boards of quangos are made by ministers with a clear party-political bias. There is overrepresentation of Tory supporters while representatives of other parties' supporters are excluded (Dunleavy and Weir, 1995, 55). It has also been suggested that many of the appointees had been donors to the Conservative Party (Fisher, 1997, 240). Likewise, boards of public-sector firms and newly-privatized firms have often been staffed with politicians from the government party. Overall, the vast majority of Conservative Party income comes from donations, but it is not possible to assess the relative importance of large donations from wealthy individuals and corporations (Pinto-Duschinsky, 1994, 14–15).

These appointments create a web of loyalties between commercial firms, the Conservative Party and large spending quangos. Although major scandals have not appeared, there has been a degree of suspicion in some quarters. Thus Dunleavy and Weir's (1995, 58) three years' search of the words 'ministers, minister, Cabinet' in the early 1990s resulted in the discovery of 806 cases of a total of 3479 mentioning 'sleaze' in most British newspapers.

Germany

Although Germany has had some major patronage-related scandals, for instance the Flick affair in the 1980s, patronage is not a central feature in the realm of national government. This has less to do with the relevance of patronage in German politics than with the fact that Germany is federal and with the division of tasks and powers between central and Land governments. Indeed, the bulk of patronage resources discussed above is at the disposal of Land governments and it seems that Land politicians do not refrain from using them (König and Liebert, 1996). At the national level, however, Germany clearly belongs to the group of countries where patronage is not central, though not insignificant.

Patronage is relevant for top civil service jobs. Some officials at the very top come to be temporarily retired, specifically state secretaries and division heads in the ministries, as well as further down in the foreign and intelligence services (Derlien, 1995, 76). Derlien (1991, 255) counted a total of 111 *political* civil service posts in 1969 and 140 in 1982. In these years major government changes occurred with the coming to power of the SPD–FDP under Chancellor Brandt in 1969, and the CDU/CSU–FDP coalition under Chancellor Kohl in 1982. In both cases every second state secretary and every third division head were retired, but most vacancies were staffed from within the civil service (Mayntz and Derlien, 1989). Party patronage is also significant in connection with positions below the two highest levels. A survey of the three highest levels of the civil service showed that political party membership increased from 28 per cent in 1970 to 36.7 per cent in 1972, to 51.7 per cent in 1981 and to 57.3 per cent in 1987 (Mayntz and Derlien, 1989). In all cases the government parties increased their share.

Top positions in government agencies and quangos, which are not numerous, are also filled on a patronage basis. These positions include the federal labour office, the Bundesbank, the federal cartel office and the telecommunications regulation authority. The same applies to public sector firms, which, however, are not numerous.

The other forms of patronage may not be very developed in the German federal government, but they are not wholly absent either. The most spectacular case was unquestionably the Flick scandal of the 1980s:

the Flick trust had given substantial donations to parties in exchange for a massive tax exemption. This scandal involved the chairmen of the three most important parties, the CDU, SPD and FDP. The chairman of the FDP, Count Lambsdorff, was indeed found guilty of tax evasion by the courts (Seibel, 1997; Jeffery and Green, 1995, 131–2).

France

Patronage became highly relevant in France from the 1980s. The factors which account for its development include frequent changes in government and the policy reversals which accompanied these changes. After more than two decades of predominance of the Right, there was a move from Right to Left in 1981, from Left to Right in 1986, from Right to Left in 1988, from Left to Right in 1993 and from Right to Left in 1997. All patronage resources have been used in a strictly majoritarian way: the winner takes all.

Although non-material status improvements can be achieved for instance by means of decorations, they are not important in terms of patronage. Appointments to top civil service positions and ministerial cabinets are small in number but very important. According to Rouban (1995, 50) 500 civil servants' posts are 'at the government's discretion'; and according to another count there are about 1000 positions in the more extensively defined patronage category (Morel, 1997, 55). When the Socialists (PS) came to power in 1981, they replaced over half of the central administration's 139 directors in their first year of government (Suleiman, 1984, 112). These changes were of the same order of magnitude as those which took place when Giscard d'Estaing became president in 1974 and a shift took place within the non-socialist camp from Gaullists to 'Centrists'. Most of these appointments were made from within the civil service, however, rather than by bringing in outsiders (Rouban, 1995, 50). Moreover, according to Rouban (1995, 50),

> politicization is increasingly significant below high civil service ranks, disturbing middle-level managers and clerical staff who find themselves suddenly confronted with a new rule of the game where seniority is challenged by revolving-door politics.

The politicization of the civil service's top layer and of the ministerial *cabinets* helps to improve the government parties' policy-making capacity. It may violate the bureaucratic merit system, but it can be legitimised by a broad interpretation of the democratic principle. This is especially true if the bureaucracy is not neutral in party political terms and may endanger the implementation of the government's programme. However, the French politicisation of the top administration has been linked to other aspects besides policy-making and party programme implementation by Yves Mény (1997, 16):

> The inner circle, the private office, increasingly and at every level replaces the normal administrative authorities which it controls, commands and sometimes short-circuits. A dedicated collaborator takes on a task that an independent civil servant would refuse.

Since French parties are comparatively weak in organisational terms while elections have become expensive, there is a great need for money; hence the temptation to abuse public office is always present, a temptation which French parties do not appear to have been able to resist. Consultancy agencies have bridged the gap between the government and business firms:

> the main providers to the PS (or PCF) as a rule had little liking for those on the receiving end of their generosity but were obliged to bite the bullet so as to have access to procurement contracts.
>
> (Mény, 1997, 13)

Making use of these consultancy agencies guaranteed firms a greater chance of success when competing for government contracts. As Mény (1997, 14) put it: 'In effect, public decision-making is auctioned off.' The most prominent example was Urba, the consultancy firm which had made powerful contributions to the presidential elections of 1974, 1981 and 1988, and the national activities of the PS as a whole. Thus 'corruption was at the heart of Mitterrand's strategy for political conquest' (Mény, 1997, 20; Fay, 1995, 118).

To be sure, patronage and corruption was not limited to the Socialist party, as the *Carrefour du Développement* affair (Fay, 1995, 116) and other scandals had seemed to indicate. Amnesty laws were passed in 1988 and 1990 to cover 'all breaches of the law committed before 15 June 1989 in relation to the direct or indirect funding of election campaigns or political parties or groups'. These laws were enacted by the Socialist majority with part of the right-wing opposition abstaining or voting in favour of it (Fay, 1995, 118). Not only did the former Socialist prime minister Pierre Bérégovoy commit suicide in 1993, but several ministers from the non-socialist government of prime minister Edouard Balladur had to resign. Government patronage had thus become a significant feature of French politics in the last decades of the twentieth century.

Austria

Party patronage has been notorious in postwar Austria (Secher, 1958; Müller, 1989). Given the breadth of government activity, parties can draw on a full menu of patronage goods. In a country where titles have traditionally been held in high esteem, impressive titles such as *Ökonomierat* for farmers, *Kommerzialrat* for businessmen, or even *Professor* (to be distinguished from *Universitätsprofessor*) for all kinds of intellectuals or artists, have an intrinsic value. These titles are regularly awarded by the cabinet minister in charge of the relevant portfolio. It has become standard practice that interest groups and professional associations make proposals for the bulk of these awards. Many of these organisations have close links with political parties and normally a kind of quota system renders the awarding of titles a relatively smooth and consensual process. Only in the early 1980s did the then Vice-Chancellor Norbert Steger of the Freedom Party attempt to use the resource of non-material status improvements more strategically: rather than following the proposals of the the People's Party-dominated business chamber for the bulk of awards, he distributed titles according to his own political considerations, attempting in this way to satisfy the needs of his own party.

Jobs in the civil service and in the public sector at large have traditionally been used for patronage purposes (Müller et al., 1996, 103–8; Dobler, 1983; Fehr and Van der Bellen, 1982). It has also often taken for granted that patronage has some influence on government contracts and licenses. On the one hand there are major banking and insurance trusts, which in turn control all kinds of other firms, which are generally labelled 'black' or 'red'. The most important are the Raiffeisen organisation, which is closely linked to the farmers organisations ('black') and the Wiener Städtische/Bank Austria group, which has been controlled by the Vienna city government ('red'). Likewise, the Erste Bank is generally referred to as part of the non-socialist empire, while the Bawag, the bank of the Trade Union Congress, belongs to the left. The major parties take care of the interests of the firms which are 'politically close'. This was especially clear in the context of the privatisation or selling off of the nationalised banks in the 1990s, but the game became increasingly complicated by various 'cross-party' alliances of firms competing with each other for the government's favour, as when licences for mobile telephone systems and private radio companies where given out in the 1990s.

Meanwhile, parties are assumed to be engaged in a give-and-take relationship with firms. There has hardly ever been an arms purchase by the Austrian army which has not resulted in allegations of illegal party finance (Gehler and Sickinger, 1995). Indeed, those firms which obtain government contracts, for instance to build roads, are more likely to place expensive advertisements in party publications than business firms which do not get these contracts (Sickinger, 1997, 48–56). Those deals which indeed were proven, however, have not occurred at the national level. Party political considerations are probably also present when it comes to the allocation of government subsidies and grants, although not much is known about this, apart from grants to genuinely political organisations such as youth organisations and to newspapers (Sickinger, 1997, 191, 195–6). Likewise, pork-barrel legislation is still an understudied phenomenon, which does seem to exist: as this chapter was written, for instance, the government was engaged in an attempt to sell the state's housing cooperative, the value of which had been estimated at 18 billion ATS, for 180 million ATS to the housing cooperative of the SPÖ-dominated trade unions.

Italy

The 'First' Italian republic, to which the following discussion is confined, was a classic case of party patronage. All potential patronage goods were available to the national government and all were indeed used in the patronage mode. There were differences, however, in the relative importance of these goods and the degree to which they served patronage purposes. Moreover, changes occurred over time as a move took place from majoritarian to consensual patronage.

Italy gives out hundreds of decorations and titles every year and political patronage is highly relevant in this context. Interestingly, appointments to the high civil service are not markedly affected by party patronage. According to Cassese (1984), the higher civil service pays the price for not being part of the patronage system by being less influential than its counterparts in most Western European countries. At the lower levels of the civil service, party patronage, particularly of the Christian Democrat party, was an important feature of the so called 'First' Italian Republic, in particular in bypassing regular recruitment procedures. Between 1973 and 1990, 350 000 persons were recruited into the public service outside regular procedures, as against some 250 000 recruited regularly (Cassese, 1993, 324–5). Jobs in public institutions and in the roughly 1500 public-sector firms, most of which are held by the state holding-companies IRI, ENI and

EFMI, were largely filled by patronage (Leonardi and Wertman, 1989, 236–8).

Government contracts and licences are believed to have been widely used for the purpose of patronage in Italy, although few cases were proven before the 1990s, the oil scandal of the early 1970s being an exception (Rhodes, 1997, 56–8). The investigations against the political class of the so-called 'First' Republic by the *Mani Pulite* inquiry brought to light many more spectacular examples. These included the payment of four billion lire from the state holding company ENI to the Socialist Party for a contract on a power station, and kickbacks to Christian Democrat and Socialist politicians worth 130 billion lire from the Montedison trust in exchange for the purchase of a bankrupt firm's shares at an inflated price (Rhodes, 1997, 68). In addition to these peaks, both the Christian Democrat and the Socialist Party received at least 40 million lire per month directly from ENI (Rhodes, 1997, 69). Members of the national government were also involved in transactions of this kind at the local level. The former Prime Minister and national leader of the PSI, Bettino Craxi, for instance, personally directed the affairs of the Socialist party's Milan organisation: this organisation, in turn, played a leading part in extracting bribes from those firms which obtained contracts for building the local underground system. The bribes to all parties added up to 4 per cent of the contract's overall value (Gundle, 1996, 87). Likewise, all remaining goods were used for patronage purposes.

Cazzola (Rhodes, 1997, 65) estimated that Italian parties received on average at least 60 billion in 1986 lire per year in illegal funding between 1979 and 1987. According to an update by Cazzola the amount obtained illegally by parties was 3400 billion lire per year in the remaining years of the 'First' Republic (Rhodes, 1997, 71). This was at least ten times the total official income of all Italian parties, including those, such as the Radicals, the Greens and the Italian Social Movement, which were not part of the corruption circuit (Rhodes, 1997, 71–2). If these parties are excluded, the Socialist party leader Craxi was right when he stated in parliament in July 1992

> that no-one was innocent, that everyone knew about the system of bribes and rake-offs and that it was common knowledge that the funding of parties was largely irregular or illegal.
>
> (Gundle, 1996, 88)

This is reflected by the fact that in 1993 a third of the deputies and a quarter of the senators were under investigation, and that by the end of 1994 a total of more than 7000 politicians were under investigation, about 4000 of whom had been taken into preventive custody (Della Porta and Vannucci, 1996, 354).

Belgium

Belgium has the dubious honour of sharing the lead with Italy among the eight countries analysed here and in Western Europe in general in terms of party patronage. However, in contrast to Italy, the system did survive. While non-material status improvements are either rare (knighthoods) or irrelevant (decorations) in respect to patronage, all kinds of material goods are involved in patronage exchanges. Jobs at the top of the public sector are generally allocated according to party patronage (De Winter *et al.*, 1996, 172–5). To begin with, more than 2500 staff positions are available in the personal *cabinets* of ministers (De Winter, 1996, 332). The civil service is wholly colonised by political parties, with recruitment and promotion depending on party patronage. This applies even to the judiciary (De Winter, 1996, 336; Van Outrive, 1996, 376). Jobs in public service and public-sector firms, 'ranging from the janitor in a public kindergarten to the chairman of the board of directors of SABENA' (De Winter, 1996, 336) are to a large extent allocated through patronage. Scandals have brought to light the fact that government contracts are also used as patronage goods. Other evidence, such as the occurrence of meetings of ministers with businessmen on the basis that these contributed to party finance, suggests that the scandals revealed only the tip of the iceberg. Finally, pork-barrel legislation, designed to provide collective benefits to local constituencies, is a common feature of Belgian politics (De Winter, 1996, 337).

Comparative summary

The information on patronage at the national level in individual countries is mainly qualitative: it is therefore difficult to draw precise comparisons. However, an attempt to do so is made in Figure 7.1 on the basis of seven dimensions and an overall classification of the countries has been obtained as a result.

Figure 7.1 The extent of government patronage in eight Western European countries

Indirect support for this classification is provided by the findings of four surveys among 'several thousand business executives' which took place in 1995 and was reported by Heidenheimer (1996, 338). Respondents were asked to rank countries on a 'corruption scale', ranging from very corrupt (0) to very clean (10). Italy was clearly considered the most corrupt West European country (scoring 2.99), followed by Greece (4.04), Spain (4.35), Portugal (5.56), Belgium (6.85), France (7.0), Austria (7.13), Germany (8.14), Britain (8.57), Ireland (8.57), Norway (8.61), the Netherlands (8.69), Switzerland (8.76), Sweden (8.76), Finland (9.12) and Denmark (9.32). While corruption and patronage are related phenomena, they are not identical. Nevertheless, there is a large amount of consistency between the two rankings, with the low placement of Belgium on the scale being the major deviation.

The politics of patronage

Patronage style

Given that some patronage exists in a country, what style is being adopted? Is it majoritarian, with the winner taking all, or proportional, with opposition parties obtaining a share? In the 'cartel party' concept developed by Katz and Mair (1995, 17), particular stress is placed on the continuous access of these parties to the resources of the state, irrespective of whether they are in government or opposition: '...even when a party is excluded from government...this rarely implies a denial of access to the spoils of the state, [n]or to at least some share of patronage appointments'.

Changes over time can occur along two dimensions, the government or opposition status of parties and the participation in the allocation of patronage. Italy, for instance, moved towards proportional patronage in the period analysed here. While there was no major change in the government and opposition status of the parties, the opposition Communist Party was gradually included in the 'cartel' and received minor shares of the patronage goods (Della Porta and Vannucci, 1996, 356). The move was different in Austria as it went from single-party government to grand coalition government. Although the division of spoils between the two major parties is more balanced under a grand coalition, neither of these parties had ever been excluded from access to patronage (Müller *et al.*, 1996, 105). Moreover, the Freedom Party had gradually been incorporated in patronage allocation before 1983 and fully participated in it during its brief period of government participation

(1983–87). The Freedom Party's turn towards a populist form of protest and the formation of the grand coalition of the Socialist and People's Parties in 1987 ended this development. Proportionality between the two major parties increased, but the relationship between government and opposition became majoritarian.

Figure 7.2 attempts to summarise the relevant information. Majoritarianism means that government patronage is reserved to the government parties, a proportional system means that all parliamentary parties obtain a share which is roughly proportional to their strength. No country practices a fully proportional arrangement: either not all parliamentary parties obtain their share or the shares of those which participate in the allocation of patronage are not proportional to their parliamentary strength. As a rule government parties fare better, while some parties are excluded from the allocation of patronage alltogether. Overall, however, Finland and the Netherlands are the countries where the allocation is at its most proportional: given the relatively modest amount of government patronage, this is not a major sacrifice for the government parties; Austria in the period of single-party governments, from 1966 to 1983, as well as Italy have also practice proportionality. In all other countries patronage is distributed essentially on a majoritarian basis, the opposition receiving nothing or next to nothing.

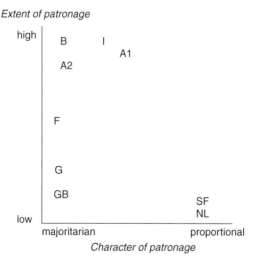

Figure 7.2 Majoritarian and proportional patronage

Patronage decision-making

Who determines who the beneficiaries of patronage will be, that is to say who really distributes patronage? If the government and its directassociates distribute it because they are officially in charge of the resources but do no more than implement decisions made by partyofficials, it is then the party, not the government which is *de facto* in charge of patronage. Admittedly, a full answer is difficult to give as the knowledge of even country specialists is limited on this aspect of covert politics. However, as can be seen from Figure 7.3, it seems that in Belgium and Italy parties tend to dominate the government while the opposite is the case in France and Britain; Austria, Finland and the Netherlands constituted intermediate cases; and no information was available for Germany in this respect.

The rationale of patronage

Patronage can serve many purposes and indeed serve several purposes simultaneously. If one proceeds from the assumption that actors are rational, the key question is that of the (expected) return for patronage. Two goals are particularly important in this respect, namely whether patronage aims at creating a competitive advantage for the party, or aims at affecting the power distribution within the party.

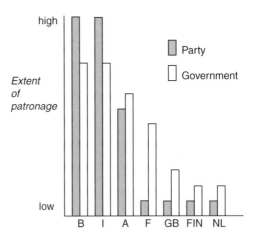

Figure 7.3 The relative importance of party and government in government patronage

Patronage may help political parties to acquire resources and to increase their power. The most important resources are money and labour, which can be turned into political power, for instance, by investing them in an election campaign, but as such they are not yet power. Political parties appeal to the public by offering candidates and policies. Voters, activists and donors may respond to these incentives (Wilson, 1973; Schlesinger, 1991). The more intense the left–right conflict is in a given party system, the more party finance will be likely to come to pro-business parties from the business community and to pro-labour parties from the trade unions. However, the official outputs of political parties – candidates and policies – are collective (or public) goods (Schlesinger, 1991). These are available to all members of a polity, regardless of whether they have helped in producing them by contributing to party finances or by providing their labour or not. To give one example, political parties which promote general business interests such as private property, low tax rates, cheap labour and generous tax reliefs for businesses, appeal to the business community at large. But why should individual firms contribute to the finance of these parties? On the one hand, in all likelihood their individual contribution would not be decisive in terms of the parties' ability to produce and market its collective goods. On the other hand, given that public goods are at stake, the individual firm would enjoy the party's outputs in any case. In short, political parties face a collective action problem (Olson, 1965).

This collective action problem can be overcome in several ways. One, group size, was discussed by Olson (1965) himself. If the group, here the number of firms, is small enough that individual contributions can be identified, group members may indeed produce the collective good. While this is unlikely in the case of the business community as such, it may hold true for specific sectors of the economy. If there are, for instance, conflicting party goals, with one party favouring military expenditure and the other expenditure on new roads, the respective economic sectors may be small enough to overcome the collective action problem. If this is not the case, group heterogeneity may provide the solution (Hardin, 1982; Marwell and Oliver, 1993). A small number of actors who know (or think they know) that they 'can make a difference' provide the required resources (Marwell and Oliver, 1993, 55). To refer to the above examples, those important arms or construction firms which would see themselves benefitting from the decisions to invest in the military or in roads and which would think that their contribution will make a difference are likely to contribute to the relevant parties.

Another solution to the collective action problem suggested by Olson (1965) is to provide, in addition to the collective good, selective incentives (private goods) which are available only to those who contribute to producing the collective good. However, rational actors would contribute to producing the collective good only if the value of the private good is at least equivalent to their costs. This argument has been criticised on the basis that

> somebody has to pay for the selective incentive, and paying for a selective incentive is also a collective action in that it will provide a benefit to everyone interested in the collective good, not just the people who pay for the incentive.
>
> (Marwell and Oliver, 1993, 8)

However, this problem can be 'solved' if the cost of the selective incentives is met with public money. In practice this means the favourable treatment of party donors in giving out government contracts, licenses, subsidies, grants and tax reliefs. Party finance is then a kickback for patronage. Except for Finland and the Netherlands, patronage by the government does indeed serve the purpose of triggering donations for political

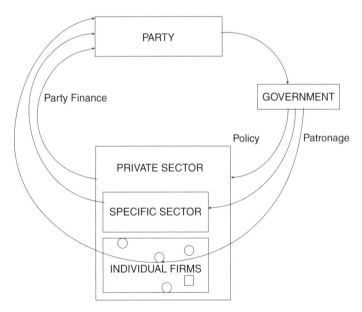

Figure 7.4 Policy, patronage and party finance

parties (Figure 7.4). Moreover, in all eight countries, though to a varying degree, patronage is used to compensate party activists for their work. Finally, the collective action problem can be solved by coercion (Olson, 1965). Government parties can abuse the powers of the state not by bribing firms to contribute to their resources, but by enforcing the law. There are ample opportunities for doing so. Firms which do not contribute may be excluded from all types of government contracts. Rather than providing 'preferential treatment' for party donors, non-donors will be punished. Examples are administrative penalties for not observing environmental standards or safety regulations; there may also be thorough inspections by the tax authorities: Chubb (1981, 76–7) gives an example at the local level. Italy and France come close to the coercion solution. The business contributions to party finance, as revealed for instance in the Italian scandals (Nelken, 1996), resemble more a tax imposed on firms than the kind of economic transaction described earlier.

Competitive advantages for the party by means of patronage can also have an effect on the power of the party. If a party can present patronage as a form of social exchange (Graziano, 1976; Eisenstadt and Roniger, 1984), thus establishing a feeling of personal obligation on the part of the client, or if it has the (illegal) means of supervising voting behaviour, patronage can help the party to win votes. In Italy, Belgium and Austria parties indeed have provided patronage to ordinary party members and/ or voters in order to improve or stabilise their electoral performance.

Finally, the power of the party can benefit from the support of those whose job it is to implement policy. Power patronage (*Herrschaftspatronage*) (Eschenburg, 1961, 12ff) aims at increasing the policy-making capacity of parties by filling key positions with people loyal to the party and its goals. This kind of party behaviour can be found in most countries, Britain being an exception as far as the civil service is concerned. Admittedly, power patronage goes against the notion of bureaucratic neutrality, but it is in tune with a broader interpretation of the idea of party government. However, these appointments may turn out to be an obstacle to party government if they are permanent and the government passes from one party or coalition to another. Yet the incumbent parties' interest in making these appointments is obvious.

Patronage can also be used in order to affect the power distribution within a party; it can have this effect even unintentionally. In this context, the relevant actors are the party factions and the government or the respective party's team in government, which, in practice, may overlap to some extent. Competing factions may be interested in using patronage in order to encourage preference voting for its candidates at general elections if the electoral law provides for such a mechanism. Likewise, they may aim at winning votes at party congresses or support in other party bodies in exchange for patronage. The government may want to increase its room for manoeuvre by providing patronage to the party: patronage is likely to be effective quickly, while policies often take time to make a difference. Finally, ministers may use patronage to build up, increase or at least maintain their standing within their party.

While it is easy to map out these strategies when discussing patronage in the abstract, it is almost impossible to verify them empirically. Two research difficulties are combined here, those of the 'black box' of intra-party politics and of the covert politics of patronage. Drawing on fragments of empirical evidence and inferring from the general features of party politics in the respective countries, one can draw the following conclusions. In the Christian Democrat parties of Italy and Belgium, factional politics have been important with respect to government patronage. As a rule, patronage goods do not only remain within the same party; they also remain within the same faction. They help to keep the factions together and to improve their position within the party, in a manner similar to the way in which patronage is used to benefit the party as a whole: in both cases the faction controls the situation. Government patronage has also served intra-party purposes in France, but the more fluid nature of French parties gives ministers the upper hand: they build up or maintain their intra-party power by using the patronage goods which come with their job.

*   *   *

Patronage and party-government relations

Patronage can be examined in the context of the types of party–government relationships which have been described in this book, namely autonomous government, dependent government, dependent party, and interdependence between government and party. However, patronage is only one dimension in the complex relationship between party and government and in most or perhaps even all countries it is not the most important one. In this case, Finland, the Netherlands and Britain have been excluded as the extent of patronage is not large enough in these countries. Any reference to these countries would therefore be misleading.

Of the five other countries of the study, Germany is the one which comes closest to the autonomous government category (Figure 7.5).

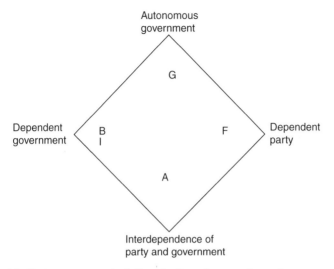

Figure 7.5 Party-government relations in the patronage dimension

Here the national government is mainly concerned with power patronage, that is to say to improve its policy-making and implementation capacity. To the extent that it engages in fund-raising via patronage activities, it moves in the direction of interdependence, since it seems that neither the party nor the government is merely a subordinate actor. Belgium and Italy are to be located in the dependent government corner: in both cases the government is the subordinate actor and it engages in patronage activities to help the parties to which it gives its support. In contrast, France leans towards the dependent party corner: intra-party power is likely to be associated to government office and government patronage has been increasingly relevant in this context. Austria is close to the interdependence corner: governments engage in substantial patronage activities, well beyond power patronage, but neither government nor party clearly dictates what is going on.

Although this chapter has been a highly tentative comparative exploration of patronage in eight European countries, a number of key aspects have come to the fore. They indicate that the matter is of great importance and this suggests that efforts have to be made to expand our knowledge both at the level of each country and comparatively.

Note

1   Patronage is naturally not confined to the national level. Sometimes resources are allocated by patronage at the local or an intermediate level, without direct involvement of national government. However, there may be indirect links such as the provision of these recources by the national government, personal links through an overlap in membership of subnational politics and the national government. Finally, kickbacks for local patronage may go to the national party.

8
Governments, Supporting Parties and Policy-making

Jean Blondel and Jaakko Nousiainen

Empirical research on cabinet formation and on party government has gradually moved towards the view that the main *raison d'être* of all governmental activity is policy-making. To quote Budge and Keman '... parties enter government to influence policy-making and to control policy-implementation', (1990, 133), a point which they subsequently test. They can thus come to the conclusion that their findings

> clearly strengthen the case for regarding parties as (a) being concerned with policy, since they exert a consistent and important influence over it, (b) being important decision-makers and actors in politics, since they move policies in the direction of their own preference and values.
>
> (*Ibid*, 158)

While both the first and the second points are valid, a third, equally important one, is not mentioned, namely that governments are also actors and decision-makers. The aim of this chapter is to begin to redress this unbalance.

Earlier research placed less emphasis on policy-making, at any rate ostensibly: office-seeking was the main object of study, either because it was believed that it was what mainly concerned parties or because office was felt to be so closely associated with policy-making that there was little point in separating the two aspects. Later, however, the goals of office-seeking and of policy-seeking began to be distinguished as they came to be viewed as pieces of either competitive or complementary bargaining strategies. Offices are indeed sometimes valued for their own sake: the need for political visibility in a mass media society can lead parties to want to belong to government whatever the cost; yet it is surely also the case that offices are by and large sought as means of advancing policy rather than as ends in themselves. Moreover, whatever motives party actors may have to join cabinets, individual ministers, as heads of departments and as members of the government, necessarily become involved at different stages in the policy-making process, a critical matter which needs to be thoroughly investigated. This is the reason why this chapter focuses on the extent to which cabinets and ministers individually enjoy a freedom of manoeuvre while also looking at the extent to which, on the other hand, these are dependent on external actors and in particular on the parties which support them.

As Sjöblom pointed out long ago, governmental policy-making can be described as problem-solving on a wide societal scale (Sjöblom, 1986, 72–119). It is therefore not surprising that there should be many different ways in which governments become involved in policy-making. One way is that which starts at the level of politically relevant groups of citizens who articulate problems and succeed in placing these problems on the public agenda, thus forcing a debate among the political actors; these matters are subsequently passed on to the government which may find that it has limited opportunities to shape the policies which are elaborated as a result. Meanwhile, other questions emerge somewhat 'higher up', so to speak, within parties or in parliament. Finally, some questions originate within the government itself, typically backed by the bureaucracy, for instance because both government and bureaucracy find that the policies they are administering need to be reformed. A comprehensive analysis of the relationship between governments and supporting parties must therefore take into account these different ways along which policies emerge and develop.

In this chapter, we shall first look at the manner in which research on policy-making has so far been undertaken. Second, we shall identify a number of characteristics which will provide yardsticks or signposts helping to look at policies comparatively. This will make it possible, third, to draw a number of conclusions about the cases which had been described on a country-by-country basis in the previous volume (Blondel and Cotta, 1996) on *Party and Government*. Admittedly, the number of cases which have been analysed for these studies is relatively small – 50 in all – and it is therefore not permissible to draw definite conclusions on this basis about the relative part played by government and supporting parties in policy-making. But what is possible is to begin to identify some trends and to suggest whether, as is widely assumed, it is correct to state that parties, not governments, are the key actors in this policy process. This analysis will therefore occupy the central part of the chapter, but, on the basis of these tentative findings, the final section will return to the questions of autonomy, government-dependence, and party-dependence, to examine the way in which contemporary European parliamentary systems appear to divide along these lines with respect to policy-making.

Current analyses of the relative role of governments and supporting parties with respect to policy-making

Efforts made to carefully examine the origins and characteristics of policy-making in parliamentary systems are recent. These efforts have mainly coincided with the renewed interest in the structures of government which has taken place since the 1980s, a renewed interest which has been given, perhaps with some exaggeration, the title of 'new institutionalism'. In this context, governments have been more closely looked at and the links between them and the other key institutions of parliamentary systems have come to be more realistically assessed. Yet this has been only a first step in the direction of the analysis of policies, as much of the work has been concerned with the examination of the nature of party competition and of coalition-building but not with the part played by policies in this context.

Some change began gradually to occur, however, in part because parties ceased to be viewed as floating freely in the political space, so to speak, and as selecting their coalition partners, when coalitions had to be built, on the basis of tactical considerations only; this had been the starting point laid down by Riker (1962) in his *The Theory of Political Coalitions*. Moreover, governments have also ceased to be viewed merely as passive objects; portfolio allocation is no longer regarded as the most important question which parties belonging to a coalition need to solve. The life of cabinets has started to be investigated, and naturally this has also meant looking at policy-making.

Subsequent research on government policy-making falls into several orientations: public policy analysis, the developing rational choice approach, empirical country studies, 'comparative realism', and research on the relationship between party programmes and government policy proclamations.

Comparative public policy analysis became a major area of western political research in the 1970s and 1980s. Its main focus was on outputs and on the impact of the social structure and social forces on these outputs; the key dependent variable was the economic performance of different political systems, this variable being typically operationalised by such means as national income, unemployment, inflation and public expenditure statistics, while the most important explanatory factor was regarded as being the distributive struggle between special-interest organisations. Given such an approach, macro-policy outputs were in turn primarily regarded as being largely determined by bureaucracies and by groups rather than by parties, parliaments and national executives. This 'input–black-box–output' view of the public policy-making process did not give government much of a part to play; as a matter of fact, the mechanisms by which inputs were transformed into coherent policies were generally not specified at all (Paloheimo, 1984; Castles, Lehner and Schmidt, 1988; Sharpe and Newton, 1984). Klaus Schubert's concise summary on the 'political market of government' reads:

> It is the model which is basically postulated by the pluralist theory of democracy, and which assumes that policies are the direct output of the interactions among interest groups. Government as a functional and processual institutional structure does not exist. Rather, government is considered to be effectively a process of log-rolling among organised interests.
>
> (1988, 171)

A significant move within the game-theoretic tradition took place when work started to be undertaken on the policy dimensions on which coalitions are based. It came to be recognised that, alongside the left–right divide, one had for instance to take into account the opposition between centre and periphery or the contrast between foreign and domestic policy (Budge and Laver, 1985; Austen-Smith and Banks, 1988; Miller, Grofman and Feld, 1989; Krehbiel, 1988; Laver and Shepsle, 1990). On this basis, a policy space was elaborated within which party competition could be analysed and the position of the various actors located. The cabinet itself could be one of these actors, but the concentration on coalition bargaining concealed its identity as an autonomous policy-making agent. Laver and Shepsle complain about the fact that 30 years after Riker's inspiring work we still lack an authoritative theoretical account of coalition government in parliamentary democracies:

> The reason for this is that government coalitions have been treated as a special type of legislative coalition, and the study of government coalitions has been treated as an extension of the theory of voting in legislatures. This has meant that discussions of government coalitions have concentrated almost exclusively on the fact that they

are *coalitions* and more or less ignored the fact that they are also *governments*. Little attention has been devoted to what happens *after* a government has been formed or how rational expectations about what will happen influences the formation process itself.

(Laver and Shepsle, 1990, 873)

Meanwhile, the methodology did also become more diverse, with systematic comparative endeavours attempting to discover broad types of formation and functioning of governments. An attempt to test coalition theories led to large databases and to comparative research arrangements, as in the work of Budge and Keman (1990). At that point, differences in policy-making conditions and differences in the policy space among countries and coalitions began to be considered, but, as noted at the outset of this chapter, the focus was almost exclusively on the behaviour of parties in government and the transformation of party policies into government policies, not on the process of policy-making as a whole. These studies were therefore more analyses of the extent to which parties steer the state than analyses of cabinet policy-making in general. Individual case studies, as collected by Richardson (1982), Bogdanor (1983) and Pridham (1986), moved easily from the formation phase to policy-making, but they tended to describe policy-making in a country rather than policy-making within a coalition or in a cabinet.

Francis G. Castles (1982) had already published at the beginning of the 1980s a volume which attempted to identify the specific role of political parties in shaping policy outputs and to specify the circumstances under which party politics mattered. In this context a major contribution was made by the study known as the 'Party Manifesto' project, the aim of which was to discover how far the electoral programmes of political parties related to the policies of governments. By using coalition agreements as indicators of policies, the research also aimed at assessing how far, in the context of coalitions, governmental policies differed from the objectives of the individual supporting parties (Budge, Robertson and Hearl, 1987; Laver and Budge, 1992).

The findings of the 'Party Manifesto project' constituted a major step forward. It was found in particular that there were substantial variations from country to country in the part played by policies in the coalition-building process. While the emphasis was mostly on 'office-seeking' in Ireland and Italy, policy motivations played a major part in Scandinavian countries and the Netherlands. Contrasts were also found with respect to the impact of supporting parties on governmental policy. Even if it is true that, in general, the parties supporting a given government are closer to the programmes of that government than are the parties which do not support it, there are also marked differences: the relationship is strongest in the Scandinavian countries, where the left–right dimension dominates the political scene and where, as a result, the governmental policy space is restricted by the existence of well-defined blocks. In Belgium, the Netherlands, and Italy, on the other hand, the relationship between the policies of the supporting parties and the policies of the governments is tenuous. It is to be noted that Italy, Belgium and the Netherlands are countries where Christian Democrat parties have played a pivotal part in government formation.

Above all, perhaps the most important finding was that the links between supporting party positions and governmental policies are rather limited, even where these ties are closest:

> One major conclusion is unlikely to be reversed. That is, that party policy, influential though it obviously is in coalition bargaining, still has less consistent and strong effects than those assumed by policy-based spatial models.
>
> (Laver and Budge, 1992, 429)

This could indicate that cabinet policy declarations do not reflect 'real' government policy positions but are in many cases a collection of promises and good aims hastily put together to justify the decisions of the party leaders to go into coalition. It can also mean that party leaders – potential ministers in the new cabinet – already assume at that point a new role conception and policy positions which diverge from pure partisan standpoints. While the analyses which stemmed from the 'Manifesto project' thus contributed to a better understanding of the policy-making process in parliamentary systems, the question of what goes on in the black box continued to be unanswered. The best way to proceed appears to see what takes place in the government after it has been formed.

The basic characteristics of the policy-making process

The premise: policy-making tends to be undertaken jointly by governments and supporting parties

We need, therefore, to enter this black box to find out more accurately the nature of the relationship between governments and supporting parties in policy-making. It is indeed natural that such an inquiry should be made given that there is a major difference between what the parliamentary system is formally and what it is in fact. Formally, the government is controlled by the legislature, parliament being the principal and the government the agent. A more realistic description consists in stating that parliamentary government has become party government, the principal being the majority party or the bloc of parties which constitute the majority and the cabinet being the agents: this is the model adopted by the studies which have been referred to. Yet even this model is far from being always realistic: in some countries, Britain in particular, the roles of principal and agent are almost reversed, the prime minister and the cabinet being the principal. The same is true in a number of other parliamentary systems. The 'pure' party government model needs, therefore, to be revised and the substantial policy-making role of the government has to be fully recognised. The government is visible and influential; it constitutes a decision-making system in which inputs are reviewed, processed and eventually transformed into policies.

Expectations, demands and programmes become public policies only through decisions taken by those who are authorised to do so. Thus the socioeconomic inputs have to go through the governmental machine, when they are not created by it, as it is not axiomatic that parties should always have the agenda-setting role: the government may be the initiator. There may be cases in which parties are fully autonomous, matters of conscience and 'moral' issues, for instance, as these can be handled by means of parliamentary initiatives without cabinet interference. But governments, too, may also be able to act autonomously – seemingly more powerful presidents than cabinets – especially but not exclusively in the foreign policy field. Beyond these situations which may be regarded as limit-cases, governments and supporting parties are likely to work together in parliamentary systems: parties need governments to transform their programmes into legal rules and to implement these rules, while governments need the votes of the supporting parties to see their proposals adopted by parliaments and the organisational networks of these parties to defend their policies among the electorate. Thus both sides participate in varying proportions in the initiation and the development stages of policies and, especially in a multi-party context, the relationship often takes the form of a complex set of interactions.

There is a varying degree of personnel overlap between government and supporting parties, but, even in the case of 'fusion', when the top party leadership becomes the government, the two sides retain and quickly increase their different political identities. Political visibility is important for both, as are electoral considerations, although it is primarily towards the end of the inter-election period that these play a major part in determining the behaviour of cabinets. Deep down, the characteristics of government and of supporting parties are different, as we saw in Chapter 4. Parties primarily have an ideological dimension, which manifests itself through policy demands; governments rule the nation and this inevitably constrains their behaviour. All governmental actions are affected by the interaction between these two functions: ministers are strongly cross-pressured as a result, although politically-appointed officials may constitute intermediaries in this respect.

These pressures come from many quarters, in particular from the bureaucracy, market forces, trade unions or foreign powers. As a result, even single-party governments are forced to take positions which diverge markedly from 'pure' party positions; this is true *a fortiori* of executives which do not have a substantial majority in parliament, though such changes may in this case be the result of the influence exercised by parties which are not in the government on the party or parties in government, and therefore constitute a form of party influence. Empirical analyses have shown, for instance, that the policy positions of postwar Swedish governments have tended to be somewhat to the right of those of the supporting parties: because of party competition and because of 'economic realities', most Swedish social democratic cabinets have been unable to advocate some of the policies which the party had promoted (Strøm and Bergman, 1992, 109–50). The cabinet's policy-making ability to act is even more constrained in coalitions, as neither the overall line nor individual measures can derive directly from any single party position; on the other hand, these constraints may constitute a resource for the government which may become an arbiter as a result. Thus public decision-making is a dynamic process: it takes many forms and involves many institutions in a varying capacity.

The phases of the policy-making process: initiation, elaboration, and outcome

In this dynamic process, the relationships between governments and supporting parties are likely to differ widely from country to country and from policy to policy. One must therefore identify a number of general characteristics on the basis of which it will be possible to describe comparatively the respective role of governments and supporting parties. This analysis has to be based on a detailed examination of cases which will provide the required information about the extent to which the two 'sides' are involved in the long process of gestation of policies from the moment an idea is suggested to the moment when that policy is adopted or rejected. Yet it is worth examining these cases only if we can draw conclusions about general trends, even if these conclusions have to be tentative: hence the need to search for characteristic stages or phases of the process and for yardsticks suggesting that one side may be playing a greater part than the other.

A number of characteristics of this kind can be identified by following the suggestions of Steiner and Dorff (1988, 142–68). First, the policy-making process can be divided into three broad phases, origin, development and conclusion. These correspond to an agenda-setting or initiation phase, an elaboration phase and an outcome phase. By looking at the cases we can discover which 'side', of the government and of the supporting parties, is involved in the initiation phase and in the elaboration phase; by looking at the outcome, we can then see whether the original policy has been adopted, rejected or amended and find out whether there is any relationship between the nature of the initiation and elaboration processes and the form which the outcomes take.

This broad categorisation is not sufficient, however. To begin with, as was suggested earlier, some policies are initiated by a common effort of the government and the supporting parties: a category of joint or co-initiation has to be added to those of government initiation and party initiation. Moreover, the elaboration phase, which is often likely to be long and complex, needs to be 'decomposed', so to speak. It would be an impossible task to attempt to identify in detail all the elements of the intricate and convoluted process through which governments and supporting parties are likely to go in the context of major policies; but four characteristics can be assessed relatively easily, even if these cannot be, at least as yet, strictly speaking measured. These four characteristics are

1. whether both sides participated and also whether other bodies participated in the process,
2. whether the elaboration was conflictual or not, the positions of the two sides being or not being markedly distinct,
3. whether the process was protracted or rapid and
4. whether this process was 'harmonious' and based on a desire to achieve a compromise or, on the contrary, whether one side was adamant to impose its views on the other, a distinction which comes under the general label of the 'style' of the decision-making process.

If we add these four characteristics of the elaboration phase to the characteristics of the other two phases, initiation and outcome, we have six attributes which can help to describe the relationship between governments and supporting parties in the policy-making process.

The initiation phase

A policy cannot be said to be initiated merely because it is mentioned in an electoral programme or in a government declaration: it is often then just an idea and its content may be vague. Especially in a multi-party context, a question becomes truly a policy only when there have been discussions and negotiations either in the cabinet or outside it. Thus initiation often needs a long preparation: as some key foreign policy decisions may have to be taken quickly within a small group, the initiation phase may naturally also be quick, while large-scale economic or social reforms may well take years to be prepared and develop, with many organisations being involved. At the limit, an idea may take such a long time to mature that it is difficult to say when it began – or indeed when the initiation period ends!

The initiation phase is crucial, as there would be no policy if there was no proposal. It might therefore seem to follow that the side which initiates an idea is the one which dominates the situation, while the side which develops the matter subsequently has to be classified as dependent. This is indeed why governments are typically regarded as dependent. It seems that ideas often emerge within parties, formally at least; they come from the research departments of the parties, from ginger groups close to these, even from meetings of sections of the rank-and-file or at national congresses. This is the view which is more or less consciously adopted when the policy-making process is regarded as consisting primarily of ideas mentioned in the party programme and subsequently implemented by the government. As was pointed out in Chapter 2, such a sequence also seems the correct one from a democratic standpoint, the party or the coalition of parties being the bodies which are held to be representative of at least a majority of the electorate.

Such a view leaves little room for ideas which might emerge within the government, although these might well be numerous. In this respect four points need to be taken into account before this conclusion is reached, even if only in principle: two of these points suggest that governments may be less influential than might appear at first sight, while the other two go in the opposite direction. First, there may be government initiation, but it may be due to external constraints, not merely in the foreign affairs field, but in relation to economic or even social policies as well. Second, the government may be formally the initiator of a particular policy but it may be under strict guidance from the supporting party(ies): thus the government may appear to initiate, but in reality be faithfully following the party(ies) line. In such a case the party is the real originator. On the other hand, third, there is party initiation if, but only if, the party idea is formulated precisely and concretely. It is not sufficient for a party or a section of that party to state that 'something must be done' in a particular field for the conclusion to be drawn that the idea germinated within the party or within that section of the party, although it is also sometimes the case that the party or party section which asks for some action may trigger within the government specific proposals which might well not have occurred otherwise. This means that one has to pay attention to the extent to which suggestions made within the party can be regarded as serious proposals. Finally, fourth, sometimes and possibly often the government as a whole or some of its ministers may use a supporting party as a springboard for their own ideas, for instance by passing on some ideas to friends within the organisation and asking them to endeavour to see that these ideas be officially adopted by the party. Government members may do so to see their proposals sanctioned in a more authoritative manner, in particular in the context of election programmes. To treat cases of this kind as instances of party initiative is obviously wrong; indeed, if such practices were found to be used frequently, it would follow on the contrary that parties would have to be regarded as being manipulated by governments markedly more than is typically recognised.

The distinction which has just been made between cases of 'real' and of apparent party initiatives, as well as between cases in which the initiative is shared by the two sides and cases where one side alone initiates proposals, suggests that the picture of the relationship between governments and parties which support them is more complex than is often recognised. All three modes of initiative can be expected to occur: the examination of specific policy cases will provide evidence for the relative importance of each of these modes.

The elaboration phase

Little needs to be said about three of the four characteristics which monitor the elaboration phase of the decision-making process. Participation, first, has two aspects: on the one hand, it helps to assess whether both sides have been involved; on the other, it aims at registering whether interest groups, such as trade unions, employers' organisations or other types of bodies have played a part in the process. Second, the extent of conflict which is being assessed relates exclusively to the tension between governments and supporting parties with respect to a given policy, not to all the conflicts which that policy may generate, for instance between the government and the opposition. Admittedly, some of these conflicts may well affect the relationship between the government and the supporting parties, for instance if the latter are worried about the impact which conflicts between government and opposition may have on their electoral chances; but it is only to the extent that the tension between government and supporting parties materialises that the matter becomes a conflict in the sense which is relevant here. Third, the duration characteristic helps to distinguish between policies which are resolved quickly, slowly or even very slowly, that is to say, in practice, over a period of a few months or less, over a period of one year or two, or after many years elapsed. It is to be expected that these three characteristics – participation, conflict and duration – will be to an extent correlated: where participation is large, conflict will tend to be widespread; policies which are conflictual or about which participation is very wide will tend to develop at a slow pace. Yet the relationship between these three attributes must be assessed empirically: the concepts are analytically distinct and policies therefore need to be monitored with respect to all three independently.

The fourth characteristic of the elaboration phase is constituted by the policy style. However, while each policy has its style, the notion of style also transcends individual policies and may constitute, to an extent, a framework within which many policies take place. This framework is likely in turn to be in large part the product of the political culture of a country and therefore to shape to an extent the relationship between a given government and the party or parties supporting that government. The policy style manifests itself for instance in the manner in which ministers and party officials communicate with each other. Ministers may have regular meetings with the national executive of their party and use such opportunities to present and discuss their proposals. Alternatively, they may rarely see party leaders; or discussions may be confined to internal party matters. Ministers may also have frequent meetings with backbenchers of their parliamentary party and even with the party rank-and-file; alternatively, meetings of this kind may be exceptional.

Thus the style of government–supporting party relationships can be regarded as being in a sense 'above' the specific policies and to char- acterise the decision processes of a particular government in relation to supporting parties and vice versa. This style is likely to be rooted in long- standing traditions, either in the polity as a whole or within particular parties, for instance traditions of trust or of mistrust between the leadership and the rank-and-file of these parties. The style can therefore be regarded as constituting an intermediate or at least an intervening variable which may help to shape the characteristics of government–supporting party relationships over a series of cases. Factors such as the structure or the ideology of the parties and the presence or absence of coalitions play a part in determining the style of government–supporting party relationships, alongside the record of previous governments. The style will in turn affect the way in which government and supporting parties relate to each other in the context of the development of policies: if members of the government seldom meet party officers, for instance, discontent may be rife in the party and objections to government policies may be greater than otherwise.

There are manifestly many types of policy styles; but two extreme positions can be recognised relatively easily. These correspond to a tendency to impose solutions to decisions, on the one hand, and, on the other, a tendency to collaborate in the decision process. These tendencies are distinct from the notions of 'adversarial' and 'consensual' politics which were eferred to in Chapter 5, as they relate, here, not to the whole political system but to the narrower relationship between the government and the supporting parties. These two sets of characteristics are somewhat linked, admittedly: there is a greater likelihood that decisions will be imposed in the context of government–supporting parties relationships if the political processes are generally 'adversarial', though this may not always be the case. There is even greater likelihood that collaboration will prevail between governments and supporting parties if the political process is 'consensual' overall, but there may be exceptions.[1] By drawing a contrast between these two extreme modes of behaviour one can identify in broad terms the manner in which the two sides relate to each other.

There might appear at first sight to be a close correlation between the style of decision-making and the other three characteristics of the elaboration phase. This may be so empirically – a point which needs to be tested – but analytically the concept of style is distinct, not just from those of participation and of pace of decision, but of conflict. There may or may not be a conflict in the sense that the two sides disagree: but the important point is that the style of decision-making does not prevent conflicts. What it does is ensure that the conflict is handled 'calmly' and 'peacefully' or, on the contrary, in a 'brutal' and 'rough' manner. The style of the policy is thus a characteristic which is inherently distinct from the other three: it must therefore be assessed independently, whether or not the empirical association is strong between this characteristic and one or more of the others.

Outcome

During the elaboration phase, the policy may sail through without problems; it may encounter difficulties but remain unscathed; it may have to be markedly modified; it may even be blocked altogether. The analysis of the elaboration phase does tell whether the passage is smooth or rough; but it is by looking at the outcome that one can discover whether, ultimately, the policy is adopted or not and, if it is adopted, whether this takes place after substantial modifications have been introduced.

The aim should of course be to describe the decision-making process with precision on the basis of these six characteristics. This is not in theory impossible as the indicators which have been described here could allow for fine rankings; but we still do not know enough about how to 'measure' policies to go in practice beyond dichotomous or trichotomous distinctions. However, even these distinctions provide elements of a concrete picture on the basis of which policy developments can be examined jointly and, when necessary, contrasted to each other.

The independent variables: three explanatory factors

These six characteristics aim at providing a description of the policy-making process. Meanwhile, three other variables, drawn from the analysis of Chapters 3, 4 and 5, aim at giving at least some idea of the factors which might account for the shape of the decision-making process. One of these factors is the style of parliamentary government in each country on the basis of the distinction drawn in Chapter 5 between political systems of a 'bipolar' character, with a majority ruling against an opposition (in this study the countries concerned are Britain, France and, as an intermediate case, Germany), and political systems in which there are large coalitions or medium-sized coalitions including a 'pivot' party and which are consequently 'not bipolar' (in this study the countries concerned are Finland, Belgium, the Netherlands, Austria and Italy). The second explanatory factor relates to the degree of 'partisanship' of policies, some of these being ideologically highly-charged while others are more designed to solve an 'administrative' problem which the country encounters. This is not a sharp dichotomy, to be sure, but it is at least uusally possible to assess whether a given policy has more of a 'partisan' or an 'administrative' character. Finally, the third explanatory factor is constituted by the field of policy-making: it is often felt, for instance, that governments are more able to initiate policies in foreign policy than in home affairs, because in foreign policy governments seem sometimes suddenly confronted with a problem to which an urgent solution must be given and they are therefore less likely to be guided by or even consult supporting parties on the matter.

Types of government–supporting party relationships in the policy-making process: an analysis based on 50 policies in eight countries

The general picture

To begin to have a concrete picture of the policy-making process, 50 policies were analysed in the eight countries covered in this volume, Britain (8), France (5), Germany (3), Belgium (6), Italy (7), Austria (8), the Netherlands (5), and Finland (8). In our earlier work (1996) work, *Party and Government*, these cases were described on a country-by-country basis: the aim here is to look at these cases together and to draw some comparative conclusions.

Let us first summarise the subject-matter of these 50 policies (Table 8.1). There are 11 foreign affairs cases, which include four policies relating to the European Union (two in Britain and one each in Austria and Finland), three relating to NATO defence, specifically on the nature of possible nuclear retaliation and on the location of nuclear missiles (two cases in Belgium and one in the Netherlands), and four other matters, the Finnish peace treaty, the unification of Germany, the 'Achille Lauro' affair, which led to tension between the Italian and American governments over the landing of a plane carrying a Middle Eastern terrorist and

Table 8.1   Distribution of policies studied by field and by country

	FOR	ECO	SOC	OTH	TOTAL
Britain	2	4	2	0	8
France	0	2	1	2	5
Germany	1	1	1	0	3
Belgium	2	2	0	2	6
Italy	2	3	1	1	7
Austria	1	5	2	0	8
The Netherlands	1	1	1	2	5
Finland	2	2	3	1	8
Total	11	20	11	8	50

Note: FOR denotes foreign affairs case; ECO Economic affairs; SOC social affairs; OTH other.

the decision of the Italian government to introduce development aid for the Third World.

There are 20 policies in the economics field. These include eight cases of privatisation (in Britain, France, the Netherlands, Austria – with three cases – in Finland and Italy), one case of nationalisation (France) and one somewhat parallel case which aimed at introducing 'planning agreements' in Britain; there are six cases of tax reform (Britain – on local government finance, Belgium and Austria – two cases each, and Finland), one budget law (Italy) and one budgetary reform (Germany); finally, the last two cases are an anti-inflationary policy in Britain in the second half of the 1970s and the setting up of an anti-trust agency in Italy.

There are 11 policies in the social area. They relate to industrial democracy (Britain), industrial relations (Britain and Finland), a special minimum wage scheme (France), employment assistance (Germany), wage indexation (Italy), gender equality at work (Finland), welfare provisions (the Netherlands), occupational health care (Finland) and maternity leave and housing (Austria): there is thus a variety of topics scattered over seven of the eight countries.

The last eight policies include three proposals for constitutional reform (Belgium, the Netherlands and Finland), two abortion laws (Belgium and the Netherlands), a proposal to reform the nationality code (France), a proposal to grant amnesty to military personnel having been involved in a rebellion (France) and a proposal to regulate television (Italy). Appendix I summarises these policies.

Policy initiation: the important part played by governments

The conclusions which can be drawn from the examination of these 50 cases have to be tentative: what, nonetheless, clearly emerges and contrary to expectations is that governments played a very large part in policy initiation, to some extent jointly with parties, but markedly more often on their own (Table 8.2). Twenty-two of the 50 policies analysed were initiated by governments, and 12 were co-initiated by governments and supporting parties: only 16 were initiated by the supporting party or parties alone. While, to an extent by implication, the literature and general impressions about the nature of government–supporting party relationships suggest that governments are likely to intervene during the elaboration phase in order to implement and perhaps to modify what parties had conceived, but not to intervene as frequently during the initiation phase, the examination of at least a substantial number of important policies across eight countries shows that governments did initiate policies alone in almost half the cases and have co-

Table 8.2   Distribution of policies studied by field and initiative

	FOR	ECO	SOC	OTH	TOTAL
Government initiative	8	8	5	1	22
Both government and party initiative	3	4	4	1	12
Party initiative	0	8	2	6	16
Total	11	20	11	8	50

initiated policies with the supporting parties in a further fifth of the cases, leaving the parties to be the initiators in a minority of situations only. Appendix II gives a summary of the characteristics of each case.

This finding is thus unexpected in itself; so is the country distribution of government-initiated, party-initiated, and co-initiated cases. Government initiatives prevailed in Italy, the Netherlands and Germany, while party initiatives prevailed in France and were on a par with government initiatives in Britain, Belgium, Austria and Finland. This breakdown is surprising: one would have probably expected governments in bipolar political systems to play a large part, as in the case Britain and France, where parties would seem to be more 'dependent'; but one would not have expected the same in the case of political systems which are not bipolar, such as those of Belgium, the Netherlands, Austria or pre-1992 Italy, these countries having often been labelled as 'partitocratic', while, on the contrary, France at least is traditionally regarded as having had weak parties.

The breakdown of the fields in which policies were government-initiated, supporting-party-initiated and co-initiated is also somewhat surprising (Table 8.2) To be sure, as is consistent with what appears to be the nature of the field, government initiative is most widespread in foreign policy. Out of 11 policies studied here, eight were initiated by the government and the other three were initiated jointly by government and supporting party; none was initiated by the party alone. However, and this time more surprisingly, the proportion of both economic and social policies initiated by the government alone is also substantial; as a matter of fact, it is also surprising that this proportion should be about the same in economic and in social matters, as the government might have been expected to be less likely to initiate policies in the social than in the economic field. In both cases, policies initiated by the party alone are a minority (respectively eight out of 20 and two out of 11). Only among the 'other' policies –

Table 8.3 Participation, bipolar/not bipolar, field of government and origin of the policy

	One 'side' only	Both 'sides'	Also groups	Total
Bipolar	1	6	6	13
Intermediate	0	2	1	3
Not bipolar	5	16	13	34
Field of government				
foreign	3	4	4	11
economy	2	11	7	20
social	1	3	7	11
other	0	6	2	8
Initiative				
government	6	11	5	22
joint	0	4	8	12
party	0	9	7	16
Total	6	24	20	50

from institutional reform in Belgium and the Netherlands through proposals on abortion in the same two countries to the proposal to grant amnesty to rebels having supported 'French Algeria' in France – is the proportion of policies initiated by the supporting party or parties markedly larger than that of policies initiated by the government (six against one).

In the foreign policy field, the three policies jointly initiated by governments and supporting parties concerned the EEC (as it then was): these were the 'renegotiation' of the Treaty by Britain in the mid-1970s and the beginning of the process of application made by Austria from the late 1980s and by Finland in the 1990s to enter the Union. In all three countries, the concrete policy was initiated by the governments concerned, but discussions took place within the parties at the same time. The other eight policies in the foreign policy area, all of which were initiated by the governments, are of two types. There were four instances in which the cabinet was obliged to act because it was under some pressure from external bodies: these were in Belgium and the Netherlands the 'dual track' proposals and the decisions to agree to locate nuclear missiles in the country concerned, which were triggered by agreements within NATO and, in Italy, the 'Achille Lauro' affair which was triggered by an American action. The government could be said to be bound to be the initiator in these cases, since the problem was forced on the country from outside: although these questions were highly sensitive, they were 'administrative' at least in the sense that a decision had to be taken by the country concerned and the government was therefore unavoidably confronted with the problem.

This was not the case with the other four foreign policies examined here, on the other hand, as these originated within the country concerned and the government had the choice to act, not to act or to act differently. These policies relate to the setting up of a programme of development aid in Italy, to the demand made by Britain to modify the extent of its EEC contributions, to the decision to force the immediate reunification of Germany, and to the Finnish decision to renegociate the peace treaty. While the first of these cases can be deemed to be budgetary in character, the other three were clear foreign policy matters. In all cases the government and especially the head of the government played the key part: the party was left to react subsequently, which it did in fact in a limited manner only.

There is therefore no doubt that parties are only minor agents in the field of foreign policy and that the government is a key initiator. Yet governments often also initiate in the economic and social fields as well. In the economic field, it might perhaps have been expected that the government would be markedly involved in budgetary and taxation matters, these being to an extent administrative and not (primarily or at least in most cases) partisan in character; the surprise, here, is that this should not be the case. Out of seven policies analysed in these areas, only two were initiated by the government alone, the effort to comply with the Maastricht criteria in Belgium and the 1992 budget in Italy; three policies originated within the supporting party: these were the reform of local government finance in Britain, the introduction of 'ecotaxes' in Belgium and tax reform in Finland; and the last three, the two tax reforms in Austria and the budgetary reform in Germany, were jointly-initiated.

The other main sub-field of economic policy covered here and covered here because of its obvious importance in the 1980s and 1990s is privatisation, together with a case of increase of public ownership in France in 1981–82 and an indirect attempt to achieve the same goal by way of 'planning agreements' in Britain in the mid-1970s. Given the weight of ideology in the context of these issues, one would have expected parties to be at the origin of all of them: in fact, they were the initiators in five cases only, those relating to nationalisation and privatisation in France, to planning agreements in Britain and to two rounds of privatisation in Austria. The government was the initiator in four cases: privatisation in Britain was started by the Conservative government in the early 1980s without any significant discussion in the party. It was subsequently supported by that party, but in the manner in which an actor receives applause after a performance. Privatisation was also essentially a governmental affair in the Netherlands, where indeed little occurred, and in Finland and Italy, where little occurred in the first instance either. The last of the ten cases, a third round of privatisation in Austria, was a joint government–supporting party initiative.

Thus, out of ten cases relating to the problem of public ownership, five originated in the supporting party – a substantial but not an overwhelming proportion, especially given the nature of the topic – one was a joint government–party initiative and four were exclusively government matters. Furthermore, the last two economic policies studied here also originated in the government: the setting up of an anti-trust body in Italy might be regarded as being a relatively 'administrative' matter, but the anti-inflationary policy of the British Labour government in the second half of the 1970s was manifestly a political issue.

The 11 policies within the social field divide five to two between those which were initiated by the government and those which were initiated by the supporting party or parties, while four further topics – gender equality at work and occupational health care in Finland, the industrial policy of the British Conservative government and the scheme for a special minimum wage in France – were jointly initiated. In the first of these four cases, the policy was started by the government as a result of some pressure to comply with international conventions; the second was started with some interest in the parties, but it dragged on for a very long time before it did mature and the government intervened in a major way. The British policy on industrial relations was based, on the one hand, on a demand made by the Conservative Party rank-and-file for legislation designed to reduce the power of trade unions but, on the other, on the determination of the government to proceed slowly in the area, at any rate in the first instance. Finally, the French policy of introducing a special minimum wage for those being given a temporary job was discussed in the Socialist Party but its effective launching was the result of the efforts made by the prime minister of the time.

The policies initiated by the government alone concerned the reforms of welfare provisions in the Netherlands, of housing and of maternity leave in Austria, of employment assistance in Germany and of wage indexation in Italy, while those which were initiated by the supporting party or parties were the policy of industrial democracy by the British Labour Party and the reform of industrial relations in Finland. Governments thus initiated major social policies to the same extent as they initiated economic policies. Only in the other fields – institutional reform (Belgium and the Netherlands), the law on nationality (France), abortion (Belgium and the Netherlands), the regulation of television (Italy), and the amnesty to French Algerian rebels (France) was a clear majority of cases (six out of eight) initiated by the supporting party. One case was jointly initiated by government and supporting parties, constitutional reform in Finland, while the case which was initiated by the government was the amnesty law in France.

Overall, three conclusions emerge from the analysis of policies with respect to initiation. First, unexpectedly, the evidence accumulated strongly indicates that governments are key actors in the initiation process. Second, governments are particularly likely to initiate policies in the foreign policy field, including in aspects of foreign affairs in which they are not pressed to do so by foreign governments and organisations; they also play a substantial part in initiating economic and social policies. Third, there is little difference, if any, in the extent to which governments initiate policies in the two types of party systems analysed here: political systems based on a bipolar distinction between government and opposition are not more likely to be characterised by government initiatives than political systems which, not being based on a bipolar type of party system, might have been expected to be more party-dependent.

The nature and style of the relationship between governments and supporting parties in policy elaboration

Participation

While there are many governmental initiatives, few policies appear to be elaborated by one side alone. On the one hand, the government is always involved: in none of the policies studied here was the government bypassed altogether during the elaboration phase. This is perhaps not surprising in the context of economic and social policies, but it is more unexpected with respect to the two 'conscience' issues, both relating to abortion, which were examined in Belgium and the Netherlands. In these two countries, while the outcome was in the end a 'free vote' in Parliament, the government steered the progress of the policy as this policy would otherwise have been (and indeed was at times) buried by opponents. One cannot extrapolate from this finding to all conscience issues and conclude that governments are always involved even in these matters: there is circumstantial evidence that this is not always the case, for instance in Britain, but there is also circumstantial evidence to support the view that governments have been involved in some issues of this type, as in the case of the abolition of the death penalty in France. What the process followed in the two abortion reform cases suggests is that, if an area of autonomy of supporting parties exists at all, it is rather small in contemporary European parliamentary systems.

Governments do not often appear to be fully autonomous either: there were only six cases out of 50 where they were found to elaborate policies alone or almost alone, for instance only with the help of a commission of experts or with very few politicians from outside the cabinet. Three of these, not surprisingly perhaps, relate to foreign affairs – the British Conservative government action to modify its contribution to the EEC, the revision of the Finnish peace treaty and the original solution of the Italian conflict with the United States over the 'Achille Lauro' episode; two cases were in the economic field, the setting up of the antitrust agency in Italy and the (very small) round of privatisation in the Netherlands; the sixth case, that of the reform of wage indexation in Italy, was in the social field.

Overall, out of 50 policy cases analysed, there was joint involvement in 44 of them. A rather small minority – 12 cases – of joint initiatives became an overwhelming majority (almost 90 per cent) in which both 'sides' were involved at some point. The parliamentary systems of contemporary Western Europe therefore organise a very strong linkage between government and supporting parties. Parties thus exercise an important function in the policy-making process, even if that function tends to take place at a second stage, during the process of policy elaboration, rather than at the initiation stage (Table 8.3).

Supporting parties are not the only bodies which are involved in the elaboration phase, however. In 20 of the 44 cases in which governments did not act alone, groups other than parties were involved: these groups often, though not always, belonged to the same ideological camp as the government and the supporting parties.

The distribution of the participation of groups by field and by type of political system has interesting features. On the one hand, it is in the social field that the number of cases in which groups are involved in the elaboration phase is largest (seven out of 11), while it is lowest in the economic field (seven out of 20), where the proportion is apparently equal to that which is found in the foreign affairs area (four out of 11). The distribution in the social field is the expected one, since it is in that field that the 'partners' are most likely to be active. What may well characterise the social field is thus not so much the fact that the supporting parties are especially involved – since, as we saw, they are not more involved in this field than in the economic field – but the fact that there is a broad involvement of organisations beyond the parties. Meanwhile, perhaps surprisingly, groups appear to be involved in the process of policy development a little more where the political system is bipolar than where it is not. There are differences among the countries of each group, however. Britain and Italy occupy, in this respect, the two extreme poles of the continuum: there is, at any rate with respect to the policies which are examined here, a large involvement of groups in single-party-government Britain while there seems to be a relatively small involvement of groups in Italy, although that country was regarded up to the 1990s as practicing continuous compromises, at least among the government parties. Even if these policies are not entirely representative of the overall trend in the two countries, they do provide an indication about the nature of policy-making.

Levels of conflict

The question of the level of conflict between governments and supporting parties is difficult to assess comparatively: what is regarded as serious conflict in one country may be regarded in another as a mere passing disagreement. A common standard is still lacking and the breakdown given here is therefore tentative. Specifically, while in nearly half the cases (24) the level of conflict seems to have been relatively high, the level of conflict in the other half is more uncertain: it appears to have been truly low in nearly a third of the cases (15) and it was probably rather low in nearly a quarter (11) (Table 8.4).

On this basis, little difference emerges between the political systems which are 'bipolar' and those which are not, in part perhaps because the assessment of the level of conflict in some of the latter group of countries seemed particularly difficult to achieve. However, the proportion of policies over which conflicts were high appears to have been smaller in the foreign and economic fields than in the social field and in relation to other policies: indeed, the economic field is the one in which the proportion of policies over which conflict was low is the largest (nine out of 20). The foreign policy field is thus not one where controversy between government and supporting parties is particularly low, as appears indeed impressionistically to be the case when one notes that the policies covered include the location of nuclear missiles and the relationships between the countries concerned and the European Union. Finally, the proportion of cases in which conflict was high is somewhat lower among policies initiated by the government or initiated jointly by both 'sides' than among policies initiated by parties.

Table 8.4   Conflict levels, bipolar/not bipolar, field of government and origin of policy

	Small	**Medium**	**Large**	**Total**
Bipolar	4	2	7	13
Intermediate	1	1	1	3
Not bipolar	10	8	16	34
Field of government				
foreign	3	4	4	11
economy	9	3	8	20
social	2	2	7	11
other	1	2	5	8
Initiative				
government	8	4	10	22
joint	3	4	5	12
party	4	3	9	16
Total	15	11	24	50

Pace of decision-making

The pace of decision-making appears somewhat affected by the various characteristics of policy-making which we have examined so far. Governments in bipolar political systems tend to take decisions somewhat more quickly than those in political systems which are not bipolar, but the difference is not very large, perhaps surprisingly (slightly under half vs a little over a third). There is also a relationship between the field of policy and the pace of the decision: foreign policy issues took the smallest amount of time to be decided on whilst economic policies took somewhat longer and policies in the social and 'other' fields took longest. Finally, party-initiated policies tended be decided slowly and government-initiated policies tended to be decided rapidly; indeed, among these, the policies developed by the government autonomously were resolved particularly quickly (Table 8.5).

Policy style

Policy style appears to play an important part in the characteristics of policy-making. Thus 'imposed' decisions are more likely to be found where the political system is bipolar (nine cases out of 13) than where it is not (ten cases out of 34) (Table 8.6). In Belgium, decisions were 'imposed' in foreign affairs and in relation to institutional matters; in

Table 8.5   Pace of decisions, bipolar/not bipolar, field of government and origin of policy

	Quick	**Slow**	**Very slow**	**Total**
Bipolar	6	4	3	13
Intermediate	2	1	0	3
Not bipolar	12	11	11	34
Field of government				
foreign	7	2	2	11
economy	8	8	4	20
social	3	4	4	11
other	2	2	4	8
Initiative				
government	12	7	3	22
joint	4	4	4	12
party	4	5	7	16
Total	20	16	14	50

Italy, it was also manifest in foreign affairs and over the reform of wage indexation. As these examples suggest, an imposed policy style seems rather widespread in foreign affairs.

Perhaps the most striking feature relates to the relationship between policy style and the origin of policies: rather surprisingly, policies initiated by governments tend subsequently to be elaborated in a more collaborative manner than those initiated by supporting parties or policies initiated jointly by governments and supporting parties. Governments seem to have to pay more attention to and negotiate more with other bodies when they initiate matters; when confronted with policies emerging from or also emerging from the supporting parties, they may be less reluctant to impose a solution if they do not like aspects of these policies.

The relationship between policy style and other characteristics of the elaboration phase

It was noted in the previous section that policy style might well be closely associated with the level of conflict as well as with the extent of participation in the elaboration process and the pace of decision-making. Conflicts might be lower, participation broader, and the pace of decision-making slower when the policy style is based on collaboration. While the first of these expectations appear validated, the last two

Table 8.6 Policy styles, bipolar/not bipolar, field of government, origin of policy, levels of conflict, extent of participation and pace of decision-making

	Imposition	Collaborative	Total
Bipolar	9	4	13
Intermediate	2	1	3
Not bipolar	10	24	34
Field of government			
foreign	6	5	11
economy	7	13	20
social	4	7	11
other	4	4	8
Initiative			
government	8	14	22
joint	5	7	12
party	8	8	16
Conflict levels			
large	14	10	24
intermediate	5	6	11
small	2	13	15
Participation			
one 'side' only	2	4	6
both 'sides'	8	16	24
groups as well	11	9	20
Pace of decision-making			
quick	10	10	20
slow	5	11	16
very slow	6	8	14
Total	21	29	50

are not: conflicts are indeed more often low when the policy style is collaborative, but participation is not much larger when the style is collaborative than when it is based on imposition. Both very slow and very quick decisions are also equally likely to occur whether the policy style is based on imposition or is collaborative. Only when policies are elaborated slowly, but not very slowly, is a collaborative style likely to prevail. The pace of decision-making and the extent of participation are thus not controlled by the policy style, while the extent of conflict does appear to be correlated with the character of the policy style.

Table 8.7   Outcomes, bipolar/not bipolar, field of government, origin of policy, level of conflict and pace of decision-making

	Rejected	Amended	Adopted	Total
Bipolar	3	1	9	13
Intermediate	0	0	3	3
Not bipolar	1	11	22	34
Field of government				
foreign	0	1	10	11
economy	1	6	13	20
social	1	4	6	11
other	2	1	5	8
Initiative				
government	0	6	16	22
joint	0	1	11	12
party	4	5	7	16
Conflict levels				
large	4	8	12	24
intermediate	0	2	9	11
small	0	2	13	15
Pace of decision-making				
quick	0	2	18	20
slow	1	5	10	16
very slow	3	5	6	14
Total	4	12	34	50

Outcomes

The very large majority – 46 out of 50 – of the policies analysed in this study were adopted in some manner, but 12 of these 46 were substantially amended before being passed (Table 8.7). This pattern reflects one of the main features of contemporary European parliamentary systems: policies which do emerge and are seriously discussed tend to be adopted, although in some cases only after substantial modifications.

The pattern of outcomes is revealing, however. First, the success rate of initiatives is larger in the foreign policy area than with respect to economic and social issues, not so much perhaps because policies in the foreign area are more likely to be adopted, but because they are likely to be adopted without any amendment. Admittedly, there is sometimes little scope for governments to change decisions which have been negotiated internationally: yet changes occur occasionally, as was shown in the context of the 'dual-track' policy in the Netherlands, a decision which was in any case never put to the test so that it is therefore not certain that the policy, while adopted on paper, would eventually have been implemented. Policies are also more likely to be adopted without change in countries in which the political system is bipolar, while, where it is not, many policies are substantially amended before being passed.

Given the general characteristics of contemporary European political systems, it is perhaps not surprising that all the policies which were rejected should have been initiated by the supporting parties. The four party-initiated policies which were rejected were two of the British Labour Party, those on 'planning agreements' and on 'industrial democracy' which the Labour government succeeded in avoiding implementing, the proposal to reform the nationality law which had emerged from one of the conservative government parties in 1986 in France – only to be taken up again in the following decade and this time adopted – and the proposal of institutional reform in the Netherlands which some coalition parties had put forward but which was entirely abandoned.

Not surprisingly, too, the policies which were not adopted and most of those which were markedly amended are found among those characterised by a substantial amount of conflict. Moreover, while none of the policies which were settled rapidly was abandoned or even substantially modified, the majority of the policies which were abandoned had previously undergone a very long process of attrition and those which were strongly amended underwent either a long or a very long process before maturing.

The main characteristics of the policy-making process thus appear to be the following:

1. Government initiatives are numerous, but, during the elaboration phase of these policies, supporting parties nearly always intervene and groups and organisations intervene in many cases.
2. A significant minority of policies is substantially amended during the elaboration stage.
3. Policies initiated by governments tend to be handled more quickly; they are also more conflictual but are often characterised by a collaborative style, as governments often appear to have to listen to the views of parties and groups to ensure that their policies are adopted.
4. Where the political system is bipolar, individual policies are often decided in a spirit of imposition between the government and the

supporting parties, although this occurs also to an extent in systems which are not bipolar.

Types of government–supporting party relationships and policy-making

Since governments are prominent in the initiation and elaboration phases of policy-making, it seems at first sight correct to conclude that, by and large, in Western Europe, supporting parties tend to depend on governments rather more than might have been expected; moreover, as there is apparently little difference in the proportion of policies initiated by governments whether the party system is bipolar or not, it also seems correct to conclude that the supporting parties' dependence on the government does not vary markedly, contrary to what had been expected, according to the type of party system. This point needs to be looked into more carefully, however; it also needs to be related to the other explanatory factors being considered here, namely the type of policy fields concerned and the primarily 'partisan' or 'administrative' character of the policies involved.

The categorisation of liberal-democratic systems as 'autonomous', 'dependent-party' and 'dependent-government' was based on two hypotheses. The first was that, by and large, while presidential systems would result in greater autonomy of governments from supporting parties, the parliamentary-cabinet system would tend to lead to an interdependence between governments and supporting parties; the second suggested that in countries where a bipolar party system prevailed, the supporting parties would tend to be more dependent on the government than where the political system was 'not bipolar'. The first of these two hypotheses appears corroborated by the evidence relating to policy-making in European parliamentary systems: the number of cases in which the government was 'autonomous' with respect to the supporting parties was, as we saw, very small and supporting parties were never autonomous from the government, as we also saw. Meanwhile, there seemed to be *prima facie* little support for the second hypothesis. This was so for two reasons: first the two countries studied here in which the political system is bipolar – Britain and France – were characterised by a *higher* proportion of party-initiated policies than the other countries. Second, in general, the elaboration of policies tends to take place on a joint basis in all types of parliamentary systems. It would therefore seem that the political systems which are bipolar are neither more nor less likely to be party-dependent than those which are not bipolar.

While this conclusion seems ostensibly valid and before considering the other explanatory factors, it must be noted that out of the 50 policies studied only four were abandoned or rejected and that all four had been initiated by the supporting parties. Moreover, three of these four failed policies occurred in countries where the political system was bipolar and only one was found in the other group of polities. This does not by itself mean that parties are more dependent in countries of the first group, but it indicates that, in this group, party endeavours to make a mark on policy are in a number of cases thwarted by governments while this outcome appears to occur less frequently in other types of parliamentary systems.

More generally, both the nature of the policy fields and the partisan or administrative character of the policy appear to play a part. We saw that the field of foreign affairs was one in which government initiatives were numerous, in part at least because this field is one in which a quick reaction is expected in many cases from other governments or from international organisations: only the government is in a position to do so and parties are obviously at a disadvantage, which is likely to occur whether the political system is bipolar or not.

The distinction between partisan and administrative policies also appears to play a part, although it is difficult to disentangle the two elements of that distinction from each other in some cases. Yet, while it does appear that the policies pursued by governments in bipolar polities are often highly partisan, the evidence is appreciably more mixed for polities which are not bipolar. One reason for the difference may be that, where complex coalitions have to be built, governments cannot afford to be as partisan as when they lead a single party or a coalition dominated by a party. This means that, in polities which are not bipolar, either matters are negotiated in a collaborative fashion until a solution acceptable to all (that is, less partisan) is found, or matters which are highly partisan are simply not discussed and are relegated to being non-decisions. There seems to be an element of both in the countries studied here. Moreover, governments even appear sometimes to be regarded as potential 'arbiters' with respect to problems which are very sensitive but are not usually considered as having a 'party' character: the abortion issues in which the governments of Belgium and of the Netherlands came to be involved might be regarded as instances of such a role.

This does not indicate that there is not a profound government involvement in policy-making in both types of party systems. It means only that the involvement of the government differs appreciably in character depending on whether the system is bipolar or not: the nature of the party system does therefore have marked influence in the type of policies which are likely to be examined and decided on. Bipolar systems lead to partisan governments which seem to take over the leadership of the party in terms of policy development from the rest of the party. Systems which are not bipolar also rely on governments for policy initiation and elaboration, but they do so in a more neutral manner, as is consistent with the character of polities in which it is less possible in view of the nature of the party system for the government to conduct partisan crusades and in which governmental action has to be ostensibly more technically administrative than aggressively political.

*   *   *

The study of the role of governments and supporting parties in initiating and elaborating policies is still at a very early stage of development. A certain lack of interest in the part played by governments, first, and the major difficulties posed by the comparative analysis of policies, second, has resulted in limited progress having been made in the area, despite its importance, not just from an academic standpoint but from the point of view of the working of democracies. Given this background, a preliminary inquiry such as the present one could only lead to tentative conclusions; these remain to be corroborated by further evidence.

Two points can be advanced, however. First, governments are involved in a major way, not just in the elaboration of policies but in their initiation, while supporting parties are involved in the elaboration of nearly all the policies which governments initiate. Second, while the picture is not as clear as might perhaps have been expected, there is at least some support for the view that, in political systems which are bipolar, policies initiated by governments are more likely to be partisan; while, in political systems which are not bipolar, policies are somewhat more likely to be initiated by the supporting parties and, when they are initiated by the government, they appear to be on the whole less partisan and more administrative.

Given the preliminary and limited character of the inquiry on which this volume has necessarily been based, the fact that these conclusions could be reached, however tentatively, is of some significance. The study of the relative involvement of governments and supporting parties *can* be undertaken, and can lead relatively easily to comparative conclusions.

Appendix I: the 50 policies on which the study is based

Britain

Labour government: 1974–9

Party proposal to introduce industrial democracy (not adopted);
Party proposal to introduce planning agreements (not adopted);
Government counter-inflation policy;
Party–government policy to renegotiate the terms of entry in the EEC and to hold a referendum.

Conservative government: 1979–90

Party–government policy to alter industrial relations in Britain by reducing the powers of trade unions;
Government policy to privatise a series of firms;
Party proposal to abolish local government rates;
Government policy designed to change the basis of British contributions to the EEC.

France

Socialist government: 1981–86 and 1988–93

Government proposal to grant amnesty to officers involved in rebellions in Algeria;
Party–government policy designed to give a minimum wage to persons being given a temporary job (RMI);
Party proposals to nationalise a large sector of the economy.

Gaullist–conservative government: 1986–8

Party policy to privatise firms;
Party proposal to make it more difficult to obtain French nationality (not adopted).

Germany

Government/party policy to reform the budget;
Government policy with respect to employment assistance;
Government policy towards reunification.

Belgium

Party policy to reform the institutions;
Government policy to introduce dual-track arrangements;
Government policy to locate missiles in Belgium;
Government policy to implement the Maastricht criteria;
Government policy on abortion;
Party policy on ecological taxes.

Italy

Government policy on wage indexation;
Government policy on development aid;
Government policy to set up an anti-trust agency;
Government policy on privatisation;
Party policy to regulate television;
Government policy on the 1992 budget;
Government policy on the 'Achille Lauro' affair relating to a Middle Eastern terrorist which United States forces effectively kidnapped in order to bring him to the United States for trial.

Austria

Party policy on privatisations, round 1;
Party–government policy of tax reform, round 1;
Party–government policy on the EEC;
Government policy on housing;
Government policy on maternity leave;
Party–government policy of tax reform, round 2;
Party policy on privatisations, round 2;
Party–government policy on privatisations, round 3.

The Netherlands

Government policy to privatise some firms;
Government policy in the field of welfare;
Party policy on abortion;
Government policy to introduce dual-track arrangements;
Party proposal to reform the institutions (not adopted).

Finland

Party–government policy on occupational health;
Party policy on industrial relations;
Party–government policy on constitutional reform;
Party–government policy on gender equality at work;
Party–government policy on tax reform;
Party–government policy on privatisation;
Party–government policy on the EEC;
Government policy on the Paris peace treaty.

Appendix II: characteristics of policies

	(1)	(2)	(3)	(4)	(5)	(6)	(7)	(8)
Britain								
Lab: ind. dem.	BIPOLAR	SOC	P	L	L	VS	I	N
Lab: plann.	BIPOLAR	ECO	P	L	L	VS	I	N
Lab: anti-infl.	BIPOLAR	ECO	G	L	L	QU	I	Y
Lab: EEC	BIPOLAR	FOR	G/P	L	L	SL	I	Y
Con: ind. rel.	BIPOLAR	SOC	G/P	L	?	SL	I	Y
Con: privat.	BIPOLAR	ECO	G	2	S	SL	C	Y
Con: loc. fin.	BIPOLAR	ECO	P	2	L	VS	I	Y
Con: EEC	BIPOLAR	FOR	G	1	S	QU	C	Y
France								
Soc: Amnesty	BIPOLAR	OTH	G	2	L	QU	I	Y
Soc: sp. min. wage	BIPOLAR	SOC	G/P	2	S	QU	C	Y
Soc: nationalis.	BIPOLAR	ECO	P	2	?	QU	I	AM
Con: privat.	BIPOLAR	ECO	P	2	S	QU	C	Y
Con: nationality	BIPOLAR	OTH	P	L	L	SL	I	N
Germany								
Budget reform	INTERM	ECO	G/P	L	L	QU	I	Y
Empl. assist.	INTERM	SOC	G	2	?	SL	C	Y
Reunification	INTERM	FOR	G	2	S	QU	I	Y
Belgium								
Const. ref.	NOT BIPOLAR	OTH	P	L	L	VS	I	Y
Dual-track	NOT BIPOLAR	FOR	G	2	L	QU	I	Y
Missiles	NOT BIPOLAR	FOR	G	2	L	QU	I	Y
Maastricht crit.	NOT BIPOLAR	ECO	G	L	?	SL	C	Y
Abortion	NOT BIPOLAR	OTH	P	2	S	QU	C	Y
Ecotaxes	NOT BIPOLAR	ECO	P	2	S	SL	C	AM
Italy								
Wage index.	NOT BIPOLAR	SOC	G	1	S	QU	I	Y
Devel. aid	NOT BIPOLAR	FOR	G	2	?	QU	I	Y
Antitrust	NOT BIPOLAR	ECO	G	1	S	QU	C	Y
Privat.	NOT BIPOLAR	ECO	G	2	L	VS	C	AM
TV regul.	NOT BIPOLAR	OTH	P	2	?	SL	C	Y
Fin 92	NOT BIPOLAR	ECO	G	2	L	SL	C	AM
'Achille Lauro'	NOT BIPOLAR	FOR	G	1	?	QU	I	Y
Austria								
Privat. 1	NOT BIPOLAR	ECO	P	L	L	SL	C	Y
Tax 1	NOT BIPOLAR	ECO	G/P	L	L	SL	I	Y
EEC	NOT BIPOLAR	FOR	G/P	L	?	VS	C	Y
Housing	NOT BIPOLAR	SOC	G	L	L	SL	C	Y
Maternity leave	NOT BIPOLAR	SOC	G	L	L	SL	C	AM
Tax 2	NOT BIPOLAR	ECO	G/P	2	S	QU	C	Y
Privat. 2	NOT BIPOLAR	ECO	P	2	S	QU	C	Y
Privat. 3	NOT BIPOLAR	ECO	G/P	2	S	QU	C	Y

Appendix II (*Cont.*)

The Netherlands								
Privat.	NOT BIPOLAR	ECO	G	1	S	SL	C	AM
Welfare	NOT BIPOLAR	SOC	G	2	L	QU	C	AM
Abortion	NOT BIPOLAR	OTH	P	2	L	VS	I	AM
Dual-track	NOT BIPOLAR	FOR	G	L	L	VS	C	AM
Const. ref.	NOT BIPOLAR	OTH	P	2	L	VS	C	N
Finland								
Occup. health	NOT BIPOLAR	SOC	G/P	L	L	VS	C	Y
Ind. rel.	NOT BIPOLAR	SOC	P	L	L	VS	C	AM
Const. ref.	NOT BIPOLAR	OTH	G/P	2	?	VS	C	Y
Gender equality	NOT BIPOLAR	SOC	G/P	L	L	VS	I	AM
Tax reform	NOT BIPOLAR	ECO	P	L	?	SL	I	AM
Privat.	NOT BIPOLAR	ECO	G	2	S	VS	C	Y
EEC	NOT BIPOLAR	FOR	G/P	L	?	SL	C	Y
Peace treaty	NOT BIPOLAR	FOR	G	1	S	QU	C	Y

(1)   Polarity: BIPOLAR (Britain, France): INTERM (intermediate) (Germany); NOT BIPOLAR (Belgium, Italy, Austria, The Netherlands, Finland).

(2)   Field: foreign (FOR); economic (ECO); social (SOC); or other (OTH).

(3)   Initiative: government (G); party (P); or both (G/P).

(4)   Participation: one side only (1); both sides (2); or groups as well (L).

(5)   Conflict: large (L); small (S); or intermediate (?).

(6)   Pace of decision: quick (QU); slow (SL); or very slow (VS).

(7)   Style of the policy: imposition (I) or collaboration (C).

(8)   Outcome: adopted (Y); rejected (N); or modified (AM).

Note

1   It is because there appear to be cases of polities, or situations in the life of individual polities, when the relationships between governments and supporting parties are truly collaborative while the political processes are not consensual overall that the distinction was drawn in Chapter 5 between 'true consensual' polities (such as the Scandinavian countries) and those 'non-bipolar' polities in which agreements take place among the parties of the coalition, but typically not beyond these parties (as, seemingly, in Austria and Belgium). See note 1 to Chapter 5.

9
Conclusion: From the Simple World of Party Government to a More Complex View of Party–Government Relationships

M. Cotta

The two faces of party government

At the end of a conceptual and empirical exploration of the relationship between executives and the parties supporting them, we need to draw some conclusions about this crucial aspect of contemporary democratic regimes. By relationship, as we have repeatedly pointed out, we mean a two-way process by which parties influence the executive and the executive influences the supporting parties. The inquiry in this volume has been restricted to parliamentary systems, while the 1996 volume (Blondel and Cotta, 1996) also examined the case of the American presidential government (Katz, 1996), which gave an opportunity to explore the 'periphery' of party government and to discover the limits of this concept in the context of a different institutional regime. As a matter of fact, by restricting the analysis to parliamentary systems, that is to say to systems where the link between governments and supporting parties is rather tight, we are likely to be able to better understand the nature of the reciprocal influence which exists between the two sides.

To begin with, a major surprise comes from the fact that the amount of research in the field is rather limited. Parties have been widely recognised as central features of contemporary democracy in political science and increasingly in legal studies, as can be seen from the vast number of empirical studies about the internal organisation, electoral roots, developmental trends, and patterns of competition among parties in democratic countries (Bartolini, Caramani and Hug, 1998). On the basis of these studies the interpretation of democracy has been reformulated to incorporate party competition as one of its central features (Downs,

1957; Linz, 1978; Sartori, 1987). Yet the evaluation of the meaning of the role of parties for the daily workings of the institutions of government (and as a consequence for the daily workings of democracy) lags behind. The concept of 'party government' which links parties with the institution of government was for a long time implicitly accepted more than systematically discussed in the literature. At most, limited aspects of the relationship between parties and government have been explored in depth. Among these, coalition-building and government formation and duration have received the largest amount of attention.[1] This is understandable: the formation of governments is obviously a key moment in the life of the executive and the role of parties is crucial at that point; yet it is only 'one' moment. Works explicitly devoted to an overall assessment of party government are on the contrary relatively rare (Schattschneider, 1942; Rose, 1969; Castles and Wildenmann, 1986; Katz, 1986 and 1987; Calise 1989; Budge and Keman, 1990), and in many cases they deal mainly with one country only (Schattschneider, 1942; Rose, 1969; Calise, 1989). In fact the first work which discussed at length and within a general perspective the theme of party government and which also attempted to render its meaning more precise is the four-volume study initiated in the 1980s by Wildenmann (Castles and Wildenmann, 1986; Katz, 1987; Castles, Lehner and Schmidt, 1988; Lessmann, 1987). Moreover, these works have analysed the relationship between party and government essentially from the point of view of the party, as if the only topic worth studying was the influence exerted by parties upon the institutions of government. The opposite perspective, namely the possibility that the institutions of government might exert an influence on the parties, did not seem to require much attention: only in the context of the examination of party types, as for instance the 'catch-all' party (Kirchheimer, 1966), or the 'cartel party' (Katz and Mair, 1995), can one find occasional references to the effect on parties of their support of the government.

   This state of affairs has undoubtedly to do with the fact that it is easier to assess the characteristics of partial aspects of government rather than of government as a whole. It also has to do with the visibility of parties which are involved in the most public aspects of political life, such as elections and parliamentary activities, a visibility which is greater than that of governments. This is only part of the explanation, however: the tensions between our normative views and the reality of democratic government have played a significant part in the way party–government relations have been examined. As it was difficult in the past for traditional conceptions of the state to accept the idea that parties were in government, because they brought, as it was then believed, their 'factionalism' inside the centre of national sovereignty, it later became difficult to accept the idea of a relatively autonomous role of government in the democratic age. When democracy becomes the key interpretation of political life and is conceived as a bottom-up process by way of which the people, through the electoral process, express their views about how the government should act and send their delegates to govern the country, all the attention is understandably concentrated on the parties. Because of their electoral role, parties are seen as the instruments of the people: they are thus naturally entrusted with the function of governing. In this perspective there is little normative space for the government as an autonomous entity. Where electors are the principal and parties the agent, the government should be but an instrument in the hands of its agents.[2]

If we leave the realm of normative conceptions and move into that of empirical reality, the shortcomings of an approach to the study of democratic government that adopts only the perspective of the influence of parties soon become apparent. Indeed, suggestions to take a less simplistic view come from various directions. On the one hand, a long tradition of studies of the state bureaucracy has alerted us to not consider it as a purely dependent variable (Lipset, 1950; Mayntz, 1978; Peters, 1978). State bureaucracies do not merely execute what they are told to do by party politicians holding the positions of government: they are often able to oppose and resist these directives. The 'Yes, Minister!' syndrome[3] is not merely a TV joke: it is real-life experience. In fact, ministerial bureaucracies play an active part as policy initiators in the defence of their own interests and/or of their views of the national interest. Government cannot therefore be seen as a one-way operation only: it is at the crossroads of different flows of influence, one at least of which comes from a direction that cannot be immediately incorporated in the bottom-up view of democracy.

Some party studies also support the need to take into account this perspective. It has often been noticed, for instance, that parties change when they come into government. This is the case in particular with socialist parties: once they ceased to be merely in opposition, they significantly watered down their traditional commitments (Kirchheimer, 1966; von Beyme, 1984). It follows that being in government affects parties.

Yet we continue to lack a systematic and balanced account of the two faces of the party–government relationship, at a time when there are signs that the age of parties with strong membership organisations and well-defined ideological identities also appears to be over in Europe (Katz and Mair, 1995). Since it was precisely that age which supported the classic party–government model whereby parties could dominate the executive, the exploration of other aspects of the party–government relationship becomes mandatory.

It seemed therefore essential to systematically explore the influence that the government exerts on the parties which support that government, alongside the influence that the parties might exercise on the government (Blondel, 1989). It became immediately apparent, however, that in order to do so the two phenomena of government and party had to be identified and analysed with precision and, beyond such an analysis, party and government had to be related to the two spheres of society and state. What the government *is* becomes clearer once the links existing between this institution and the state are established: if the government is understood as being at the head of a huge politico-administrative apparatus which combines the monopoly of legitimate use of force (Weber, 1972) with a marked involvement in the economy typical of the Keynesian state and the redistributive mechanisms of the welfare state (Rose, 1976), it becomes obvious that the government cannot be reduced to being merely a 'dependent' variable.

The linkage between government and state also suggests that there will be major variations in the features and weight of the government: the variable strength of the state and the different extent to which the government controls the state are likely to alter the scope and resources of the government. A more interventionist vs. a leaner and more *laissez-faire* state, an internationally outward-looking and expansionist vs. an inward-looking and timid state should make also for different governments. Yet this is only one, albeit crucial, aspect. The relationship of the government with the state leads to another dimension: within a given state type the steering capacity of the government *vis-à-vis* other authorities that are not part of the government may vary: it suffices to mention the different part governments may play in relation to the Central Banks or the role of independent authorities in regulating markets.

A more or less symmetrical situation can be found with regard to party and society. If parties can be viewed as the politicised projection of society, significant variations in their possible role *vis-à-vis* the government will occur both because of the degree of articulation and autonomy of society, and as a consequence of the extent to which parties monopolise the political representation of society. An active society will make for different types of parties from a passive society. Yet it is also possible to envisage within the same type of society different parts played by parties *vis-à-vis* other bodies, in particular pressure groups or social movements, with regard to the political representation of societal interests and demands. The weight of parties in society and *vis-à-vis* the government will be greater where unions and other interest organisations are under party control than where these act independently: in this last case the government may be able to play one actor against another.

The relationship between party and government thus reflects the relationship between society and state, as well as the relationship between state and government on the one hand, and the relationship between society and party on the other. The 'partyness' of governments and the 'governmentness' of parties are ultimately linked to these basic aspects of the organisation of the polity.

After having examined in general terms the place of party and government within the polity, the next aim of this volume was to analyse in some detail the true significance of the two terms. These two concepts are often taken for granted; and the phenomena to which they relate are frequently viewed as monolithic. In reality, behind the same words, different meanings and different empirical phenomena are often implied: hence the need to unpack the two concepts. With respect to party, three principal sub-components, namely the parliamentary party, the party as an extra-parliamentary organisation and the 'party in government' were described. These different elements share, of course, many points in common – the same name, the same symbols and the same traditions, as well as personal and organisational links. But the 'logic' of their action can be very diverse: their interests and their goals are not identical, nor are the constraints and incentives under which they operate and the resources they control: the party as a whole must therefore be viewed as a system of interactions rather than a monolithic actor. This means that party–government relationships are rendered complex by the fact that different parts of the party can play different games. As a matter of fact, these relationships must be regarded as being to an extent intra-party relationships, with one component of the party (the party in government) facing one or more of the other components of the same party (the parliamentary party, the party as an extra-parliamentary organisation). Yet it would be reductive to say that the party–government relations are just intra-party relations. In fact these intra-party relationships are significant precisely because the government is more than just a part of the party and is an independent source of resources, responsibilities and constraints for that component of the party which is in government. The 'party in government' is still 'party', although it is at the same time somewhat less 'party' than the other components. Moreover, as many studies about parties have abundantly shown, the importance, autonomy and resources of the different components of a party may vary very significantly over time, across countries and across party families. Party–government relationships are presumably affected by these variations.

A detailed analysis shows that the government also has a complex reality. This is primarily because it is the key institution where the two main sides of the democratic polity, the democratic or representative side and the state or administrative side, are brought together: indeed, the government sits on top of both. While the democratic side of the government is under pressure from the mechanisms of popular accountability and answers to the shifting waves of public opinion and to the interests which are mobilised in the electoral processes, the administrative side is under pressure from the internal and external commitments which the state machine has accumulated over decades or even centuries and which are embodied in its bureaucratic organisation. Directly or indirectly, the government is thus involved in different games, where resources, constraints and stakes vary. This explains why on the one hand the control of the executive by parties has so often proved elusive (and partymen once in government tend to become different from what they were before), and why on the other hand the administrative side of the government soon finds it has to come to terms with the guidance which representative politicians exercise.

The nature of the government changes significantly as a result of the variations corresponding to these two sides: thus the representative role of the government may vary from being direct and dominant to being rather indirect and subordinate. On the other hand, the administrative capabilities of governments may be stronger or weaker and cabinets may be more or less autonomous in the choice of goals to be pursued and of the means to be adopted.

The dimensions of the relationship: empirical findings

Assessing empirically the relationships between parties and government entails specifying the domains of these relationships. Studies of party government had originally tended to privilege the domain of appointments to ministerial positions. Understandably, given the visibility of these appointments and the conflicts that often surround them, the influence of parties on governments tended to be measured by the ability of these parties to appoint partymen as members of the government. Yet the need to also study policies soon became manifest, in the first instance in relations to coalition-building: thus Katz includes the control of the elaboration of policies as one of the central features of party government (Katz, 1987). A third dimension needed to be added, however, that of patronage, as the distribution of particularistic benefits can be a very important political instrument over which parties and government compete and/or cooperate.

Distinguishing between the three domains may not always be very easy in practice. The difference between policies and patronage can often be a matter of degree rather than of kind; some policies have such a limited scope and such a specific target that they borderline acts of patronage. Appointments also may be close to patronage: to appoint a person to a political or administrative office may often mean distributing a benefit rather than selecting the most competent person. Moreover, there is also a significant linkage between policies and appointments: the appointment of someone to the government may be associated with a specific policy or set of policies. Yet an analytical distinction does exist between the three domains. In most cases the difference between appointments, policies and patronage is indeed clear: each of these domains is characterised by specific types of relationships between parties and government and therefore deserves a specific treatment.

An attempt has been made in this volume to undertake a comparative examination of the forms which party–government relationships take in each of these three planes. A major aim of the analysis has been to assess whether, alongside the well-known influence of parties on government, signs of influence in the opposite direction could also be discovered. A further goal was to discover factors that would account for variations among countries and, within countries, among governments of a different political complexion.

Evaluating the three domains

Appointments

The analysis of appointments covered both the selection of cabinet members and the selection of members of party executives to see how far both parties and governments exert influence on each other. Three elements were taken into account to evaluate appointments: the identity of the nominees, the identity of the nominators, and the degree of control which nominators exercise on nominees. On this basis, it was possible to draw a number of tentative conclusions.

First, as was to be expected, the high degree of partyness of the nominees indicates that parties do exercise a major influence on the recruitment of ministers: with very limited exceptions the cabinet is the preserve of partymen and partywomen, the exceptions (mainly concentrated in Finland and in Italy in the early 1990s) being linked to periods of crisis or to difficulties experienced by the political system. Parties maintain a dominant control of the mechanisms of democratic legitimation of the executive and it is normally through parties that one can become a member of a democratic executive. It must be added, however, that in some countries the process of recruitment and socialisation within the party may be long and intense, while in others (the Netherlands being a good example) it may have much less weight.

Second, however, the picture becomes somewhat more complex when we consider the nomination process. In some countries the parties dominate this process, as in Belgium, Finland, and Italy before the 1990s, while in others the government and more specifically the head of the government has a leading role, perhaps with the assistance of his or her close collaborators as in Britain, Germany, France and to some extent Austria and increasingly Italy in the 1990s. Up to a point this contrast is attenuated by the fact that in the first group of countries outgoing ministers often exercise substantial influence either in re-selecting themselves or in contributing to the composition of subsequent governments. When this is taken into account the dependence of ministerial appointments on the party appears less strong than often implied.

In the interpretation of this contrast between party-controlled and government-controlled appointments we must take into account that the difference between a party 'nominator' and a government 'nominator' can be viewed to some extent as a difference between two types of party actors. What is normally called a party-controlled appointment means, in fact, an appointment made by the leaders of the membership or of the parliamentary party. On the other hand a government-controlled appointment is in most cases an appointment made by the leader or leaders of the 'party in government'. The two types of appointment procedures therefore indicate that different sections of the party exercise influence on the nomination process. In the second case, however, some party actors (mainly the party leader who is also the government leader) are using their government role and the resources it implies to assert their predominance over other party actors.[4]

British prime ministers, to use the best-known example of government-controlled ministerial appointments, are obviously at the same time government actors with powers deriving from the position they hold in the government, and party actors (leaders of the 'party in government' and indeed leaders of the party *tout court*). When nominating ministers they use their double authority to assert their government leadership but also to reward party friends, placate opponents and in general to maintain their control of the party. Where, as in Belgium and Italy, appointments are predominantly party-controlled, the game is played essentially within the membership or the parliamentary party. The government is not a very significant actor in itself nor an important resource to be used for intra-party purposes. If viewed in this manner, differences among countries and among governments with regard to appointment modes are also to be seen as differences in the relative weight of the various party components – parliamentary, extra-parliamentary and governmental.

To evaluate where influence truly lies with respect to appointments, *ex post* controls over the nominees also have to be examined: if no such controls exist, the nominees in practice become independent from the nominators. If one considers only the extent to which ministers can be recalled during the lifetime of a government, the influence of the party or, to be precise, the influence of the parliamentary and extra-parliamentary parties generally appears smaller than that of the government or of the 'party in government'. Reshuffles of ministers are more frequently provoked by the government leader (particularly when he or she is also the party leader) than by the parties supporting the government. This seems to suggest that parties have difficulties in prolonging their influence beyond the initial appointment: such an interpretation is, however, oversimple. Ministers know that nominators will exercise influence primarily when the government is dissolved and a new one is being set up. The true *ex post* control over nominees depends therefore on what ministers believe about which actor – party or government, parliamentary or extra-parliamentary party or 'party in government' – will dominate this process. As a result, where cabinets do not last long and the same kind of coalition patterns prevail over time, as in Belgium and Italy, cabinet changes tend to be the equivalents of reshuffles: the parliamentary party or the extra-parliamentary party are then typically in a stronger position with regard to *ex post* controls than the 'party in government'.

Who appoints whom to party leadership positions has been rarely examined so far, although the question is important if one is to obtain an overall picture of party–government relationships. In principle these appointments are internal party matters: nominators, nominees and *ex post* controls should all be within the parties and the government would not seem to have any part to play. In practice, however, government influence does exist. There are few cases where (as in the British Conservative Party) the government leader is formally entrusted with the power to nominate members of the party leadership (and even then only a section of the party leadership is involved); but it is more frequent that prime ministers and some senior ministers contribute *de facto* openly or behind the scenes to the selection of some of the party leaders. That the government should be induced to meddle with internal party affairs should not be surprising when one considers the extent to which the life of the government will be affected by party behaviour. Moreover, here too if we adopt the same approach as the one just adopted in the context of ministerial appointments, the role of the government can be interpreted at least in part as being that of a specific component of the party, the 'party in government'. Formally or informally, that component will want to take part in appointments in the parliamentary party or in the extra-parliamentary party. The greater the resources the party in government can derive from the fact that it constitutes the government, the greater should be its impact upon the choice of the leaders of the parliamentary party or of the extra-parliamentary party, other things being equal.

The degree of 'governmentness' (that is, the fact that they have held beforehand one or more ministerial positions) of the nominees to the positions of leadership in the parliamentary party or of the extra-parliamentary party is generally lower than the degree of 'partyness' of those appointed to ministerial positions. This probably reflects the fact that parliamentary and membership parties remain the main pool from which the personnel of the whole party–government subsystem is recruited. It is therefore understandable that a career in the parliamentary party or in the extra-parliamentary party, more than one in the government, should be a prerequisite for access to the party leadership. Yet this might also mean that a position in the party leadership is sometimes less important than a ministerial post: the lack of ministerial experience would then be due simply to the fact that access to the former positions takes place at an earlier stage in the career of politicians. This seems confirmed *a contrario* by the fact that countries in which the degree of 'governmentness' of party leaders is greater (Italy and Belgium being the clearest cases) are also those where party leadership positions have more weight and are therefore the preserve of more seasoned politicians.

The impact of the government on party appointments is to a great extent the impact of the 'party in government', and this results above all from the role of the party leader which combines the position of prime minister and secondarily from the role of those party influentials who are at the same time senior ministers, especially in coalitions. This aspect of the party–government relationship is therefore to an extent a 'within party game': yet we should not forget that the 'party in government' is able to exercise such an influence only because the government offers, to a greater or lesser extent admittedly, resources of prestige, power and legitimacy. Moreover, the politicians in government when playing this party game are also guided by the specific needs and perspective of the institution they belong to. Influencing the selection of the (external) party leadership is also a means for making the life of government easier.

In the field of appointments, situations of real autonomy of the government *vis-à-vis* the party are therefore rather rare. They can be found at moments of serious crisis of the political system (Italy) or at the time of an impasse in the coalition-making process (Finland) or in a limited area of government (a ministry with an especially technical role). If the definition of autonomy is relaxed to mean that although the party has an influence in ministerial appointments the positions in the two institutions are thereafter rather separate, the Dutch case is probably the nearest to government autonomy. Overall, one can say that the party is generally more autonomous *vis-à-vis* the government than vice versa, although here too the links that exist below the surface are stronger than is often suggested.

In the cases examined here the interactions between party and government tend on the contrary to be quite strong and not unidirectional: the flow of influence is not merely from party to government but from government to party as well. We have also seen that these interactions must be viewed as instances of relationships between groups of politicians who, whether in the parliamentary or extra-parliamentary party or in the government, share the fact that they all belong to the same encompassing party. These interactions are therefore to some extent at least cases of 'within-party' relations. They can be seen as cooperative, competitive or conflictual interactions between the extra-parliamentary party, the parliamentary party and the 'party in government'. These interactions reflect the existence of different equilibria between the components of the party. It does remain true, however, that in this 'within-party' game the 'party in government' derives its relative autonomy and its influence from the fact that in Western European democracies the government is more than a party appendage and that it can therefore become a real player in the relationships among the various components of the parties.

The signs of change which can be detected in the field of appointments go primarily in the direction of greater government influence, Italy being the clearest example: to some extent already in the 1980s and more clearly in the 1990s, the influence of government leaders increased both on the appointment of ministers and on the selection of the parliamentary and extra-parliamentary party leadership. In Germany, too, the influence of the chancellor has increased in relation to appointments: this was true not only during the long reign of Helmut Kohl but also recently under Gerhard Schroeder, who once installed as chancellor quickly forced (in 1999) the resignation of Lafontaine, the leader of the extra-parliamentary party. Developments in Austria are not altogether dissimilar. Those who control the government appear to be better able than in the past to also control from that position the whole party.

Policies

Both government and parties are involved in policies. Because of its specific powers of policy-making, because of its role of initiator with respect to those policies which require parliamentary approval and because it heads the civil service, the government naturally occupies a key position in this domain. On the other hand, parties, too, have a vested interest in keeping this domain under their control, because of the part they play in the electoral process as well as because of their many links with groups in society. The popular support they enjoy depends at least in part on their ability to deliver the policies that their followers prefer. Government and parties are thus both involved; what remains to be seen is what is their relationship.

That relationship is difficult to gauge, however. The sheer number of policies developed within a given time span, the complexity of most of the processes of policy-making and the number of actors involved render a systematic evaluation most problematic. The analysis undertaken here, on the basis of 50 policies spread over the eight countries, does not constitute a representative sample: caution therefore has to be exercised in drawing general conclusions. Yet these 50 policies cover a rather wide range of policy sectors, and provide at least enough empirical evidence to suggest broad directions in which the relationships take place.

The most significant finding is that the ideal-typical view of party government according to which parties dictate policies to the government which then faithfully executes them is clearly not the best representation of reality: the government plays a highly significant part. This is particularly true of the first stage of policy-making: initiation. The government is far from being a passive subject in this field waiting for the directives of the parties: it has an important role either on its own or in combination with the parties. There are variations in this respect according to policy fields: as was expected, foreign policy is more 'governmental' than economic or social affairs, but the difference is not as large as one might have supposed. Moreover, even in countries which are normally considered 'partitocratic' and where the analysis of appointments confirmed this view, the role of the government in initiating policies is far from marginal and that of parties far from overwhelming. Should one conclude that partitocracy does not relate to policies? We shall return to this point later in this chapter.

The importance of the role of government is confirmed when we move from policy initiation to policy elaboration, as in none of the policies studied was the government bypassed altogether. Meanwhile, the role of parties is also significant in most cases: policies developed fully autonomously by the government are very few. The central part of the policy process thus sees a great deal of interaction between the two sides of party government.

A more realistic image of party–government relationships follows as a result. Contrary to the model which views parties as institutions where policies are conceived and then transmitted to government, which has by then been conquered and dominated by the parties themselves as a result of party appointments to ministerial positions, real-life experience is less simple, even in those countries which have traditionally been regarded as truly partitocratic. Parties do not have the monopoly or even a predominant role in setting new policies in motion, and the government does not wait for their guidance to play a part in this field. The fact that the intervention of parties increases in the next stage suggests that to a significant extent their role has more a reactive and defensive character: they intervene to stop or correct policy developments often put forward by others which they see as being at least in part contrary to the ideas and the interests they stand for. To a significant degree the actions of parties consist in defining the boundaries within which policy-making (promoted by other actors) is permissible: their role is therefore often conservative. It aims at ensuring that an existing policy paradigm (which they concurred to shape) is not altered fundamentally but only adapted.

This is perhaps not surprising: parties are organisations with often broad ideological orientations, with activists who are sometimes strongly motivated by a collective identity, with an electoral following which at least in part is stable and has a lasting identification. They are bound to bring to political life a strong element of continuity (Converse and Dupeux, 1962; Converse, 1969; Lipset and Rokkan, 1967). Innovation in the policy field is therefore more often the consequence of governmental action, as the government has the institutional obligation to face and solve the problems posed (internally and internationally) by everyday life or resulting from the pressure of specialised interest groups.

This obviously modifies not only the idea of party government but also the simplified bottom-up interpretation of democracy which sees voters and parties as the prime-movers in the system. The more realistic view of democratic politics suggested by our findings is that the role of elections and parties is more modest, though not insignificant: it consists in checking rather than dominating the other bodies which affect political life, whether the interest groups and the movements on the one hand, or the bureaucracy on the other.

Yet we need to understand better the real role of the government as a policy initiator. This meaning does vary in a significant way: it can consist in an institutional responsibility to fulfil the functions that the state has to assume internally or internationally. This responsibility at the same time constrains the freedom of action of the government and provides for its legitimation. This is manifest in a number of foreign policy cases or in budgetary and economic policies. The action of the government is then generally backed by those sections of the central administration which can be described as the institutional guardians of these responsibilities, specifically the ministries of Foreign Affairs, Defence and Finance. Yet the action of the government can also be more political and partisan. The party in government is then more clearly behind the government. It aims at achieving political goals in the democratic arena at large, including fulfilling the political and electoral mandate which propelled it to power and maintaining or even strengthening its support in the country and that of the parties which sustain it in view of the next election. It may also aim in a more limited way to achieve goals in the intra-party arena: the party leaders that are in government may thus wish to strengthen their position *vis-à-vis* other components of the party.

Thus, as for appointments, party–government relationships are at least in part within-party relationships where different internal components of the party are at play. However, much more than in the case of appointments, the non-party face of government is highly significant in the context of policies. Possibly the clearest example of the difference between the two aspects – highly political and partisan, administrative and technical – is offered by the privatisation policies in Britain in the

1980s and in Italy. In both countries privatisation policies were promoted by the government rather than by the supporting parties (Conservatives in Britain, Christian Democrats and Socialists in Italy). However, in Britain, after an initial stage when the predominant goal was to obtain resources for the national budget, the policy became part of an ideological platform that the government leader with her political advisors (the 'party in government') was exploiting to renovate the Conservative Party image in the country and to win electoral support (for the party and for herself): it became then a highly partisan policy and the government behind it was also a highly partisan government (Blondel, 1996). In Italy, the privatisation policies which emerged between the end of the 1980s and the beginning of the 1990s were predominantly motivated by budgetary needs. The Treasury administration and the Finance ministers of this period (who were not partymen but technocrats in most cases) had a prominent role in promoting these policies against the resistance of the parties supporting the government. The parties in government tolerated the policy when they could not oppose it (Cerboni and Cotta, 1996; Cotta and Verzichelli, 1996). The government was in this case more the expression of the state and of its institutional responsibilities than of the parties.

The party and the non-party faces of government may, depending on the cases and the situations, cooperate or conflict. The party in government may to some extent use (or even manipulate) the constraints under which the administrative government works to strengthen its hand in intra-party conflicts. On the other hand, while the partisan government may want to press for a policy direction to gain an advantage on the terrain of democratic competition, it may have to face constraints resulting from its internal or external administrative obligations. This is a situation that seems bound to emerge increasingly in some areas of social policy. The wish of left-wing (but also often Christian Democratic) parties in government to preserve or change only marginally social expenditure in order not to antagonise their traditional electorate conflicts increasingly with government obligations to implement rigorous budgetary guidelines set by the European Union. Choosing between these options is a difficult dilemma for the parties in government.

Overall, the distinction between the different faces of government – partisan and administrative – may also help to explain to an extent some surprising findings of our research such as the fact that countries known for their partitocratic character do not show a clear predominance of party over government in the policy field, and particularly in policy initiation. There is in fact some evidence that in such cases the autonomous role of the government in the field of policies derives predominantly from its institutional and administrative responsibilities. As if the parties satisfied with their control of appointments and, as we shall see, of patronage were willing (or perhaps could not avoid) leaving the administrative government in charge of at least some of the policy problems. Paradoxically, in less-partitocratic countries (as in Britain) the government tends to play a more partisan role in the field of policy-making. The leadership of the party in such countries is in fact more clearly in the hands of the leader of the government and thus it is understandable that he/she uses in a direct way the government institution to pursue his/her policy preferences.

Patronage

Patronage is the most difficult of the three domains to assess. This is in part because it is the least 'legitimate' of the three aspects of party-government. As a result, factual information is problematic to obtain, patronage often being concealed or disguised. Moreover, patronage generally consists of a large number of small deeds that are not easy to observe.

The opportunity to distribute patronage goods (titles, jobs, contracts, procurement, subsidies and so on) is to a large extent in the hands of governments. In spite of all normative restrictions and regulations designed to prevent the particularistic use of public resources, the great expansion of state intervention in economic and social life has substantially increased the potential for patronage. Not all of it is controlled by the national government, to be sure: local authorities and parliament have their share and, in this way, opposition parties may gain an access, albeit smaller, to patronage. However, the fact that national governments can obtain the largest proportion of these resources is obviously an element that leads parties to want to be in power. The control over patronage provides parties with a resource for rewarding members and followers and for enhancing and preserving the internal cohesion of the membership party (but also of the parliamentary party and of the party in the electorate). Patronage can in fact prove an important complement or substitute of ideological faith and of policy successes.

The relationship between the domains of patronage and policy is complex. On one hand, some policies may be seen as the preconditions for patronage: they create the opportunities and the instruments for its implementation. On the other hand, patronage may be a substitute for policy. Where the approval of innovative and universalistic policies may prove (or simply appear) difficult – for instance in a fragmented institutional system with elusive majorities – political actors (parties and governments) will probably find patronage a useful substitute for winning support. Distributive coalitions for the allocation of patronage are generally easier to build than majorities for more controversial policy measures.

The level of patronage varies appreciably from one country to another: even though the information available about the eight countries in this study is qualitative, a distinction can be drawn between the polities where patronage is low (Finland, the Netherlands and Britain), those where it is intermediate (Germany and France) and those where it is high (Austria, Belgium and Italy). This suggests that patronage cannot be overlooked in the assessment of party–government relationships in the third group of countries and probably in the second group as well, while it could perhaps not be concerned in detail for the countries of the first group. This also suggests that 'governing' does not have the same meaning everywhere.

There is a clear asymmetry in this context. Formally, patronage is predominantly distributed by the government: as in the context of policies, parties do not have direct access to it. It follows that there cannot be 'pure' party autonomy in this domain, while one can imagine pure government autonomy, as well as party dependence, government dependence and interdependence between party and government.

Empirical evidence suggests that there are a variety of patterns in the distribution of patronage. The two countries where the level is highest, Belgium and Italy, offer ample evidence of a dependent government. Patronage, although materially handed out by the government, is closely controlled by the parties, which use it to reward their members and followers. In some cases, for instance for bank and television appointments in Italy before 1994 or for lower rank promotions in the Belgian public service, this control is so strict that the government simply rubber stamps decisions taken by the parties (Cotta and Verzichelli, 1996; De Winter, Frognier and Rihoux, 1996). This would almost be party autonomy if it were not for the fact that parties need to be in government to exercise this power. Moreover, even in these cases of strong party influence, there is evidence that ministers obtain their own share of patronage and can in this way enhance their influence on the party at large.

The weight of government seems greater in the other countries, whether in those where patronage is small (Britain, Finland and the

Netherlands) or in those where it is intermediate (Germany and France), but also in a country where it is decidedly high (Austria). Prime ministers and ministers (to whom should be added the French presidents) are in such cases more independent in distributing patronage goods, while the party as such has less influence and is more a recipient than a decision-maker. France represents probably the extreme case of government dominance over party in this field and is therefore at the opposite extreme to Belgium or Italy. French presidents and prime ministers pull the crucial levers with the help of their collaborators and are not under the control of the party at large. This is also the situation in Britain, albeit in a context of a lower amount of patronage.

Yet what constitutes the 'government' in this case needs to be more closely looked at, as we did for appointments and for policies. By and large, the government does not so much mean here the 'institution', but rather a number of individuals – presidents, prime ministers or ministers – who play their own game if they have margins of autonomy *vis-à-vis* the party. When playing this games, they operate to an extent as party actors: they are often politicians with a strong stake in the party from which they originate. In the government where they are temporarily located they can use the patronage resources at their disposal to strengthen the popular following of their party, to consolidate their leadership in the party and stave off challenges to it. In the cases where ministerial tenure is short and uncertain they can also use these resources to prepare the ground for their return to the party when they lose their ministerial status. The government at work here is basically the 'party in government', but rather as a collection of individuals and not as a team.

Yet these governmental actors do not just play a party game: they have institutional aims as well. Patronage is used to keep the parties happy while the ministers govern, and to reward civil servants and other political or administrative collaborators who contribute to the efficient working of the government. The more the government plays an independent part in patronage, the more this is likely to be due to the fact that party identities and party links with governmental actors are weak and overshadowed by the personal entrepreneurship of ministers. Party is then an instrument more than an end in itself.

A final remark on the ambiguity of party–government relationships has to be made with regard to this domain: where parties are clearly at the helm and the government is in a dependent position, parties are also, in a sense, 'dependent' on the government. They *must* be in government in order to have access to the key resources needed for their activities. The most extreme case in this respect was probably that of

Italy: parties that had lived off patronage for decades abruptly collapsed when they lost control of these resources (Cotta and Isernia, 1996).

A comprehensive evaluation of the three dimensions

If we now consider jointly the three dimensions of government–supporting party relationships – appointments, policies and patronage – we have to conclude, on the basis of the evidence collected in this study, that nowhere are the parties fully in control and the governments fully dependent. The government has always some autonomy and always exercises some influence on the supporting parties. Thus the 'party government' model (Katz, 1986) or, as we prefer to define it, the 'party-dependent government' model is a polar extreme from which real-world situations are distant, albeit more or less.

There are nonetheless significant variations among the eight countries that have been analysed here. The most striking concerns patronage, which is widespread in some countries but not in others: indeed, its scope may be so reduced that, where this is the case, it need not be considered at all, while this is never so for the other two dimensions, appointments and policies. Patronage and policies are to an extent alternative to each other: where patronage plays a large part, policies are less far-reaching or they tend to have some of the characteristics of patronage activities. Appointments complement the other two dimensions, at least in part: thus they may be closely connected to policies by helping to produce the desired policies, or to patronage by providing a mechanism to control the distribution of patronage. They are also an important resource in their own right for politicians (whose motivations to seek ministerial jobs and/or leading positions in the parties are well-established).

When we attempt to provide a comprehensive view of party-government relations which takes into account the three different planes a crucial problem arises immediately. To which unit of analysis do our representations of party–government relationships apply? To the country, to the individual government, to the individual party, to different planes of action or going even further down the scale to specific acts? If our model applies to the country level, that would mean that it applies to every government and every party involved in the government and to all the actions of all these governments and parties in a given country. Or in any case that deviations from the norm should be rare. Only exceptionally would a government or a party in its relations with the government, and only for a limited number of actions, conform to a different model. At the other extreme, the model might change from cabinet to cabinet, from party to party or even from action to action. The answer to this question is empirical: the unit to be chosen is the one that enables the most parsimonious description of reality. The implications of different answers are obviously also important for our causal explanations: if only variations across countries are significant we will be able to disregard as explanatory factors all those variables which vary within countries (be they the political composition of the government, the type of party or the policy sector, and so forth) and concentrate on the contextual variables (such as the institutional setting, the party system, for example). If, on the contrary, we find significant variations within countries the explanatory power of the contextual variables will have to be questioned.

The empirical findings of this book, for all their limitations, provide a picture that indicates rather clearly the importance of cross-country differences. In a first very parsimonious and global representation it is permissible to say that our countries – typically all their cabinets and the common practice of governance – show a fairly stable pattern of party–government relations. Of these countries some are nearer to the model of the party-dependent government model than others. However in none of our countries it can be said that the government is purely dependent, that it is just an obedient tool in the hands of parties.

Two main models apply to the countries analysed here. One of these fits Italy, before the crisis of the 1990s, and Belgium as well as, in broad terms, Austria: these are countries where the parties are strong and their impact is pervasive. The membership and/or the parliamentary components of these parties are in control of ministerial and party appointments. They are also in control of what is, in these cases, extensive patronage. On the other hand the appointments of the highest party officers are done within the party. Government dependence on parties would be complete if parties also dominated policies, but this is, somewhat surprisingly, not the case: either because they are not interested, or because they do not have the technical skills to deal with such matters or because they prefer to escape the risks involved, supporting parties leave a significant space to the government to initiate and elaborate policies. The model of the party-dependent government thus has to be modified to incorporate some autonomy for the government. We propose to call it *patrimonial party government*: parties tend to conceive the government as a treasure chest to be conquered and used for distributive purposes rather than as an instrument aiming at changing society. To the extent that in some situations a steering function has to be exerted, parties are prepared to leave some scope to the government viewed in its administrative capacity and to confine themselves to a guardianship role. Austria differs from Italy and Belgium mainly in that, as a result of the greater fusion between government and party leadership in that country, the government tends to have a stronger say over appointments. Probably, in Austria, a more streamlined party system which resulted either in single-party governments or in stable coalitions of the two main parties rendered the cabinet more central in the context of an overall party-patrimonial system.

In the other model the government is the centre of gravity of party–government relationships. The cabinet – in effect the prime minister, helped by a few influential ministers or counsellors that form his or her entourage – has substantial autonomy in making and unmaking governmental appointments. It also exercises a significant influence over appointments to the leading positions of the membership and parliamentary party. Its weight in the initiation and elaboration of policies is predominant (but this does not exclude some counter-influences from the external party), and the same can be said for the field of patronage (although this is typically less extended than in other cases). Britain (especially under Conservative governments), Germany (under the long CDU/CSU–FDP governments) and France are the countries which correspond best to this model.

While it has a leading role the government in these countries is anything but non-partisan or 'technocratic'. In fact one could argue that the political and partisan nature of the government is in such cases even stronger because of the fusion which exists of party leadership and government leadership: the true leaders of the party sit in the government, while this is not the case in party-patrimonial situations, where political authority is located in the external party and where the government, being more dependent, maintains at the same time a more administrative character. Yet, in countries where the party leadership is squarely in the institution of government rather than being inside the membership party, the leadership style does seem to alter somewhat as a result of this situation: it is not ostensibly wholly party-oriented and acquires a kind of 'statelike' character. Although these party-cum-government leaders cannot forget their party supporters, they also have to play for a larger audience: there is more of a tendency than in party-patrimonial cases for leaders to go beyond the party. Indeed, once in government, leaders, especially when they remain in office for a long period, are likely to increasingly consider the (other components of the) supporting parties as instruments designed to help their governmental actions rather than as ends in themselves. They come to identify themselves with their governmental role because of the institutional prestige and legitimacy associated with this role. Hence some distance from the party, a distance which is typically perceived by both sides: the leader is often irritated by requests coming from the membership and parliamentary parties, which make the running of government less easy, while these bodies feel frustrated because 'their' government is often not faithful to the party platforms. That explains why the government in its policy-making activity may face from time to time the protests of its supporting party(ies). Appointments, some degree of accommodation in the content of policies, and the distribution of patronage are the instruments the government will use to avoid more costly confrontations with its supporters. This model should therefore be referred to as being a *partisan government*, both because the role of the government is central and because the government is strongly political and dominated by the party leader(s).

The two remaining cases – the Netherlands and Finland – fit less well in either of these models. Both countries differ markedly from the party-patrimonial model in that patronage plays a very limited part. In the context of appointments Finland comes rather near to the model of the party-dependent government: appointments to the cabinet are strictly controlled by the party, while the cabinet has little or no influence over party appointments. In the policy field, evidence of a strong party role can be found in the importance and rather detailed contents of coalition agreement: yet the dependence of the government on parties is far from complete. Not only is the government obviously a prime mover in transforming relatively vague party proposals into fully-fledged legislative bills, but it also initiates new policies with the support of the administrative branch. For these reasons Finland could be defined as a case of *limited party-dependent government*.

The case of the Netherlands is different; in the domain of appointments both sides are relatively autonomous. The government has little say over party appointments. Parties play some part in ministerial appointments, to be sure, but those who are appointed do not necessarily have a long party career and *ex post* party controls over them are weak. Over policies, despite increasingly detailed coalition programmes, the cabinet appears rather autonomous. The case of the Netherlands could therefore be referred to as one of *semi-autonomous government*.

Yet a picture based exclusively on differences at the country level does not fully correspond to the reality of party–government relations. Variations within countries also play a part. First, party does make a (some) difference: party–government relationships tend to change somewhat

when a different party comes to power. Strong membership organisations and well-defined ideological platforms have an effect, which
means that parties of the Left tend to exert a greater pressure on 'their'
government and on 'their' ministers with respect to appointments,
policies and patronage. This has been the case in Britain with Labour
governments and in Germany with SPD-led cabinets; it is also the case in
the Netherlands and Belgium when the behaviour of Socialist parties
with respect to the governments they support is compared to that of
Liberal or Christian Democrat parties. Yet these variations across parties
do not completely overshadow the country characteristics: party–government relationships in a British Labour cabinet differ from party–
government relationships in a British Conservative cabinet. However,
these two forms are more similar to each other than they are, for
instance, to the way in which Belgian parties behave with respect to
the governments which they support. Moreover, such differences
among parties may also be declining in view of the fact that the ideological and organisational decline of Left parties is making them more
similar to their bourgeois counterparts.

Some variations are also associated with the political cycle. While the
administrative side of governments is by its nature lasting, the political
side of (democratic) governments is by definition non-permanent. Cabinets are formed, live for a more or less extended time-span and then
die. We may easily expect some consequences from the juxtaposition of
these two different 'clocks'. The stages of the government cycle are in
part linked to the electoral cycle, in part to other political events that
may take place between elections both inside the supporting parties and
outside. The influence of parties is in general more marked in the initial
phase of cabinets. The appointment of new ministers is often done
directly by the parties; and the first policies initiated by the government
tend to follow the party programmes and/or the coalition agreements
reached among parties during government formation. Afterwards, the
influence of parties generally declines. In some cases the role of parties
may be quickly overshadowed by that of the government. Where the
government emerges directly from elections the government leader
immediately wins a strong dominance over appointments and policy-
making. As in such cases the government leader is also the leader of the
party we can say that the 'party in government' rapidly takes over to the
detriment of the external party. The party has won but, paradoxically,
the victory immediately creates a rather sharp separation between the
'party in government' and the rest of the party that does not directly
enjoy the glory of office.

Where elections do not have such a decisive impact the process takes longer, but after some time in office the distance between the government and the supporting parties generally tends to grow. This process is less noticeable when the time perspective of cabinets is very short: ministers have scarcely had time to acquire autonomy from the external components of the supporting parties before a crisis brings back to the helm the external components of the supporting parties in the context of the negotiation process leading to a new government. When cabinets are more stable, on the other hand, the grip of the external party loosens. Even if they are appointed by the party, ministers are rarely subjected to very strong *ex post* controls. A 'recall' by the party is not a very common occurrence since such a move may endanger difficult coalitional agreements, and policy-making is, as we have seen, conducted under a number of different pressures and constraints, among which those coming from the supporting parties are only one component. Examples of the growing autonomy of government are provided not just by the U-turn in economic policy of the French Socialist governments in the 1980s, but also by the rather autonomous policies of the long Craxi government in Italy between 1983 and 1987.

Finally, variations in the party–government relationships are also associated to differences among policy fields. As expected, the probability of government autonomy is higher in the field of foreign affairs, particularly during the initiation stage, than in the economic and social fields, as parties are more likely to launch policy initiatives in these fields either on their own or jointly with the government, and to participate in the elaboration of these policies.

Explaining variations

On the basis of these empirical findings we may now return to our initial hypotheses. We expected first of all that the party system, and in particular the distinction between bipolar or non-bipolar systems, would be a major explanatory variable of variations in the government–supporting parties relationships. The basis for this hypothesis are the effects that this feature of the political system has upon the role of the government and of the parties in the representative game: in bipolar systems the government tends to take the lead in the representative game and the prime minister, strengthened by the electoral legitimacy he or she has received, will exert the leadership over the party. In non-bipolar systems, on the contrary, as electoral results are seldom decisive for the formation of governments, parties remain the crucial dispensers of democratic legitimacy and can thus assert their right to control the cabinet.

Our findings indicate, in fact, that the most marked differences in the relationships between governments and supporting parties exist between countries that belong to the two different party-system categories. Countries in which the party system is bipolar do display a significantly greater degree of government autonomy in ministerial appointments and a greater dependence of party appointments on the government. However, in these countries, the role of the government in policy-making is associated with a substantial amount of (cooperative or conflictual) initiatives and interventions of the parties in the elaboration phase. This is in part because, although directly legitimised electorally, the government does nevertheless emerge from the party and before its first electoral victory the government leader was the party leader; moreover, the external components of the party – membership and parliamentary party – that are not directly involved in the government may not feel entirely happy with its decisions and are in a position to exercise some pressure, for instance in parliament.

The picture is less clear in countries where the party system is not bipolar as there are more variations. The most striking element of variation concerns, as we have seen, the balance between the three planes of the relationship, and in particular the fact that in two of the five cases patronage plays little or no role. Finland and the Netherlands are two rather clear examples of what we have called an 'incomplete' relationship: patronage is almost irrelevant and the two planes of appointments and policies are predominant. In Austria, Belgium and Italy, on the contrary, party-dominated patronage is very large and it reduces the weight of policies. This contrast requires an explanation that goes beyond the party system variable. The explanation is probably to be found in the relationship between parties and the state, and in the character of the public sector. A weak state with a penetrable civil service and parties that have come to consider themselves as superior to that state and are in need of short-term resources for their followers provide, perhaps, the combination of factors which explains the party-patrimonial cases. Factors leading to a relatively weak state exist in fact in Austria – which has had an uncertain national identity throughout the first half of this century – in Belgium – with its tensions among linguistic groups – and in Italy – where to a relatively recent state unification is to be added the breakdown of the state apparatus and external occupation when fascism collapsed. Meanwhile, in all three countries parties acquired a dominant position. In the Netherlands, on the contrary, we have a state with a longer tradition and a more solid authority which has kept the parties somewhat at the margins while a more technocratic pattern of government autonomy developed. The Finnish case, where parties have indeed acquired a strong role but with a programmatic rather than patrimonial orientation (that is, stressing policies rather than patronage), is a bit more puzzling. The recent (and troubled) history of the Finnish state was perhaps compensated in this case by stronger bureaucratic traditions and by a more competitive party system which have contained the potential for patronage.

The fact that even in the party-patrimonial cases the government enjoys a relatively autonomous role in the field of policy-making, confirms the importance of compensation among the three dimensions of government–supporting parties relationships. This also means that there are clear limits to the action and interests of parties, while the role of the government is strengthened on the policy dimension by the need to respond to international, economic or budgetary challenges. Critical situations and the consequential responsibilities which fall upon governments are thus to be seen as another factor contributing to the explanation of government–supporting parties relationships.

We have also seen, throughout our analysis of cases, that two other variables are associated with variations in government–supporting parties relationships: the internal structure of parties – the strength or weakness of membership organisations in particular – and the phases of the political cycle – early or later stages of a government, proximity or distance from elections being the main aspects involved. The explanatory potential of these variables derives from the fact that both can affect in a significant way the resources and the needs of parties and governments. Parties with a strong membership organisation are better able to influence 'their' ministers than less-structured parties: they have a greater impact on the recruitment of politicians and have more to offer to them when they leave office. They also have more staff able to contribute to the elaboration of policies. At the same time they need to obtain more from the government to satisfy their members. With regard to the impact of the political cycle, the crucial aspect is that the weight of the democratic mandate of the parties or of the government varies appreciably from one moment of the political cycle to another.

Relationships between governments and supporting parties are, as we have seen, more complex in their outlook and in their explanation than simple models often imply. Current findings are partial: yet they provide some important clues for understanding the complexities of this relationship. Governments and parties are at the intersection between state and society, between bureaucratic administration and democratic representation, and inevitably the relationship between the two sides or faces of party government reflects all the tensions and problems that derive from this political marriage. In a democratic state, neither of the two sides can be expected to entirely dominate the other: but within these boundaries the potential for variations across countries and within countries remains substantial. The important transformations underway in all European countries in the mechanisms of political mobilisation and in the organisational structure of parties, compounded with the changing constraints and opportunities under which national governments operate as a consequence of the growth of supranational integration and international globalisation, also suggest that the relationship between government and supporting parties will be subject to further changes in the future. The topic discussed in this book is thus far from exhausted.

Notes

1   During the 1960s and 1970s a large body of writings blossomed on this matter. Among these we can remember Riker 1962, Leiserson 1966, De Swaan 1973, Taylor and Laver 1973.
2   Along these lines of reasoning Müller and Strøm (1997) apply the principal/agent scheme to the relationship between parties and governments.
3   As it is well known to viewers of the British TV, 'Yes, Minister!' is the title of a satirical serial where the secretary of a British Minister always says yes to his minister's wishes but in the end manages to do exactly the opposite, i.e. what pleases himself.
4   One should not forget, however, that the government role as it is an asset can also be a liability: government failures can have negative consequences for the leader of the government, for the ministers and for the 'party in government' in general and weaken their authority in the party.

References

Adonis, A. (1997) 'The UK: Civic Virtue Put to the Test', in D. Della Porta and Y. Mény (eds), *Democracy and Corruption in Europe* (London: Pinter).

Alber, I. (1982) *Vom Armenhaus zum Wohlfahrtsstaat* (Frankfurt: Campus).

Almond, G. and Powell, G. B. (1996) *Comparative Politics: a Developmental Approach* (Boston: Little, Brown & Co.).

Almond, G. and Verba, S. (1963) *The Civic Culture* (Boston: Little, Brown & Co.).

Andeweg, R. B. (1996) 'The Netherlands. Parties between Power and Principle', in J. Blondel and M. Cotta (eds), *Party and Government* (London: Macmillan).

Andeweg, R. B. (1996) 'Elite–Mass Linkages in Europe: Legitimacy Crisis or Party Crisis?', in J. Hayward (ed.), *Elitism, Populism, and European Politics* (Oxford: Clarendon Press), 143–63.

Austen-Smith, D. and Banks, J. (1988) 'Elections, Coalitions and Legislative Outcomes', *American Political Science Review*, LXXXII, 405–22.

Bagehot, W. (1963) [1867] *The English Constitution* (London: Oxford University Press).

Bakema, W. E. (1991) 'The Ministerial Career', in J. Blondel and J. L. Thiébault (eds), *The Profession of Government Minister in Western Europe* (London: Macmillan), 70–98.

Bartolini, S., Caramani, D. and Hug, S. (1998) *Parties and Party Systems* (London: Sage).

Bendix, J. (1992) 'Going Beyond the State? Comment to Mitchell', *American Political Science Review*, LXXXCXVI, 1007–10.

Beyme, K. von (1985) *Political Parties in Western Democracies* (Aldershot: Gower).

Blondel, J. (1987) *Political Leadership*, (London and Los Angeles: Sage).

Blondel, J. (1989) *The Political Factors Accounting for the Relationship between Governments and the Parties Supporting them* (Florence: European University Institute), mimeo.

Blondel, J. (1991) 'The Post-Ministerial Careers', in J. Blondel and J. L. Thiébault (eds), *The Profession of Government Minister in Western Europe* (London: Macmillan).

Blondel, J. (1996) 'Britain: A Textbook Case of Government–Supporting Party Relationship', in J. Blondel and M. Cotta (eds), *Party and Government. An Inquiry into the Relationship between Governments and Supporting Parties in Liberal Democracies* (London: Macmillan), 22–39.

Blondel, J. and Cotta, M. (eds) (1996) *Party and Government. An Inquiry into the Relationship between Governments and Supporting parties in Liberal Democracies* (London: Macmillan).

Blondel, J. and Müller-Rommel, F. (eds) (1993) *Governing Together* (London: Macmillan).

Blondel, J. and Thiébault, J. L. (eds) (1991) *The Profession of Government Minister in Western Europe* (London: Macmillan).

Bodiguel, J.-L. (1983) 'A French-Style "Spoils System"?', *Public Administration*, LXI, 295–300.

Bogdanor, V. (ed.) (1983) *Coalition Government in Western Europe* (London: Heinemann).

Brosio, G. (1988) 'Patronage and Bureaucratic Efficiency', *European Journal of Political Economy*, IV, 95–104.

Bryce, J. (1981) *The American Commonwealth* (New York: Macmillan).

Budge, I. (1996) *The New Challenge of Direct Democracy* (Cambridge: Polity Press).

Budge, I. *et al.* (1976) *Party Identification and Beyond* (London: Wiley).

Budge, I. and Keman, H. (1990) *Parties and Democracy: Coalition Formation and Government Functioning in Twenty States* (Oxford: Oxford University Press).

Budge, I. and Laver, M. (1986) 'Office Seeking and Policy Pursuit in Coalition Theory', *Legislative Studies Quarterly*, XI, 485–506.

Budge, I. and Laver, M. (1992) 'Coalition Theory, Government Policy and Party Policy', in M. Laver and I. Budge (eds), *Party Policy and Government Coalitions* (Basingstoke: Macmillan), 1–9.

Budge, I., Robertson, D. and Hearl, D. (eds) (1987) *Ideology, Strategy and Party Change* (Cambridge: Cambridge University Press).

Burke, E. (1770) *Thoughts on the Causes of the Present Discontents*.

Calise, M. (1989) *Il governo di partito* (Bologna: Il Mulino).

Cassese, S. (1984) 'The Higher Civil Service in Italy', in E. N. Suleiman (ed), *Bureaucrats and Policy Making* (New York: Holmes & Meier).

Cassese, S. (1993) 'Hypotheses on the Italian Administrative System', *West European Politics*, XVI, 316–28.

Castles, F. G. (1982) *The Impact of Parties: Politics and Policies in Democratic Capitalist States* (London: Sage).

Castles, F. G., Lehner, F. and Schmidt, M. G. (eds) (1988) *Managing Mixed Economies* (Berlin: de Gruyter).

Castles, F. G. and Wildenmann, R. (eds) (1986) *Visions and Realities of Party Government* (Berlin: de Gruyter).

Cerboni, A. and Cotta, M. (1996) 'Le privatizzazioni: i partiti e la crisi finanziaria', in M. Cotta and P. Isernia (eds), *Il gigante dai piedi di argilla. La crisi del regime partitocratico in Italia* (Bologna: Il Mulino).

Chodak, S. (1989) *The New State; Etatization of Western Societies* (Boulder: Lynne Rienner).

Chubb, J. (1981) 'The Social Bases of an Urban Machine: The Christian Democratic Party in Palermo', in S. N. Eisenstadt and R. Lemarchand (eds), *Political Clientelism, Patronage and Development* (London: Sage).

Converse, P. E. (1969) 'Of Time and Partisan Stability', in *Comparative Political Studies*, II, 139–71.

Converse, P. E. and Dupeux, G. (1962) 'Politicization of the Electorate in France and the United States', in *Public Opinion Quarterly*, XXVI, 139–71.

Cotta, M. and Isernia, P. (eds) (1996) *Il gigante dai piedi di argilla. La crisi del regime partitocratico in Italia* (Bologna: Il Mulino).

Cotta, M. and Verzichelli, L. (1996) 'Italy: Sunset of a Partitocracy', in J. Blondel and M. Cotta (eds), *Party and Government. An Inquiry into the Relationship between Governments and Supporting Parties in Liberal Democracies* (London: Macmillan); 180–201.

Daalder, H. (1992) 'A Crisis of Party?', *Scandinavian Political Studies*, XV, 269–88.

Dahl, R. A. (1971) *Polyarchy. Participation and Opposition.* (New Haven: Yale University Press).

Dekker, P. (1995) 'Civil Society als partij-ideologie?', *Socialisme en Democratie*, n.2, 62–73.

Della Porta, D. (1997) 'The Vicious Circles of Corruption in Italy', in D. Della Porta and Y. Mény (eds), *Democracy and Corruption in Europe* (London: Pinter).

Della Porta, D. and Pizzorno, A. (1996) 'The Business Politicians: Reflections from a Study of Political Corruption', *Journal of Law and Society*, xxiii, 113–31.

Della Porta, D. and Vannucci, A. (1996) 'Controlling Political Corruption in Italy: What Did Not Work, What Can Be Done', *Res Publica*, xxxviii, 353–69.

Derlien, H.-U. (1991) 'Regierungswechsel, Regimewechsel und Zusammensetzung der politisch-administrativen Elite', *Leviathan*, xii, 253–70.

Derlien, H.-U. (1995) 'Public Administration in Germany: Political and Social Relations', in J. Pierre (ed.), *Bureaucracy in the Modern State* (Aldershot: Edward Elgar).

De Swaan, A. (1973) *Coalition Theories and Cabinet Formation* (Amsterdam: Elsevier).

De Winter, L. (1991) 'Parliamentary and Party Pathways to the Cabinet', in J.Blondel and J. L.Thiébault (eds), *The Profession of Government Minister in Western Europe*, London, 1991, 44–69.

De Winter, L. (1993) 'The Selection of Party Leaders in Belgium: Rubber-stamping the Nominee of the Party Elites', *European Journal of Political Research*, xxiv, 233–56.

De Winter, L. (1996) 'Party Encroachment on the Executive and Legislative Branch in the Belgian Polity', *Res Publica*, xxxviii, 325–52.

De Winter, L., Frognier, A.-P. and Rihoux, B. (1996) 'Belgium: still the Age of Party Government?', in J. Blondel and M. Cotta (eds), *Party and Government. An Inquiry into the Relationship between Governments and Supporting Parties in Liberal Democracies* (London: Macmillan), 153–79.

Dobler, H. (1983) 'Der persistente Proporz: Parteien und verstaatlichte Industrie', in P. Gerlich and W. C. Müller (eds), *Zwischen Koalition und Konkurrenz. Österreichs Parteien seit 1945* (Vienna: Braumüller).

Doig, A. (1996) 'From Lynskey to Nolan: The Corruption of British Politics and Public Service?', *Journal of Law and Society*, xxiii, 36–56.

Downs, A. (1957) *An Economic Theory of Democracy* (New York: Harper & Row).

Dunleavy, P. and Weir, S. (1995) 'Media, Opinion and the Constitution', in F. F. Ridley and A. Doig (eds), *Sleaze: Politicians, Private Interests and Public Reaction* (Oxford: Oxford University Press).

Duverger, M. (1964) *Political Parties* (London: Methuen).

Duverger, M. (1980) 'A New Political System Model: Semi-Presidential Government', in *European Journal of Political Research*, 8, 87–165.

Dyson, K. (1977) *Party, State and Bureaucracy in Western Germany* (London: Sage).

Dyson, K. (1987) 'State', in V. Bogdanor (ed.), *The Blackwell Encyclopaedia of Political Institutions* (Oxford: Blackwell), 590–3.

Easton, D. (1981) 'The Political System Besieged by the State', *Political Theory*, ix, 303–25.

Easton, D. (1990) *The Analysis of Political Structure* (New York: Routledge).

Eisenstadt, S. N. and Roniger, L. (eds) (1984) *Patrons, Clients and Friends* (Cambridge: Cambridge University Press).

Eschenburg, T. (1961) *Ämterpatronage*, (Stuttgart: Curt E. Schwab).

Fay, C. (1995) 'France', in F. F. Ridley and A. Doig (eds), *Sleaze: Politicians, Private Interests and Public Reaction* (Oxford: Oxford University Press).

Fehr, E. and Van der Bellen, A. (1982) 'Aufsichtsräte in öffentlichen Unternehmen. Skizzen zur politischen Ökonomie Österreichs', *Zeitschrift für öffentliche und gemeinwirtschaftliche Unternehmen*, v, 123–50.

Ferrero, G. (1988) *Pouvoir. Les génies invisibles de la Cité* (Paris: Livres de poche).

Fisher, J. (1997) 'Donations to Political Parties', *Parliamentary Affairs*, L, 235–45.

Flora, P. and Heidenheimer, A. J. (1981) *The Development of Welfare State in Europe and America* (New Brunswick: Transaction Books).

Gauchet, M. (1995) *La Révolution des pouvoirs. La souveraineté, le peuple et la représentation* (Paris: Gallimard).

Gehler, M. and Sickinger, H. (eds) (1995) *Politische Affären und Skandale in Österreich* (Thaur: Kulturverlag).

Giglioli, P. P. (1996) 'Political Corruption and the Media: the Tangentopoli Affair', *International Social Science Journal*, XVII, 381–94.

Gordon Walker, P. (1970) *The Cabinet: Political Authority in Britain* (New York: Basic Books).

Graziano, L. (1976) 'A Conceptual Framework for the Study of Clientelistic Behavior', *European Journal of Political Research*, IV, 149–74.

Gundle, S. (1996) 'The Rise and Fall of Craxi's Socialist Party', in S. Gundle and S. Parker (eds), *The New Italian Republic* (London: Routledge).

Hamilton, A. *et al.*, *The Federalist* (1787); Everyman Edition (1911), (London: Dent).

Hardin, R. (1982) *Collective Action* (Baltimore: Johns Hopkins University Press).

Heidenheimer, A. J. (1996) 'The Topography of Corruption: Explorations in a Comparative Perspective', *International Social Science Journal*, XVII, 337–47.

Heywood, P. 'Spain', in F. F. Ridley and A. Doig (eds) (1995) *Sleaze: Politicians, Private Interests and Public Reaction* (Oxford: Oxford University Press).

Heywood, P. (1997) 'From Dictatorship to Democracy: Changing Forms of Corruption in Spain', in D. Della Porta and Y. Mény (eds), *Democracy and Corruption in Europe* (London: Pinter).

Hix, S. (1997) *Political Parties in the European Union* (London: Macmillan).

Huyse, L. (1994) *De Politiek Voorbij: een blik op de jaren negentig* (Leuven: Kritak).

Jacobs, J. (1992) *Systems of Survival; A Dialogue on the Moral Foundations of Commerce and Politics* (London: Hodder & Stoughton).

Jeffery, C. and Green, S. (1995) 'Germany', in F. F. Ridley and A. Doig (eds), *Sleaze: Politicians, Private Interests and Public Reaction* (Oxford: Oxford University Press).

Jennings, I. (1961) *Party Politics*, Vol. II: *The Growth of Parties* (Cambridge: Cambridge University Press).

Jennings, I. (1969) *Cabinet Government* (Cambridge: Cambridge University Press).

Katz, R. S. (1986) 'Party Government: a Rationalistic Conception', in F. G. Castles and R. Wildenmann (eds), *Visions and Realities of Party Government* (Berlin: de Gruyter), 31–71.

Katz, R. S. (1987) 'Party Government and its Alternatives', in R. S. Katz (ed.), *Party Governments: European and American Experiences* (Berlin: de Gruyter), 1–26.

Katz, R. S. (1996) 'The United States: Divided Government and Divided Parties', in J. Blondel and M. Cotta (eds), *Party and Government. An Inquiry into the Relationship between Governments and Supporting Parties in Liberal Democracies* (London: Macmillan), 202–24.

Katz, R. S. and Mair, P. (1995) 'Changing Models of Party Organization and Party Democracy: The Emergence of the Cartel Party', *Party Politics*, I, 5–28.

Keane, J. (1988) 'Introduction' in J. Keane (ed.), *Civil Society and the State: new European perspectives* (London/New York): Verso, 1–31

Keane, J. (1998) *Civil Society: Old Image, New Vision* (London: Polity Press).

Kiewiet, D. R. and McCubbins, M. D. (1991) *The Logic of Delegation* (Chicago: University of Chicago Press).

King, A. (1975) 'Executives', in N. Polsby and F. Greenstein (eds.), *Handbook of Political Science* (Reading: Addison-Wesley), Vol. 5, 173–256.

Kirchheimer, O. (1966) 'The Transformation of the Western European Party Systems', in J. La Palombara and M. Weiner (eds), *Political Parties and Political Development* (Princeton, N.J.: Princeton University Press).

Klingemann, H. D. and Fuchs, D. (eds) (1995) *Citizens and the State* (Oxford: Oxford University Press).

König, T. and Liebert, U. (1996) 'Germany. Party Influence or Chancellor Rule?', in J. Blondel and M. Cotta (eds), *Party and Government. An Inquiry into the Relationship between Governments and Supporting parties in Liberal Democracies* (London: Macmillan).

Koole, R. A. (1994a) 'The Vulnerability of the Modern Cadre Party in the Netherlands', in R. S. Katz and P. Mair (eds), *How Parties Organize; Change and Adaptation in Party Organizations in Western Democracies* (London: Sage), 278–303.

Koole, R. A. (1994b) 'Dutch Political Parties: Money and the Message', in H. E. Alexander and R. Shiratori (eds), *Comparative Political Finance Among the Democracies* (Boulder: Westview).

Koole, R. A. (1996) 'Cadre, Catch-All or Cartel: a Comment on the Notion of the Cartel Party', *Party Politics*, II, 507–23.

Krehbiel, K. (1988) 'Spatial Models of Legislative Choice', *Legislative Studies Quarterly*, 13, 235–319.

Lasswell, H. (1930 and 1977) *Psychopathology and Politics* (Chicago: University of Chicago Press).

Laver, M. and Budge I. (eds) (1992), *Party Policy and Government Coalitions* (Basingstoke, Hants: Macmillan).

Laver, M. and Shepsle, K. (1990) 'Coalitions and Cabinet Government', *American Political Science Review*, LXXXIV, 837–90.

Laver, M. and Shepsle, K. A. (eds) (1994) *Cabinet Ministers and Parliamentary Government* (Cambridge: Cambridge University Press).

Laver, M. and Shepsle, K. A. (eds) (1996) *Making and Breaking Governments; Cabinets and Legislatures in Parliamentary Democracies* (New York: Cambridge University Press).

Laver M. and Schofield, N. (1991) *Multiparty Government* (Oxford: Oxford University Press).

Leiserson, M. (1966) *Coalitions in Politics* (Ann Arbor: Michigan University Microfilms).

Leonardi, R. and Wertman, D. A. (1989) *Italian Christian Democracy* (Houndmills: Macmillan).

Lessmann, S. (1987) *Budgetary Policy and Elections: an Investigation of Public Expenditure in West Germany* (Berlin: de Gruyter).

Lijphart, A. (1984) *Democracies* (New Haven, Conn.: Yale University Press).

Linz, J. J. (1978) 'The Breakdown of Democratic Regimes: Crisis, Breakdown and Reequilibration', in J. J. Linz and A. Stepan (eds), *The Breakdown of Democratic Regimes* (Baltimore: Johns Hopkins University Press).

Linz, J. J. and Stepan, A. (1996) *Problems of Democratic Transition and Consolidation* (Baltimore: Johns Hopkins University Press).

Lipset, S. M. (1950) *Agrarian Socialism* (Berkeley: University of California Press).

Lipset, S. M. and Rokkan, S. (1967) 'Cleavage Structures, Party Systems and Voter Alignments: An Introduction', in S. M. Lipset and S. Rokkan (eds), *Party Systems and Voter Alignments* (New York: Free Press).

Lopes, F. F. (1997) 'Partisanship and Political Clientelism in Portugal (1983–93)', *South European Society & Politics*, II, 27–51.

Luther, K. R. (1999) 'A Framework for the Comparative Analysis of Political Parties and Party Systems in Consociational Democracy', in K. R. Luther and K. Deschouwer (eds), *Party Elites in Divided Societies: Political Parties in Consociational Democracy* (London: Routledge) 3–19.

Mackintosh, J. P. (1962) *The British Cabinet* (London: Stevens).

Mair, P. (1995) 'Political Parties, Popular Legitimacy and Public Privilege', *West European Politics*, XVIII, 40–57.

Mair, P. (1997) *Party System Change. Approaches and Interpretations* (Oxford: Oxford University Press).

Manin, G. (1995) *Principes du gouvernement représentatif* (Paris: Calmann-Lévy).

March, J. G. (ed.) (1993) 'Selecting Party Leaders', special issue of *European Journal of Political Research*, XXIV, 229–359.

March, J. G. and Olsen, J. P. (1989) *Rediscovering Institutions; the Organizational Basis of Politics* (New York: Free Press).

Marwell, G. and Oliver, P. (1993) *The Critical Mass in Collective Action* (Cambridge: Cambridge University Press).

Mavrogordatos, G. T. (1997) 'From Traditional Clientelism to Machine Politics: The Impact of PASOK Populism in Greece', *South European Society and Politics*, II, 1–26.

Mayntz, R. (1978) *Soziologie der oeffentlichen Verwaltung* (Heidelberg: Müller Iuristischer Verlag).

Mayntz, R. and Derlien, H.-U. (1989) 'Party Patronage and Politicization of the West German Administrative Elite 1970–1987', *Governance*, II, 384–404

Mény, Y. (1997) 'France: The End of the Republican Ethic?', in D. Della Porta and Y. Mény (eds), *Democracy and Corruption in Europe* (London: Pinter).

Michels, R. (1915) *Political Parties* (1962 edition) (New York: Free Press).

Mill, J. S. *Representative Government* (1861; Everyman Edition 1957) (London: Dent).

Miller, N. R., Grofman, B. and Feld, S. L. (1989) 'The Geometry of Majority Rule', *Journal of Theoretical Politics*, I, 379–406.

Mitchell, T. (1991) 'Limits of the State; Beyond Statist Approaches and their Critics', *American Political Science Review*, LXXXV, 77–96.

Morel, L. (1996) 'France. Party Government at Last?', in J. Blondel and M. Cotta (eds), *Party and Government* (London: Macmillan).

Müller, W. C. (1989) 'Party Patronage in Austria; Theoretical Considerations and Empirical Findings', A. Pelinka and F. Plasser (eds), *The Austrian Party System* (Boulder: Westview Press), 327–56.

Müller, W. C. (1993) 'The Relevance of the State for Party System Change', *Journal of Theoretical Politics*, V, 419–54.

Müller, W. C. and Philipp, W. (1987) 'Parteienregierung und Regierungsparteien in Österreich', *Österreichisches Zeitschrift für Politik*, XVI, 277–302.

Müller, W. C., Philipp, W. and Steininger, B. (1996) 'Austria. Party Government Within Limits', in J. Blondel and M. Cotta (eds), *Party and Government* (London: Macmillan).

Müller, W. C. and Strøm, K. (eds) (1997) 'Koalitionsregierungen in Westeuropa – eine Einleitung', in W. C. Müller and K. Strøm (eds), *Koalitionsregierungen in Westeuropa* (Wien: Signum Verlag).

Müller, W. C. and Strøm, K. (1999) 'Conclusions: Party Behaviour and Representative Democracy', in W. C. Müller and K. Strøm (eds), *Policy, Office, or Votes: How Parties in Western Europe Make Hard Decisions* (Cambridge: Cambridge University Press), 279–309.

Namier, L. (1957) *The Structure of Politics at the Accession of George III* (Manchester: Manchester University Press).

Nelken, D. (1996) 'A Legal Revolution?', in S. Gundle and S. Parker (eds), *The New Italian Republic* (London: Routledge).

Nettl, J. P. (1968) 'The State as a Conceptual Variable', *World Politics*, XX, 559–92.

Norris, P. (1997) *Passage to Power. Legislative Recruitment in Advanced Democracies* (Cambridge: Cambridge University Press).

Norris, P. and Lovenduski, J. (1995) *Political Recruitment* (Cambridge: Cambridge University Press).

Nousiainen, J. (1996) 'Finland', in J. Blondel and M. Cotta (eds), *Party and Government. An Inquiry into the Relationship between Governments and Supporting Parties in Liberal Democracies* (London: Macmillan), 110–27.

Olson, M. Jr. (1965) *The Logic of Collective Action* (Cambridge, Mass.: Harvard University Press).

Osborne, D. and Gaebler, T. (1993) *Reinventing Government; how the Entrepreneurial Spirit is Transforming the Public Sector* (New York: Plume).

Ostrogorski, M. (1903) *La démocratie et l'organisation des partis politiques* (Paris: Calmann-Lévy).

Paloheimo, H. (1984) 'Distributive Struggle, Corporatist Power Structures and Economic Policy in the 1970s in Developed Capitalist Countries', in H. Paloheimo (ed.), *Politics in the Era of Corporatism and Planning* (Helsinki: The Finnish Political Science Association), 1–46.

Panebianco, A. (1988) *Political Parties: Organization and Power* (Cambridge: Cambridge University Press).

Payne, J. L. *et al.* (1984) *The Motivation of Politicians* (Chicago: Nelson Hall).

Peters, G. (1978) *The Politics of Bureaucracy. A Comparative Perspective* (New York: Longman).

Pinto-Duschinsky, M. (1994) 'British Party Funding, 1983–1988', in H. E. Alexander and R. Shiratori (eds), *Comparative Political Finance Among the Democracies* (Boulder: Westview).

Pridham, G. (1986) *Coalitional Behaviour in Theory and Practice: An Inductive Model for Western Europe* (Cambridge: Cambridge University Press).

Punnett, R. M. (1993) 'Selecting the Party Leader in Britain: a Limited Participatory Revolution', in *European Journal of Political Research*, XXIII, 257–66.

Putnam, R. D. (1976) *The Comparative Study of Political Elites* (Englewood Cliffs: Prentice Hall).

Putnam, R. D. (1993) *Making Democracy Work. Civic Traditions in Modern Italy* (Princeton: Princeton University Press).

Ranney, A. (1962) *The Doctrine of Responsible Party Government* (Urbana, Ill.: University of Illinois Press).

Rhodes, M. (1997) 'Financing Party Politics in Italy: A Case of Systemic Corruption', *West European Politics*, xx, 54–80.

Rhodes, R. A. W. (1994) 'The Hollowing out of the State: the Changing Nature of the Public Service in Britain', *Political Quarterly*, lxv, 138–51.

Rhodes, R. A. W. and Dunleavy, P. (eds) (1995) *Prime Minister, Cabinet and Core Executive* (London: Macmillan).

Richardson, J. (ed.) (1982) *Policy Styles in Western Europe* (London: Allen & Unwin).

Riker, W. (1962) *The Theory of Political Coalitions* (New Haven: Yale University Press).

Rockman, B. A. (1987) 'Government', in V. Bogdanor (ed), *The Blackwell Encyclopaedia of Political Institutions* (Oxford: Blackwell), 257–61.

Rokkan, S. (1970) 'Nation-Building, Cleavage Formation and the Structuring of Mass Politics', in S. Rokkan, *Citizens, Elections, Parties* (Oslo: Universitetsforlaget), 72–144.

Rose, R. (1969) 'The Variability of Party Government: A Theoretical and Empirical Critique', *Political Studies*, xvii, 413–45.

Rose, R. (1974) *The Problem of Party Government* (London: Macmillan).

Rose, R. (1976) 'On the Priorities of Government', *European Journal of Political Research*, iv, 247–89.

Rose, R. (1980a) 'British Government: The Job at the Top', in R. Rose and E. N. Suleiman (eds), *Presidents and Prime Ministers* (Washington: American Enterprise Institute), 1–49.

Rose, R. (1980b) 'Government against Sub-governments: A European Perspective on Washington', in R. Rose and E. N. Suleiman (eds), *Presidents and Prime Ministers* (Washington: American Enterprise Institute), 284–347.

Rose, R. (1984) *Understanding Big Government* (Beverly Hills: Sage).

Roth, G. (1963) *The Social Democrats in Imperial Germany* (Totowa: The Bedminster Press).

Rouban, L. (1995) 'Public Administration at the Crossroads: The End of the French Specifity?', in J. Pierre (ed.), *Bureaucracy in the Modern State* (Aldershot: Edward Elgar).

Sartori, G. (1976) *Parties and Party Systems: a Framework for Analysis* (Cambridge: Cambridge University Press).

Sartori, G. (1987) *The Theory of Democracy Revisited* (Chatham: Chatham House).

Sartori, G. (1994) *Comparative Constitutional Engineering: an Inquiry into Structures, Incentives and Outcomes* (Basingstoke: Macmillan).

Scarrow, S. E. (1996) *Parties and their Members: Organizing for Victory in Britain and Germany* (Oxford: Oxford University Press).

Scharpf, F. W. (1997) *The Problem Solving Capacity of Multi-level Governance* (Florence: Robert Schuman Centre).

Schattschneider, E. E. (1942) *Party Government* (New York: Holt, Rinehart & Winston).

Schlesinger, J. A. (1991) *Political Parties and the Winning of Office* (Ann Arbor: University of Michigan Press).

Schmitt, C. (1988) *Parlementarisme et démocratie* (Paris: Seuil).

Schofield, N. and Laver, M. (1985) 'Bargaining Theory and Portfolio Payoffs in European Coalition Governments 1945–83', *British Journal of Political Science*, xv, 143–64.

Schubert, K. (1988) 'Politics and Economic Regulation', in F. G. Castles, F. Lehner and M. G. Schmidt (eds), *Managing Mixed Economies* (Berlin: de Gruyter), 169–96.

Schumpeter, J. A. (1947) *Capitalism, Socialism, and Democracy* (New York: Harper).

Searing, D. D. (1994) *Westminster's World: Understanding Political Roles* (Cambridge, Mass.: Harvard University Press).

Secher, H. P. (1958) 'Coalition Government: The Case of the Second Republic', *American Political Science Review*, lii, 791–809.

Seibel, W. (1997) 'Corruption in the Federal Republic of Germany before and after the Wake of Reunification', in D. Della Porta and Y. Mény (eds), *Democracy and Corruption in Europe* (London: Pinter).

Sharpe, L. J. and Newton, K. (1984) *Does Politics Matter? The Determinants of Public Policy* (Oxford: Clarendon Press).

Sickinger, H. (1997) *Politikfinanzierung in Österreich* (Thaur: Kulturverlag).

Sjöblom, G. (1986) 'Problems and Problem Solutions in Politics', in F. G. Castles and R. Wildenmann (eds), *Visions and Realities of Party Government* (Berlin: De Gruyter).

Sotiropoulus, D. A. (1996) *Populism and Bureaucracy. The Case of Greece under PASOK, 1981–1989* (Notre Dame: University of Notre Dame Press).

Spruyt, H. (1994) *The Sovereign State and Its Competitors* (Princeton: Princeton University Press).

Steiner, J. and Dorff, R. H. (1988) 'Analysis of Decision Cases', in F. G. Castles, F. Lehner and M. G. Schmidt (eds), *Managing Mixed Economies* (Berlin: de Gruyter), 142–68.

Strøm, K. (1984) 'Minority Governments in Parliamentary Democracies', *Comparative Political Studies*, xvii, 199–228.

Strøm, K. (1990) *Minority Government and Majority Rule* (Cambridge: Cambridge University Press).

Strøm, K. (1994) 'The Political Role of Norwegian Cabinet Ministers', in M. Laver and K. A. Shepsle (eds), *Cabinet Ministers and Parliamentary Government* (Cambridge: Cambridge University Press), 35–55.

Strøm, K. and T. Bergman (1992) 'Sweden: Social Democratic Dominance in One Dimension' in M. Laver and I. Budge (eds), *Party Policy and Government Coalitions* (Basingstoke, Hants: Macmillan), 109–150.

Suleiman, E. N. (1984) 'From Right to Left. Bureaucracy and Politics in France', in E. N. Suleiman (ed.), *Bureaucrats and Policy Making* (New York: Holmes & Meier).

Sundquist, J. L. (1986) *Constitutional Reform and Effective Government* (Washington: The Brookings Institution).

Taylor, C. L. (ed.) (1983) *Why Governments Grow* (Beverly Hills: Sage).

Taylor, M. J. and Laver, M. J. (1973) 'Government Coalitions in Western Europe', *European Journal of Political Research*, i, 205–48.

Thiébault, J. L. (1993) 'Party Leadership Selection in France: Creating a President's Party', *European Journal of Political Research*, xxiii, 277–94.

Tocqueville, A. de (1856) *L'ancien régime et la révolution* (Paris).

Van Gunsteren, H. R. (1997) *Organising Plurality: Citizenship in post 1989 Democracies* (manuscript).

Veljanovski, Cento (1987) *Selling the State* (London: Weidenfeld).

Ware, A. (1996) *Political Parties and Party Systems* (New York: Oxford University Press).

Weber, M. (1922) (1972) *Wirtschaft und Gesellschaft* (Mohr: Tübingen).

Weller, P. (1985) *First Among Equals: Prime Ministers in Westminster Systems* (Sydney: Allen and Unwin).

Wiberg, M. (1991) 'Public Financing of Parties as *Arcana Imperii* in Finland', in M. Wiberg (ed.), *The Public Purse and Political Parties* (Jyväskylä: Finnish Political Science Association).

Wilson, J. Q. (1973) *Political Organization* (New York: Free Press).

Winter, D. G. (1987) 'Leader Appeal, Leader Performance, and the Motive Profiles of Leaders and Followers', *Journal of Personality and Social Psychology*, LII, 196–202.

Index